BECOMING

BUCKY FULLER

The MIT Press | Cambridge, Massachusetts | London, England

LORETTA LORANCE

BECOMING

BUCKY FULLER

MIT Press books may be purchased at special quantity discounts for business or sales promotional use. For information, please email special_sales@mitpress.mit.edu or write to Special Sales Department, The MIT Press, 55 Hayward Street, Cambridge, MA 02142.

This book was set in Hoefler Text by Graphic Composition, Inc. Printed and bound in Spain.

Library of Congress Cataloging-in-Publication Data

Lorance, Loretta.
  Becoming Bucky Fuller / Loretta Lorance.
      p.   cm.
  Includes bibliographical references and index.
  ISBN 978-0-262-12302-0 (hardcover : alk. paper) 1. Fuller, R. Buckminster (Richard Buckminster), 1895–1983—Psychology. 2. Fuller, R. Buckminster (Richard Buckminster), 1895–1983—Criticism and interpretation. I. Fuller, R. Buckminster (Richard Buckminster), 1895–1983. II. Title.
  TA140.F9L67 2009
  620.0092—dc22

                                                              2008029418

10 9 8 7 6 5 4 3 2 1

CONTENTS

ILLUSTRATION CREDITS

1.1–1.10, 1.12, 1.14–3.1,   R. Buckminster Fuller Papers, Courtesy of Department of Special Collections and
3.3–3.9, 3.11–3.12, 5.1, 6.1,   University Archives, Stanford University Libraries, Stanford University, Stanford,
6.4–6.15, 6.21, 7.1   CA. The works of Buckminster and Anne Hewlett Fuller © Copyright, The Estate of
R. Buckminster Fuller, all rights reserved.

1.11   Courtesy of The Frank Lloyd Wright Foundation. The drawings of Frank Lloyd
Wright are Copyright © 1954 The Frank Lloyd Wright Foundation, Taliesin West,
Scottsdale, AZ.

1.13   Courtesy of John Angeline, New York, NY.

3.2, 3.10   Avery Architectural and Fine Arts Library, Columbia University in the City of New
York. Courtesy of The Estate of Buckminster Fuller, Santa Barbara, CA.

6.2–6.3, 6.16–6.20   Courtesy of The University of South Carolina Newsfilm Library, University of South
Carolina, Columbus, SC.

6.23   Courtesy of Chicago History Museum, Chicago, IL.

PREFACE

In the 1960s and 1970s, Buckminster Fuller (1895–1983) was a popular speaker on the international lecture circuit. His untraditional way of thinking about the world and how it works was embraced by many, especially those in the counter-culture movement. They would sit through lengthy lectures of four or five or more hours to absorb Fuller's lessons on how to make the world a better place. One reason the self-styled anticipatory comprehensive designer[1] was popular was he practiced what he preached.

Fuller pursued his goal along many paths. He designed houses for industrial production to reduce the use of materials, labor, and costs. A major achievement was the development of the geodesic dome, a hemispherical self-supporting structure built of interlocking tetrahedra made from mass-produced parts. Fuller saw the tetrahedron, a pyramidal form, as the basic shape of the universe. This led him to devise a new type of geometry, synergetics, based on the 60-degree angle, or two-dimensional triangle and three-dimensional tetrahedron, instead of the 90-degree angle, or two-dimensional square and three-dimensional cube. Fuller believed synergetics described the coordinates of the Earth, an unproven hypothesis.[2] His interest in the Earth went beyond defining its geometric order to organizing a system for tracking its resources. He began tracking the planet's resources in the 1960s, which he named the World Design Science Decade. The inventory of the Earth's resources evolved into the ongoing World Game. The purpose of the World Game is to show that the "world [can] work for everyone"; it is also "an antidote to war games."[3] While these diverse accomplishments may seem unrelated, they are all components of Fuller's mission to teach people to use technology for positive purposes, not negative ones, and to treat the closed ecological system of the Earth with respectful caution.

This philosophy was well developed by the 1960s, but Fuller did not begin his career with such lofty goals. His first independent project was an attempt to found a company, 4D Corporation, to manufacture a house of his design, Dymaxion House, in the late 1920s. Although this project was never realized, it did help establish Fuller as someone who was willing to go against conventional ideas and it did propel him into the public arena. His popularity was at its height in the 1960s and 1970s when his ideas and work were seen as welcome alternatives to established social mores and conventions. Some people interpreted these as rationale to withdraw from society, to drop out. This was not Fuller's intention. He believed it was important to work to effect change from an informed position within society, not by turning one's back on it. Therefore, it is not surprising that his first independent project, the Dymaxion House, represented more than just a new design for an industrially reproduced house; it was intended to make life better for its inhabitants who would in turn be able to improve society.

The Dymaxion House was a radical departure from the traditional house design, but it was not the first design for an industrially reproduced house. In the nineteenth century, prefabricated houses were manufactured in the British Isles and the United States. A number of companies, such as Sears Roebuck & Company, E. F. Hodgson & Co., and Gordon-Van Tine, had long histories of manufacturing and marketing houses by the 1920s. Fuller's idea of the industrially reproduced house was much different from the models offered by his predecessors. He did not want to produce the structural frame, interior partitions, floors, ceilings, and exterior cladding as these companies did. He wanted to manufacture the house and sell it as a complete unit with wiring, plumbing, environmental controls, and appliances. Fuller also rejected the reliance on stylistic criteria, especially historic styles, unlike established manufacturers.

Like Fuller, Howard Fisher was also interested in manufacturing houses in a manner similar to automobile production. Unlike Fuller, Fisher successfully founded such a company, General Houses, Inc., in 1932. European modernists — especially Mies van der Rohe, Walter Gropius, and Le Corbusier — advocated using standardization and prefabrication in houses. Yet Fuller was critical of these architects because he believed they simply wanted to use technology to package the traditional house in a stylish envelope.

With the design of the Dymaxion House he reconfigured the traditional right-angled house into a radial plan with a metal and plastic exterior. The lack of ornament, crisp lines, and use of planar surfaces reflect his understanding of both International Style design criteria and methods of industrial production. Fuller's attitude toward mass production and prefabrication may have paralleled the interests of his contemporaries, but his unusual design concepts meant the Dymaxion House was relegated to the realm of fantasy or futuristic architecture instead of being understood as a viable alternative to existing types of contemporary houses.[4]

Fuller's approach to design, allowing machine processes rather than aesthetics to control his strategy, places him in an unusual position within twentieth-century architecture. Although not a trained architect — in fact, he was not fully trained in any field — Fuller regarded the Dymaxion House as a practical and marketable solution to the need for shelter. He was disdainful of most architects because he felt their designs were inhibited by their fidelity to the demands of style or tradition. In terms of the house, the only traditions to which Fuller conformed were those of providing shelter and comfort. He believed houses should enrich the physical and intellectual lives of their inhabitants. These guidelines led him to reconceptualize the house as a radial container filled with labor-saving devices capable of facilitating and easing everyday life. Fuller did not feel bound by the stylistic conventions of architecture or its history as he sought to apply the principles of industrial production to houses.

Becoming Bucky Fuller is the first in-depth study of the beginnings of Fuller's interest in industrial processes, the home-building field, and architectural theory and design in the 1920s. It is a revisionist study of the development of Fuller and the Dymaxion House. Much of the material under discussion will be known to those familiar with Fuller's activities in the 1920s and early 1930s. Of course, one must revisit familiar material in order to treat it anew, which this text most certainly does. Fuller always acknowledged that his work on the Dymaxion House initiated his lifelong mission to manufacture houses. He was not, however, completely honest about the events leading up to the beginning of the project, or about his own activities during this period, or about what he was originally trying to accomplish. This is not to intimate that Fuller fabricated the events of this time. It is, rather, to disclose that he took artistic license with some of the facts of his life and work during the period under discussion to present himself in the best possible light.

My argument in *Becoming Bucky Fuller* is based primarily upon a close reading of papers in Fuller's archives, especially the multivolume scrapbook he began in 1907, the *Chronofile*. There is very little use of secondary sources in this text, including the semi-autobiographical books and biographies on which Fuller collaborated. With few changes and additions, the story of Fuller's activities in the 1920s and early 1930s is consistent whether it was written in 1951 (Richard Hamilton's unpublished biography, "Work of R. B. Fuller: Design Initiatives and Prototype Engineering"[5]) or 1999 (Y. C. Wong's dissertation, "The Geodesic Works of Richard Buckminster Fuller, 1948–68 [The Universe as a Home of Man]"[6]). Even researchers who are critical of Fuller basically repeat the same information (Karl Conrad's dissertation, "Buckminster Fuller and the Technocratic Persuasion"[7]). The reason for the consistency is simple: by 1939 Fuller had decided how his development and activities during this period would be portrayed, and his version became the template from which later accounts were derived.[8] During his life Fuller granted very few people permission to consult his private papers. Yet he did not destroy the documents contradicting his carefully constructed story. A few Fuller scholars have consulted these papers, but they elected to fit the information the papers contain into the accepted narrative with few modifications. For me, these documents served as maps I followed as I wended my way through the truth and fiction of Fuller's biography and work. Instead of trying to fit the information I discovered in Fuller's papers into the established sequence of events, I used it to write a parallel history, connected to the original at major points.

In writing this parallel history, I use as much text from the original documents as possible. These texts are allowed to "speak" for themselves. In addition, there is no backward extrapolation from later materials. In other words, I do not use information from Fuller's later writings to explain what he was doing in the 1920s. As he continued to work on his concept for the industrially reproduced house, Fuller expanded and refined his ideas. The later materials show how the project progressed, not how it began. Although not all the first steps are known, Fuller's archives reveal a carefully planned, extensively analyzed, albeit unsuccessful, strategy to organize a corporation to manufacture and market an industrially reproduced house with a full array of mechanical accessories, the Dymaxion House.

Becoming Bucky Fuller is concerned with both the origins and development of the Dymaxion House project and Fuller's public persona. The years between 1922 and 1933 saw not only the development of Fuller's first project for an industrially reproduced house but also the development of Buckminster Fuller, the man with the vision and determination to follow the project through to completion. This is not to privilege the early work over the later work, but to thoroughly analyze for the first time Fuller's activities during this period without looking through the veil he placed over them. I have formulated my answer to why Fuller cast the events of the 1920s into a seductive narrative instead of a mundane reiteration of just the facts. "Just the facts" presents the life of an ordinary person, and Buckminster Fuller was no ordinary person.

1

BUILDING STOCKADE

In honor of moving to Chicago with her husband, Anne Hewlett Fuller began a diary. Even though she was nine months' pregnant, Anne (figure 1.1) was delighted to depart Long Island to live with her husband again. Twenty-one days later, on August 28, 1927, Anne gave birth to a girl, Allegra (figure 1.2), who was healthier than her deceased sister, Alexandra. Starting a new life together in a new city with a new baby offered the prospect of a happy future to the young couple. Anne lovingly noted that she and Bucky were now "going to stay together always as we miss each other too much."[1]

The couple's long separation—punctuated by brief visits, telephone calls, and telegrams—began in June of the previous year when Bucky, as Anne affectionately called her husband Buckminster (figure 1.3), went to Chicago to establish a midwestern subsidiary of the Stockade Building System. Stockade was a building materials and construction company started by Fuller and his father-in-law, James Monroe Hewlett (figure 1.4). The uncertainty and demands of organizing a branch of Stockade (figure 1.5) in a new territory were so great that Anne remained in New York until circumstances warranted her relocation. Fourteen months after founding the Chicago subdivision, Fuller felt secure enough to uproot his very pregnant wife.

Despite the pressure placed upon his personal life, as president of the parent company Fuller was the most logical choice for developing the Chicago territory. After all, he was young, energetic, and related to two prominent Chicago families, and he understood the psychology of sales. Fuller knew to gear his sales pitch to each audience, a technique he needed to persuade his Chicago contacts of Stockade's value. He was particularly well suited to the task because he had been involved with the company since its inception.

The Stockade Building System was incorporated in 1923. Its basis was a lightweight, fibrous block. According to Stockade brochures, during World War I Hewlett realized the need to eliminate waste and inefficient practices in the construction of buildings. He discovered architectural waste was predominantly found in the heaviness of masonry walls and resulted from building traditions,

1.1

....

Buckminster Fuller,
Anne Hewlett Fuller,
ca. 1928.

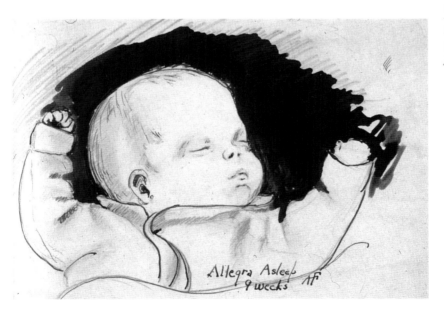

1.2

....

Anne Hewlett
Fuller, *Allegra
Asleep*, 1927.

1.3

Anne Hewlett Fuller,
Bucky, ca. 1928.

I.4

Victor White,
*James Monroe
Hewlett*, 1940.

Stockade Building
System, Inc.,
cover of *Stockade
Patented*, 1926.

not necessity. Hewlett knew masonry was valued for its insulating qualities and its durability. He also knew the tradition of building with masonry inhibited innovation in construction materials and methods. His search for an equally strong yet less wasteful alternative to masonry produced the Stockade block.

The Stockade system embedded a concrete frame within enclosing walls of cement-bonded fibrous blocks stabilized by metal clips.[2] It married the strength of an internal supporting frame with the security of masonry walls. The frame was poured-in-place concrete and the walls consisted of the company's light-weight blocks. The dimensions of the blocks, 16 inches long by 8 inches wide by 4 inches high, were based on those of the common brick "as this is the accepted module pleasing to the eye as developed through the ages of architecture."[3] Unlike bricks, the Stockade blocks have a four-inch round hole near each end. As the courses of blocks were laid, concrete was poured into the holes and the blocks served as a mold for the concrete frame. The poured concrete columns connected to concrete lintels at every floor and opening. After the concrete set, the blocks remained in place to protect the frame and function as walls (figure 1.6). Stockade provided a system for the manufacture and construction of a building's structural frame, outer shell, and interior partitions.

Even though the blocks were shaped like bricks and laid in courses like them, Stockade claimed walls made of its blocks were superior to those of masonry: "The STOCKADE SYSTEM . . . represents the last word in substantial, economical, weather resisting, heat insulated, sound and vermin-proof building construction."[4] The blocks were the most significant component of this sturdy, scientific, and economical method of building. They weighed about two pounds and were supposedly unbreakable. They were also fire-resistant and water-repellent. In addition, because the blocks had no capillary action, they did not compromise the concrete by pulling moisture out of it as it set. Embedded in the blocks, the concrete frame was well protected from accidents and weather damage. Furthermore, Stockade block walls were resistant to cracking since mortar or plaster was applied directly to their fibrous surfaces, making

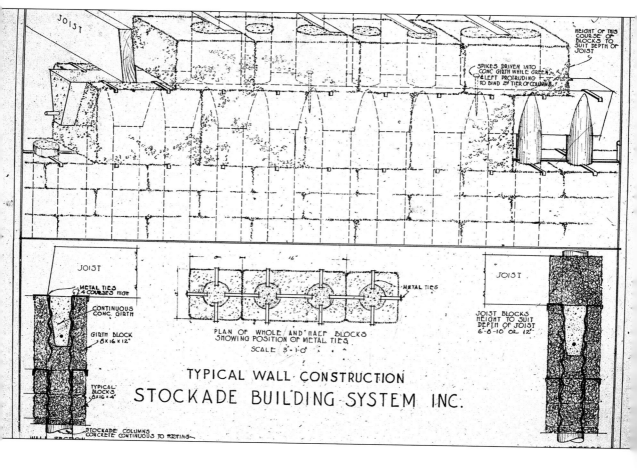

1.6

Stockade Building
System, Inc.,
typical stockade
wall construction,
1926.

the walls self-insulating. Finally, the chemical composition of the blocks made them vermin-proof. Stockade's innovative system promised clients a durable, low-maintenance structure, superior to any made of masonry.

Before such a new and efficient system could be offered to interested parties, a method for manufacturing, transporting, promoting, advertising, selling, and managing it was required. For this Hewlett called upon Fuller in 1922. At the time, Fuller was a reservist in the navy and was otherwise unemployed; therefore, the offer represented a good opportunity. Hewlett, a well-respected and well-connected architect,[5] did not enlist the services of his son-in-law in the development of this new business venture out of paternal concern. Fuller's background had prepared him to take on the diverse responsibilities required to launch a fledgling company.

Although unemployed when Hewlett recruited him, Fuller's previous job was as a national sales manager for the Kelly-Springfield Truck Company. It is not quite clear when Fuller's employment at Kelly-Springfield ended, although he was either already dismissed or told of his imminent departure shortly before Hewlett's offer. Charles Young, Kelly-Springfield's president, wrote a recommendation for Fuller to James McCarthy of Price Brothers in Quebec on June 6. Young praised Fuller's efficiency, integrity, and industriousness while regretfully noting that the national sales market for trucks was currently too slow to justify Fuller's continued employment with an annual salary of $3,600, a little more than $69 per week.[6]

Young's letter differs greatly from Fuller's explanation of why he left the company. According to Fuller's 1944 résumé, his employment ended upon "termination of that Company by voluntary liquidation, in May 1922,"[7] implying the company went out of business. Young's letter clearly contradicts this as well as Fuller's claim that he earned $100 per week as the national sales manager for trucks. Perhaps Fuller's calculation of $100 per week was based upon his expectations of sales commissions and an expense account. He mentioned these to Arthur Meeker, an upper-level executive at Armour & Company and family friend who was instrumental in persuading Armour to hire Fuller. Fuller explained that although Kelly-Springfield was offering him a better job with a higher salary, he was concerned about leaving Armour. Meeker encouraged Fuller to accept the new position since he did not foresee an equivalent opportunity for him at Armour. While Fuller's salary at Kelly-Springfield may have fluctuated between the two amounts, both were higher than the $50 per week he received from Armour.[8]

Fuller's association with Armour was long and complex. For example, one of the first sales he made for Kelly-Springfield was a 31/2-ton truck to Armour. He began working for Armour in 1915 and rose from a meat lugger to assistant cashier. His employment was interrupted in 1917 when he entered the navy, but he returned to the company two years later.[9] He then quickly resumed his climb up the Armour corporate ladder. By the time of his departure for Kelly-Springfield, Fuller was a manager of national and international accounts. His responsibilities included customer relations, troubleshooting, correspondence, tracking orders, marketing, and writing reports. Working his way through the ranks at Armour provided him with firsthand knowledge of corporate departments and their interrelationships, valuable experience he would put into use at Stockade.

Fuller also brought inventiveness as well as knowledge of machinery and factory processes to Stockade. His first "inventions" date from his childhood. Among the earliest, according to Fuller, were a playpen for his younger sister, Rosie, and a hand-operated pole to make rowing a boat easier. Fuller treated his inventiveness as a hobby until 1914. His attitude changed when his family sent him to work for a cousin in Sherbrooke, Quebec, after he substituted a week of partying in Manhattan for his first-semester midyear exams at Harvard. His job in Sherbrooke was to help install textile machines in a new cotton mill (figure 1.7). This imposed exile to the world of gritty manual labor was intended as edifying punishment, but Fuller was fascinated with the factory and its machinery.

Even though he was only an apprentice millwright, Fuller claimed that his enthusiasm caught the attention of the chief engineer who gave him the task

1.7

Workers in the
Sherbrooke Factory,
ca. 1914. Fuller is the
second from the left
(with mustache).

of finding the means to repair or replace broken parts. Some he took to local shops, some he redesigned and improved. The chief engineer also encouraged the young apprentice to keep a notebook with sketches of his ideas. Fuller described his months at Sherbrooke as "a self-tutored course of engineering exploration"[10] during which he learned about design, manufacturing, factory machinery, and the connections between machine parts.

He received additional training in mechanics and engineering at the Naval Academy in Annapolis, Maryland, during World War I. Fuller's extremely poor eyesight prevented him from enlisting in the navy, although with the help of a friendly optometrist in Bar Harbor, Maine, he was accepted into the U.S. Navy Reserve Force in 1917. He began his service as the chief boatswain of the *Wego*, his mother's boat that he volunteered to patrol the Maine coast (figure 1.8). He quickly earned the rank of ensign and was given temporary command of his own ship. He was next assigned to temporary command in Boston Harbor before being transferred to the USS *Inca*, which he sailed from Boston to Hampton Roads, Virginia.[11] He outlined his responsibilities to his mother: "Our work is to convey the airoplanes [*sic*] on long test flights + to do patrol work with them. We watch out for them if they have trouble and have to land. We then tow them ashore or give them much help as is necessary."[12] Fuller later described his job as saving training pilots from drowning when their planes flipped into the water during landing. He also claimed to have invented a crane and hook device to lift overturned planes out of the water and prevent the pilot's death, although there is no record of this in Fuller's files or the navy's records.[13] Alden Hatch, Fuller's friend and biographer, claimed that Fuller discussed his working drawings with Commander Patrick Bellinger, the officer in charge, who approved the use of Fuller's rescue winch.[14] Bellinger is also credited with supporting Fuller's application to the three-month special officer's training program at the Naval Academy.[15] Fuller's letters, however, name Lieutenant Commander Walker as the officer pushing him to attend Annapolis and supporting his application: "I have been again chosen for a course at Annapolis by my squadron Commander,

1.8

The *Wego* and its crew, ca. 1917.

Lieutenant Commander Walker, who says that if I will study and take that course he prophesies that I will graduate among the very first and should receive another promotion."[16]

With Walker's, and perhaps Bellinger's, encouragement Fuller sat for the qualifying exams in May 1918. He happily reported to his mother on the 14th: "I learned that I placed number ten on the list of fifty men to go to Annapolis from this District yesterday but have not as yet had any official orders. I am glad that I passed the exam well anyway. There were about one hundred that took it. If they do not hold me up for my eyes at the last minute I will be alright, but I greatly fear that they may, but as I am already an officer and as I passed the exam well I may have a chance. I certainly pray that I may get through as I want terribly to go through with that course."[17] A little less than a month after reporting his success to his mother, Fuller reported to the Naval Academy where he studied navigation, gunnery, seamanship, electrical engineering, and marine engineering as well as navy regulations and customs.[18] Fuller graduated in September and was promptly discharged from the naval reserves so he could enlisted in the navy (figure 1.9). He resigned a year later because he "did not want to be away from his family on assignment for long periods of time."[19] Of the subjects he studied at the Naval Academy, those about engineering were the most useful during Stockade's formative period.

When Hewlett called upon Fuller in 1922 to assist in the development of Stockade, he was not concerned that his son-in-law had no architectural training since architecture was his profession. Before the Stockade venture, Fuller's experience with construction and the building trades was extremely limited. According to Hatch, Fuller used materials left over from after the construction of the family house to build a small structure on his family's private summer retreat, Bear Island, Maine.[20] Few references to this early structure exist, and Fuller did not include it in his list of accomplishments, perhaps because he did not design it. It was "the architect's first structure, a snug little slope-roofed cabin called Birch Lodge. Fuller built it in 1908, when he was 13 years old and

1.9

Fuller as
communication
officer on board
the USS *George
Washington,* ca.
1919.

working from plans found in *St. Nicholas* magazine."[21] The Birch Lodge project gave Fuller a basic understanding of how a structure is put together and how it stands up in traditional timber construction. There was, however, little in the experience he could apply to the development of the Stockade system, a new method of construction.

One of the first steps required to transform the Stockade system from a good idea into a marketable product was to determine the best method of producing the blocks. While the patent would seem to serve as a blueprint for production, in actuality there were still many kinks to be worked out when Fuller began to tackle the problem. At first Fuller and a coworker began hand mixing and hand forming blocks to discover the correct ratio of components. Equal parts of "excelsior and lime . . . with a small amount of sugar or gluecose [*sic*] as a toughener or binder"[22] were found to be best. They also needed machinery to evenly mix the blocks. The search for machinery was futile because "no such machines were apparently manufactured";[23] they would have to be built from scratch. It is not clear where these experiments were conducted although Hatch places the company's humble beginnings in a barn on Hewlett's Lawrence, Long Island, property.[24] Once the problem of manufacturing the blocks was solved, the next step was to set up a formal corporation.

The Stockade Building System, Inc., was established in January 1923. The main purpose for incorporation was to procure enough subscriptions to guarantee a perfected manufacturing process in order to optimize profits. Subscriptions were needed because all advancements to date were financed by "the expenditure of personal capital. It became apparent that if progressive steps were to be made, more capital than could be furnished from that source would be necessary."[25] Fortunately, enough subscriptions were sold to give Stockade the financial foundation it needed to begin mass-producing blocks.

Production began slowly. The notes of the second board meeting show a vote to consult Robert McAllister Lloyd who was recommended as the best mechanical engineer. With Lloyd's assistance, the most advantageous production method was determined and some of the essential machines were purchased but most were manufactured. A factory was consequently organized in Summit, New Jersey. It was not until the fall that production "was just approaching a profitable volume."[26]

Unfortunately, just as production became profitable, the hard-won machinery was destroyed when the factory burned. Insurance covered most of the loss, except for $900 that the insurance company figured Stockade could salvage.[27] Much had been learned about perfecting the manufacturing process before the fire, and it was decided to begin again from an informed position.

This meant rebuilding the Summit factory and forming a subsidiary company, the Stockade Corporation of New Jersey. The subsidiary's purpose was to absorb the costs of building and operating the new factory as well as to insulate the parent company, Stockade Building System (SBS), from further liability. In return, the parent company supplied the necessary machinery. SBS kept control over the New Jersey company by retaining 51 percent of its stock. It was also estimated that it would now take the Summit factory two years to turn a profit. To proceed, the Stockade board decided to authorize another subsidiary in New England.

Thus, the pattern for growth was established. The parent company was based in Manhattan, and it sold the rights to manufacture and market the blocks to subsidiaries. By 1927 five franchises of the Stockade Building System were organized. Two, the New York and New Jersey branches, shared the Manhattan office with the parent company. Fuller's division, Stockade Midwest, was in Chicago and the others were in Washington, D.C., and Brookline, Massachusetts.[28] Offices and plants were sometimes in different cities. For example, the Summit factory made blocks for the New Jersey and New York divisions, and the plant for Fuller's branch was in Joliet. Possibilities for further expansion into Ohio, Florida, California, and abroad were explored.[29] In 1927 the potential for growth was promising.

A number of factors contributed to Stockade's success. Stylistic flexibility and the quality of Stockade structures were very attractive features. Contacts within the building and architectural trades provided easy access to prospective clients. Hewlett was a well-respected architect and, as the vice-president of the American Institute of Architects, had a large network of friends and business associates. He used it to his advantage to help open doors for Fuller, who was both Stockade's president and primary salesman in its formative years. He wrote a casual, but respectful, letter of introduction for Fuller, which could be addressed to different persons in different fields without text alterations. The letters to Col. Paul Starrett, an architect, and William H. Woodlin, president of the American Car & Foundry Company, are identical even though they were sent to people whose interest in Stockade structures would vary. Starrett might find the economical and adaptable method of construction suitable for a few projects. Woodlin, on the other hand, was a business executive who might find Stockade's economical and durable structures appropriate for some of his company's needs.

Quality and economy were two of the system's main selling points. Stockade advertised its structures as safe from fire and moisture as well as insulated against heat, cold, and noise. These fine characteristics resulted from the combination of the pierced Stockade blocks and the poured-in-place concrete frame. The system was based on Hewlett's original patent and augmented by technical improvements developed as theory was put into practice. Hewlett and Fuller were awarded three additional patents for advancements and improvements to the system. The first was given to Hewlett for a partition wall using the Stockade system. Hewlett and Fuller were granted a joint patent for a supporting wall made of Stockade blocks that had been implied, but not claimed, in Hewlett's original patent. Fuller received the third one for the block mold and production process.[30] The additional patents protected Hewlett's and Fuller's ideas from being co-opted by others without increasing the complexity of the Stockade system. It remained simple, with few components (blocks, clips, and concrete), and, more important, inexpensive to use.

To attract clients Stockade needed to build structures as sturdy as, but less expensive than, those made of brick, the building material most closely resembling Stockade's blocks. Its next closest competitors were the manufactured homes sold by companies like Sears, Hodgson, and Gordon-Van Tine. Like Stockade, these companies marketed the basic frame and interior divisions of houses; unlike Stockade, these companies charged extra for heating, plumbing, wiring, and fancy finishes.[31] The cost of a Stockade structure was determined by the production costs of the blocks. Fuller estimated in 1923 that blocks could be produced for about 8¢ and this would decrease as production increased.[32] In 1923 the wholesale price of bricks was slightly under 2¢ each or $19.81 per thousand.[33] Even though the cost per brick was less than the cost per Stockade block, the differences in construction methods meant a greater number of bricks than Stockade blocks were needed to complete a structure. Bricks also required skilled masons who could lay level courses bonded with mortar, whereas Stockade blocks did not. To his estimate of 8¢, Fuller added the caveat that "through estimates of contractors making firm bids on structures utilizing the Stockade Building System, it has been found that at a price of 15¢ per block we can undersell . . . the cheapest competition we will meet."[34]

It turned out Stockade was able to sell the blocks for more than 15¢ without pricing itself out of the market. Harrison Gill, an architect, quoted 20¢ a block and Theodore Skinner, a consulting engineer, noted a cost of $840.00 for 4,000 Stockade system blocks (or 21¢ each) in testimonial letters.[35] When labor costs were figured in, Stockade still claimed an advantage over its competitors. The company informed prospective clients the system was so simple that skilled labor was not required. If, however, professional contractors were used, the simplicity of the Stockade system still offered significant savings.

Construction time and costs were reduced by the omission of some steps and materials traditionally required for interior and exterior finishes. The hairy

Stockade Building
System, Inc., test of
stockade wall at the
Massachusetts
Institute of
Technology, 1924.

or rough surface of the blocks allowed direct application of plaster or stucco; no binding agent, no mesh, no lathe was needed. While direct application of a finish could potentially compromise the integrity of the resulting surface, independent testing proved it did not (figure 1.10). In 1924, the Mechanical Engineering Laboratory at the Massachusetts Institute of Technology tested a Stockade wall to determine its suitability for use in the Greater Boston area. Approval was based upon the durability and strength of the standard Stockade block wall with plaster applied directly to the blocks. It was found that the plaster surface withstood the tests without cracking, although insignificant cracking did occur after the wall was transported to a new test site. This cracking was specifically credited to mishandling, not an inherent flaw within the wall or the plaster.[36] This test verified that Stockade's ability to reduce the costs of materials and its construction process produced sturdy and reliable results.

A variety of additional tests also validated some of Stockade's other claims about its blocks and structures. Many of these tests may have been too technical to interest the layperson, but the findings would have been strong enough to convince the professional of Stockade's value. Riverbanks Laboratories found Stockade walls had an acoustic absorption coefficient of 54 percent; the blocks did keep out much unwanted sound.[37] The Robert Hunt Company validated Stockade's claims that its blocks were fire-resistant. Hunt's tests concluded the blocks "will not support combustion under anything like normal conditions, [their] tendency being to hinder and obstruct combustion."[38] No reports exist to support or contradict Stockade's assertion that its walls would remain free of moisture and vermin.

Not mentioned in promotional literature but substantiated by tests was the Stockade wall's resistance to racking, or the distortion of a right-angled wall into a parallelogram by wind or other forces. This important test was conducted at Manhattan's Grand Central Palace in 1925. It was performed on a "standard Stockade System . . . [with] a window opening in the middle of the wall which weakened its condition, especially for the test."[39] Despite its weakened state,

the wall withstood up to 4,000-pound loads with no signs of racking or of cracking plaster. In the 1920s, Fuller thought such tests and displays were important
methods to demonstrate Stockade claims were more than just words as he wrote
to Lloyd: "We are having many tests made bearing out claims . . . we have made
for Stockade by well-known authorities."[40] Different municipalities, of course,
have different building codes, and Stockade would have needed to demonstrate
its ability to meet those codes at the local level. In order to do this, many of the
same tests were repeated when the company began to develop a new territory.
Fuller would later describe the tests as reinforcing outdated building practices
and blocking progress. Although he admitted that they had been "conceived to
protect the citizenry against dangerous building practices . . . [Fuller denounced
them as] the sacrosanct means of perpetuating antediluvian techniques, backed
as they were by the enormous political power of the construction establishment."[41] There undoubtedly were resistance and skepticism toward Stockade
as a new method of construction using nontraditional materials, but the various tests helped convince skeptics. Conducting the racking test in an important
public setting like Grand Central Palace was a confident way to display the quality of Stockade walls to the trades and general public. Fuller used similar points
to convince Stockade's treasurer of the necessity of such expenditures when he
explained how they helped confirm Stockade's viability.[42]

Undoubtedly, such demonstrations gave Stockade exposure. They (and
Hewlett's involvement) may also have brought Stockade to the attention of the
editors of *The American Architect*, who were planning a fifty-year anniversary issue for January 1926. Benjamin T. Betts informed Fuller that "in the preparation on historical data on the development of the building industry during the
last fifty years . . . 1875 to 1925 . . . we are writing to leading companies like your
own" who manufacture construction materials.[43] The letter indicates Stockade
was well regarded within building and architectural circles less than three years
after it began marketing its system. The company submitted a small advertising
pamphlet that was reproduced in the Historical Advertising Section. Included

in this section were steel, heating equipment, and mosaic manufacturers. Participants in the Historical Advertising Section were chosen for their contributions to architecture; its theme was technology improves the building arts.[44] Stockade was included because it was an innovative method of construction; no other construction companies were showcased in the magazine's *Golden Anniversary Issue*.

One contemporary building technique whose principles were similar to Stockade's but whose purpose was very different was the Textile Block System associated with Frank Lloyd Wright. Although Wright did not invent this system, he adapted it to suit his needs.[45] Both Stockade's and Wright's methods involved precast blocks, a binding agent, and an internal system of metal rods. In both the blocks were laid in regular courses with metal bars running through them for strength and stability. Wright cast indentations along each side of his blocks to cradle the bars within their concrete bed. In contrast, the fibrous Stockade blocks were formed with holes near each end into which the reinforced concrete frame was fitted and poured. Another difference between the two systems was the way the walls were actually built. The walls in Wright's system were doubled, with an insulating space between the inner and outer wall. A metal tie-bar connects the inner and outer walls adding stability (figure 1.11). Stockade walls were solid, with the 8-inch thickness of the bricks providing insulation (figure 1.12). Wright designed the patterned textile blocks to be the exposed walls, effectively merging aesthetic expression and structure (figure 1.13). The Stockade blocks functioned to protect the structural frame and to provide neutral surfaces onto which exterior and interior finishes were applied (figure 1.14). The Stockade system was impersonal and stylistically flexible. It could be used, as were brick or timber frames, for buildings in any architectural style. The components of Wright's Textile Block System could also theoretically be used for a building in any style. Its structural elements were similar to Stockade's. Yet the potential for the Textile Block System to be adapted by other architects may have been lost because it was so strongly identified with Wright. Although

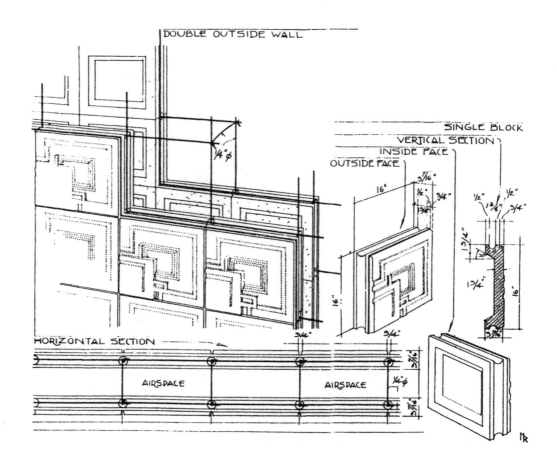

I.II

Textile Block System,
ca. 1923.

1.12

Stockade Building System, Inc., drawing of
section of stockade wall with molds cut away
to reveal reinforced concrete frame, 1926.

1.13

Frank Lloyd Wright, *John Storer House*, Hollywood, CA, 1923.

1.14

....

Stockade Building
System, Inc., *Stockade
House and House under
Construction*, ca. 1926.

the Stockade system was associated with Hewlett, it was not perceived as representing his architectural expression but as offering others with a means to realize theirs.

Those who chose to build with Stockade took advantage of its stylistic flexibility. In the 1960s, Fuller described Stockade as "good for any filler wall . . . for garages and residences or small buildings or filling in the walls of big buildings."[46] These were the primary applications of the system as period photographs illustrate. The images show buildings (figure 1.15), Stockade displays (figure 1.16), as well as houses and construction sites (figure 1.14). The buildings range from simple and utilitarian structures (figure 1.14) to cottages (figure 1.17) to multi-gabled, rambling houses (figure 1.18). When these buildings were used in advertising, the name of the architect or builder was prominently noted. Stockade was clearly communicating what its role was in the structures: it served as the frame upon which the designer's idea was crafted.

When Fuller went to Chicago in June 1926, he was extremely capable of explaining Stockade's method to prospective investors and clients. After all, he had been with the company from the beginning. One of his first tasks was to determine the most efficient manufacturing process for the blocks; then patents were filed to protect the technological discoveries. In addition to his contributions to the factory processes, Fuller had been instrumental in creating a market for Stockade in New York.

In Chicago his recent Stockade achievements and diverse background served him well as he worked to create a self-supporting subsidiary. His work may have been a little easier in a city he described as "a 'hard boiled' business section of the country [that] . . . is at the same time pretty much the center of the building and building material world"[47] than it had been in New York. Since the city was home to two significant nineteenth-century developments in construction, the balloon frame and the internal frame skeleton, Chicago architects were obviously receptive to innovations in building construction. In 1833, according to Carl Condit, "the balloon frame, a widely useful innovation in structural

1.15

Stockade Building System, Inc.,
Stockade Structure at Brookville,
Long Island, NY, ca. 1926.

1.16

Stockade Building
System, Inc.,
*Exhibition of
Stockade Wall
System*, ca. 1926.

1.17

Stockade Building
System, Inc.,
*Stockade Residence
at Joliet, IL*, ca. 1926.

1.18

Stockade Building System, Inc.,
*Stockade Residence at Lake
Wales, FL,* ca. 1926.

techniques" appeared "that was the first of Chicago's revolutionary contributions to the building arts."[48] The second important contribution was realized
in William Le Baron Jenney's Home Insurance Building, 1884–1885. Condit
champions the Home Insurance Building as coming closest to being the first
true skyscraper, with a fully developed skeletal construction.[49] Stockade, like
the balloon frame and the internal skeleton frame, was a new way to accomplish an old chore. In Chicago Fuller needed to convince a new set of investors
and builders of its usefulness.

His job was undoubtedly made easier by the positive reception Stockade
had already received. The company attracted a lot of publicity. Its inclusion
in *The American Architect: Golden Anniversary Issue* was impressive. Stockade
was also included a 1926 issue of *Scientific American* as part of a "review of the
newest developments in science, industry and engineering."[50] A very brief article, "Lower-Cost Houses Coming," in *Babson's Reports*, heralded the system as
a promising method of cutting construction costs, but failed to mention the
name of the company.[51] Publicity focused on the quality of the product that
was complemented by the fact the parent company looked like a solid investment. In three and a half years, Stockade licensed four subsidiaries and built
three factories. On paper it appeared financially stable with its liabilities equal
to its assets.[52] Correspondence between Fuller and Sam Hoffmann, general
manager of the Manhattan office, tells a different story. Their letters are primarily concerned with chronic money shortages, imminent plant closings, and
hopeful prospects of new clients. None of this information was presented to
the Chicago audience. Fuller could and did use potential sales as part of his
sales technique. He also knew utilizing Stockade's established reputation in
combination with its rapid growth was a winning strategy — one he used exceptionally well in Chicago.

Fuller immediately began to push the product and establish contacts in Chicago. His diligence was quickly rewarded: by August the subscriptions necessary
to fund the midwestern branch were sold. Hoffman sent Fuller congratulations

for his success in the middle of the month, although he deferred to Fuller's request to keep the information confidential.[53] The secret was out before too long. Fuller's brother, Wolcott, a Stockade investor and employee, sent his congratulations four days later.[54] The rapid pace continued. In early September official notice was given at a SBS board meeting in New York that Fuller had closed a contract with a group of Chicago investors. There was a slight deviation in the contract because only 25 percent of the Chicago subsidiary's stock was available to the parent company, not the customary 30 percent.[55] The notes do not reveal how the alteration was negotiated. But the terms were settled and the first meeting of the Stockade Midwest Corporation was on October 7, 1926.[56] It took Fuller less than five months in Chicago to recruit investors, negotiate a contract, organize the company, and incorporate it.

Fuller was also quick to sell the Stockade method of construction. By November 16, Stockade houses were built and inhabited in Lisle, a Chicago suburb. Two solicited testimonials show the owners were content with their new homes. Mr. and Mrs. A. C. Strong wrote simply, "[W]e are pleased with our home built of Stockade."[57] William Otterley praised his new house: "In reply to your inquiry regarding the Stockade house purchased from A. T. McIntosh Company, I take pleasure in answering it is proving much better than I anticipated at the time of purchase. This house is unquestionably the warmest house I have ever lived in and it is the only house, (excepting sod houses in the West) that the wind does not cause to crack during a hard storm."[58] These houses were built with blocks manufactured on the East Coast since the Joliet factory would not be operational until the following March.[59] Fuller had no reason to wait until local production was under way to sell the system to Chicago homeowners, architects, builders, and developers. Built homes were free advertising; the sooner they were standing, the sooner he could use them to his advantage.

The ability to use blocks made at other facilities did not deter Fuller from setting up his own factory. Just five months after the incorporation of Stockade Midwest, the Joliet plant was fully operational. Its first month's production

(March 1927) was 31,000 blocks, of which 5,483 were sold. In the following month, 44,063 were made and 15,126 sold.[60] Fuller was now in a position to develop the Chicago territory without dependence upon the eastern factories.

Manufacturing his own blocks did not mean compromising quality. It may have meant improving it. The frustrations involved in organizing the Joliet plant must have been eased by his previous experiences with Stockade and at the cotton mill in Sherbrooke. He could use his experience to figure out how to produce quality blocks with fewer growing pains. Fuller wrote to Mac in early 1928 that his production was higher and the blocks were of better quality than those produced at other factories.[61] It is not possible to corroborate Fuller's claims, but the swift growth and financial success of the new subsidiary suggests the Midwest division was at least able to meet, if not surpass, its clients' expectations.

Building on the foundation laid by the parent company and its four eastern subsidiaries, Fuller was able to achieve rapid success in Chicago. Through hard work and determination, he turned a new franchise of a relatively young company into a profitable enterprise. By November 1927, as he matter-of-factly informed Mac, Stockade Midwest made $1,000 net and sales were starting to exceed production.[62] The annual audit showed the Stockade Midwest Corporation was on solid ground with assets of $57,177.58.[63] Thus, when his very pregnant wife, Anne, left Long Island with him for Chicago on August 7, Fuller expected that his hard work had built the foundation for a secure future.

2

CORPORATE RESTRUCTURING

When Fuller went to Chicago as the sole representative of SBS, he was its president and fully supported by its board of directors. Although he was in regular contact with the New York office, the physical separation between the company's president and its office created difficulties and delays in day-to-day operations. For example, Fuller's signature was required on all checks and payments. Sam Hoffman sent checks to Fuller in Chicago for endorsement and then made payments after the signed checks were returned. Hoffman also sent Fuller reports on bank balances, sales, and administrative issues for comment, sometimes two or three times a day on the Twentieth Century Limited train. Fuller was usually dilatory in replying and Hoffman repeatedly reminded him of his obligations. Fuller may not have been as reliable as Hoffman preferred, but he did oblige the general manager by sending comments, directions, and progress reports at his own pace.[1] Fuller's accounts of his activities were not overly specific, which may have signaled concern for the SBS board.

Fuller also did not completely disclose to the board what tactics he used to organize Stockade Midwest so quickly. He neglected to secure its consent before closing the deal to incorporate the subsidiary. This may have been particularly distressing to board members because it decreased their potential earnings. He informed them the parent company was given 25 percent of the division's stock options, not the usual 30 percent, when he informed them the Chicago branch was incorporated.

As president of both the parent company and the new subsidiary, Fuller may have felt it unnecessary to keep the board informed of the individual steps leading to the latter's incorporation. This may have been especially so when he needed to make some adjustments to make the venture more attractive to midwestern investors. Although nothing in Fuller's papers explains his motives, it is easy to imagine he thought of Stockade as his company and the Midwest branch as his project. Therefore, he may have felt a sense of proprietorship that fueled an independence the New York Board found threatening.

Just twelve days after the first board meeting of Stockade Midwest in October 1926, DeCoursey Fales, an SBS board member, sent Fuller a note expressing his unhappiness with Fuller's methods and lack of communication: "I wish to impress upon you the seriousness of your following out to the letter your uniform contract; and I think you ought to let your Board know what you are doing."[2] The reprimand touched a nerve. Right before the next SBS board meeting, Fuller nervously wrote to Sam Hoffman that he did not want to make any mistakes; he needed the board's support. He mentions neither specific errors nor Fales's cautionary note.[3] The reminder about his accountability may have been strong enough to make Fuller realize that even though he was by himself in Chicago, he still answered to the parent company.

He may have worried that any dissatisfaction with him would surface at the meeting and reinforce Farley Hopkins's opinion of him. Hopkins, a Chicago businessman with significant investment in SBS and Stockade Midwest, was negative toward Fuller — in general, as president of SBS, and as president of Stockade Midwest. In November Hopkins purchased 250 shares of SBS to gain the controlling interest.[4] Before this Hopkins was a minor shareholder in Stockade Midwest, but his relationship with the parent company is unclear. He obviously considered SBS a solid company and a sound investment since he invested a lot of money and energy in it.[5] He probably began to take over the parent company in September when financial pressures compelled Hewlett to liquidate some of his Stockade holdings.

At that time Hewlett informed Fuller he intended to either sell some Stockade shares or use them for collateral against a loan:

> *I find myself in need of about $5000.00 more but am exceedingly anxious to avoid selling any more Stockade stock except possibly an odd ten shares out of the 100 share lot that I originally spoke of selling. I thought perhaps somebody out there would be interested in buying this ten shares and at the*

same time loaning me the $5000.00 for one year upon the security of 100
shares. If it should prove necessary to let any more of my stock go, I should
like it to get into the hands of someone who would back you up, so that is
the reason why I am suggesting that you find someone out in Chicago that
would take up a proposition of this kind.[6]

Hewlett's correspondence suggests a tough financial situation, and later in the same day he sent a more anxious telegram suggesting that he sell only fifty shares if the first idea was impractical.[7] Hewlett's letter indicates he previously sold stock and was now reluctant to sell more than necessary. He was also concerned about ensuring continued support for his son-in-law, perhaps another indication that the New York board was disgruntled with Fuller. Hewlett initially held the controlling interest in Stockade,[8] and his reluctance to sell stock at this time may indicate he was worried that relinquishing control could jeopardize Fuller's relationship to the company. The rapidly delivered alternative proposal, on the other hand, reveals that Hewlett's financial needs outweighed his concern about selling too much stock.

There is no record of how much stock, if any, Hewlett sold that September and who might have purchased it. The following sequence of events, however, make Hopkins the best candidate. If he did acquire between fifty and a hundred shares from Hewlett during the latter's financial crunch, the new purchase positioned him to take over SBS at the November meeting when he bought 250 shares to become the major stockholder.

Once in control Hopkins immediately began to reorganize SBS. One element of his restructuring was to elect his associates officers of the board. Hoffman wrote to Fuller in early January 1927 that his expense check was delayed because the new treasurer had not yet assumed his duties. Robert McAllister Lloyd, the original treasurer, had not resigned, which prevented E. B. Millar from taking over.[9] Not surprisingly, Hopkins's plans for reorganization also called for a new company president: himself.

Although it makes perfect sense that Hopkins would want to be president of a company he controlled, the appearance of Fuller's February 10, 1927, resignation letter is surprising. There is nothing in the records leading up to it and no indication beyond Fales's and Fuller's letters indicating problems between Fuller and the board. Yet, if his resignation letter is an accurate gauge, the board was extremely dissatisfied with him: "Being informed that it is desired by its Board of Directors, and deemed necessary to the welfare and success of the Company that I take the following action, I herewith tender my resignation as President of the Stockade Building System, Inc., to take effect immediately."[10] If Fuller was as detrimental to the company as his letter implies, it is curious he was still employed by Stockade after he relinquishing his position as president.

Fuller continued as president of Stockade Midwest and remained on the board of the parent company. He continued to work for SBS in an administrative capacity. On the day he resigned, Fuller wrote many letters dealing with various aspects of the business. In addition, six days later he reassured a concerned business associate, William McCarty: "You undoubtedly were surprised and upset at the apparent change of command. It is in line with what you, Bill Hull and I discussed upon our last meeting. Do not let it discourage you or allow it to diminish any of your faith in Stockade."[11] Fuller also gave a laudatory radio talk on a Chicago station about Stockade in the following month.[12] These actions demonstrate that despite his reduced status, Fuller's commitment to Stockade was not diminished.

Fuller, however, at some point jeopardized Stockade's commitment to him. There is no record of what happened or indication of whether it occurred before or after Fuller submitted his resignation as president. Perhaps in reference to Fuller's resignation, an unknown event, or both, Andy King, Fuller's cousin and a business associate, sent a telegram advising: "Taylor and I wish you success . . . Keep your temper, your head and your confidence."[13] Hoffman was a bit more direct when he suggested: "[I]n the meantime you have been able to straighten out the matter so as to give you, at least, some additional time."[14]

Hoffman's letter does not state what Fuller's misstep was, but it is clear the former SBS president committed some compromising error. The most persuasive evidence that Fuller brought about his problems with the parent company is a handwritten letter from Hewlett:

> *I think you realize how slow I should be to attribute to you any but honorable intentions but I don't think you realize how impossible it is to get along with one's friends and business associates on any basis but one of perfect truth and frankness and you have in your anxiety to help forward perfectly proper accomplishment been too ready to adopt what must seem to anyone on the outside as tricky methods. My acquaintance with Farley Hopkins is as you know very slight. My impression is that he intends to do the decent thing by you and all of us, but if that should not be the case it would be most unfortunate that after putting all the enthusiasm and good work that you have into Stockade you should be the means of justifying outside attack.*[15]

The correspondence hints at an act much worse than unauthorized alteration of a standard business contract. It also implies a more damaging offense than the exaggeration Frances Freeman, a secretary, mentioned in a note about the tense working conditions in the reorganized New York office. According to her, Mr. Reid, the new office manager, was small-minded, uncongenial, and contemptible. She was fired because Reid noticed "that all my loyalty and cooperation seemed to be directed to you and to Mr. Hoffman; that whenever he dictated a letter to you I seemed to look to Mr. Hoffman for approval, and that when he tried to insinuate about your making misstatements or overstatements, I was always ready to defend you."[16] Freeman provides the only specific evidence of Fuller's wrongdoing and it is in accord with Hewlett's admonition about his son-in-law's overenthusiasm. Overenthusiasm, even continuous, hardly seems a cardinal offense. Perhaps to a petty and hostile management, the combination of overenthusiasm, poor communication, and creative negotiations justified Fuller's resignation to Hopkins's new board.

Fuller was next pushed to sever his ties to the parent company. Almost a month after stepping down, he wrote to Fales, the critical former board member: "As you know or may not know Mr. Hopkins has succeeded me as President of the Stockade Building System, and I am confining my efforts to the Chicago Corporation."[17] Fuller offered no explanation, but in a July letter to O. A. Rasin he described the development of his new relationship to Stockade:

> *You probably do not know that I am no longer connected with the Stockade Building System, but am with its new subsidiary the Stockade Midwest Corporation, and am in no way able to effect any adjustments for the Stockade Building System, as control of this company has passed into the hands of Mr. Farley Hopkins, a man from Chicago who put up a considerable amount of money and reorganized the Stockade Building System. . . . All our earlier plans . . . were . . . not considered, as it is the privilege of capital to dictate its own terms, where a weak concern accepts its aid. I have but a comparatively small amount of interest left in the Stockade Building System, and all my stock represents actual cash at par value.*[18]

Except for noting the rejection of previous plans and the privilege of capital, Fuller was blandly professional. He shed no light on his relationship with Hopkins or about his own contribution to his weakened position within the Stockade hierarchy.

In October 1927, just one month short of a year after becoming Stockade's major shareholder, Hopkins created a new corporation named Stockade Structures, Inc. This new company, of which Hopkins was president, absorbed the parent company and the subsidiaries. The minutes of a special Stockade Midwest board meeting describe complete support of Hopkins's plan:

At this meeting a proposition of Mr. Farley Hopkins, President of the Parent
Company, was unanimously recommended for acceptance by the stockhold-
ers. The general substance of this proposition . . . was to exchange our stock,
share for share, to the extent of the capital put in our company for stock
in a new national company including the Parent Company and the other
subsidiaries, into which company he had proposed to subscribe $200,000.
in cash.[19]

With this move Hopkins gained complete control of Stockade and could operate the company according to his own terms.

The terms must have included Fuller's dismissal as president of Stockade
Midwest as well as the termination of his employment. Nothing in Fuller's papers offers any hint about this major restructuring. Like the sudden appearance
of his resignation as president of the parent company, Fuller's ousting from
Stockade Midwest is surprising. He was blindsided as he wrote to Mac: "I was
fighting pretty much of a lone hand and so busy trying to prove my point that
it could be made a paying business that I was unaware of (and would have had
no time had I known of it) the plans going on outside and the first thing I knew
I was forced out, of all management. That this was a shock and almost heart
breaking you may well imagine."[20] Fuller lost this battle in November 1927, just
three months after his wife joined him in Chicago, but the war involving him,
Stockade, and Hopkins was not yet over.

This war had personal as well as professional components:

Stockade . . . really looked good for the first time in 5 years. So that was the
stratigical [sic] time for the big grab and <u>Nothing</u> *was allowed to stand in*
the way of the grab. . . . Graduating from a hand nursed business to an im-
personal project there are a number of changes that will have to take place,
but I believe that all hands will come out alright. The thing that hurt most

was false statements to undermine me. It was very unnecessary as shown
a proper reason I would always concede for the good of my backers. Some
people just can't credit anyone with altruism.[21]

The false statements are not explained, although they may have referred to his work with a Stockade coworker, Martin Chamberlain, on a patent as discussed later. And, even though Fuller was no longer employed by Stockade, Hopkins's personal attacks continued. Anne's diary entries in late November discuss Hopkins's maltreatment of her husband. She recorded on the 21st that "Bucky saw Geo. Cross. They can not [*sic*] make out why Farley is so keen to get Bucky out of Chicago."[22] Two days later, she noted a more hostile Hopkins: "Bucky . . . ran into Farley at Tomlinson's — as usual most disagreeable. . . . Bucky spoke to Marti [Chamberlain] who is getting sick of Farley's cussing out Bucky. Farley told him not to let RBF in plant."[23] Many of Fuller's business associates understood the personal nature of these attacks.

A few of these associates, George Cross, Henry Tomlinson, and Chamberlain, helped him secure contacts for his new job as a flooring salesman for the F. R. Muller Co. of Waukegan. They also worked with Fuller on the development of his new project, Fuller Houses. Fuller Houses appears in the diary as a completely formulated idea; Fuller must have been working on it while at Stockade. It is first mentioned on November 22 when Anne wrote that "Bucky . . . saw Ingratiane . . . and talked about 'Fuller Houses.'"[24] Numerous diary entries note that Fuller would often pitch Fuller Houses while making business calls for Muller. This may have been similar to the dual or conflicting interests that got him into trouble at Stockade. In an uncanny recreation of the organization of Stockade Midwest when he was on his own in Chicago reporting to an office in New York, Fuller's sales territory was in Chicago and the Muller office was in Waukegan.

Although W. R. Smythe wondered if Fuller would be satisfied selling Muller flooring, he offered Fuller a job at $50.00 per week, with a commission of 1¢ per foot on all footage over 100,000 feet (figure 2.1).[25] The job may have seemed like a step backward to his Armour and Kelly-Springfield days, yet Fuller was happy to accept it. He was especially relieved that it was less demanding than his work at Stockade. Fuller welcomed the respite and the added benefit of maintaining his network within architectural circles: "[T]he job which I have taken representing a very fine and reliable old firm in the flooring business here in Chicago on a salary and commission business has the double advantage of keeping me amongst the architects etc, as well as providing a living and a great rest from the terrible responsibility that I have felt without any chance of relief for the last five years."[26] Besides, his only other prospect was a position with the Celotex Corporation, a Stockade competitor, which never materialized.[27] As Fuller explained, he accepted the Muller job since it met his immediate needs: "I had to keep my family going and I had established some status in the building trade out here and therefore started in on the first thing that offered in the building line, while making plans for my own next move."[28] The Muller job was not glamorous and did not pay exceptionally well, but it gave Fuller the opportunity to support his family without having to divert too much attention away from his more important project, Fuller Houses.

It seems safe to surmise that Fuller's salary, including commissions, at Muller was less than what he earned at Stockade. There is no exact figure given in his personal papers for his Stockade salary. He later claimed he earned $50 a week at Stockade, but this may have been a conflation of what his various other jobs had paid him. It seems doubtful that the president of one company would earn the same weekly salary as the salesman of another. Even if there were no reduction in his income, Fuller was experiencing a financial pinch. He was feeling a little insecure because, as he confided to Mac: "I am afraid I have taken an awful financial trimming for the time being as I am owed a great deal of money and stock."[29] In response to their financial situation, the Fuller family reduced its expenses in January 1928.

2.1
....

Letter from W. R.
Smythe, F. R. Muller
Co., Inc., Waukegan,
IL, to RBF, Chicago, IL,
November 22, 1927.

ESTABLISHED 1908

FRANKLYN R. MULLER, Inc.

MAIN OFFICE AND FACTORY
WAUKEGAN   ILLINOIS

SBESTONE EVERLASTING STUCCO
SBESTONE MAGNESITE TERRAZZO
SBESTONE MAGNESITE FLOORING

MULLER
ASBESTONE
GUARANTEED PRODUCTS
TRADE MARK

TELEPHONE WAUKEGAN
PRIVATE EXCHANGE TEN

November 22nd, 1927.

Mr. R.B.Fuller,
Room 824,
Hotel Virginia,
Chicago, Illinois.

Dear Mr. Fuller:

      Referring to our conversation a few days ago, I
am rather inclined to believe that you are the type of man I
want.

      The only doubt in my mind is as to whether our
type of business will appeal to you. However, if you care to
try it out, we are willing to try you out on a salary of $50.00
per week, with a commission of 1¢ per foot on all footage
secured by you above, 100,000 feet.

      You would primarily be representing us in Chicago
and district, with Waukegan as head-quarters, but you, of
course, understand whenever and wherever it might be desirable
to give you the opportunity to secure some real worth-while
business in other parts of the country, we would expect you to
make trips and we in turn would pay your expenses.

      If this proposition appeals to you, I would
appreciate your ringing me up tomorrow, so that we can arrange
an appointment for an interview.

      Very truly yours,

      FRANKLYN R. MULLER, INC

WRS:AB.

When Anne joined Fuller in Chicago, they lived in number 922 of the Virginia Hotel at the corner of Rush and Ohio Streets in the near north side of Chicago, close to the Loop, Chicago's business district. At some point they moved into room 823. Anne provided a brief description of their lodgings (which could be of either room) and neighborhood in a mid-September letter to her father: "I'm back at the hotel now and everything is awfully nice and comfortable in spite of the terrific heat (96°). It's the first warm weather we've had and if it had to come this is the best time as our rooms here are way up looking toward the Lake. . . . It's so beautifully kept up in this section and everyone seems to be working so hard to make it more beautiful and efficient and finer in every way."[30] The Virginia Hotel also looked onto the recently completed Tribune Tower, which Anne drew from one of their windows (figure 2.2).

The Virginia was an apartment hotel offering the convenience of private quarters combined with modified butler services, somewhat like a Manhattan doorman building in the early twenty-first century. Among the benefits of apartment hotel living were a sense of security, screened guests, access to a handyman, furnishings, utilities, package handling, and telephone usage for a weekly or monthly fee. This type of accommodation was acceptable to Anne and Fuller, both of whom belonged to the upper echelons of East Coast society and were listed in the New York Social Register.[31] Anne first suggested the possibility while preparing to move to Chicago. About a month later, she agreed with Fuller's idea of staying in his hotel: "I think your idea about living at the Virginia is the best too. During the hot weather and all we wouldn't want to struggle over getting settled and cooking etc."[32] Anne may have been encouraged by her mother-in-law who lived in an apartment hotel. Hatch reported that Fuller's mother lived in a Manhattan apartment hotel on East 31st Street in 1915 where he stayed with her when he first began working at Armour.[33] Thirteen years later Fuller noted in his holiday letter to Uncle Waldo that his mother and younger sister were "living this winter at 995 Fifth Avenue, New York City, an apartment hotel."[34] The Virginia Hotel may not have been of the same caliber

2.2
....
Anne Hewlett Fuller,
Tribune Tower, 1927.

2.3

Allegra taking her first
steps in Lincoln Park,
Chicago, 1928.

as 995 Fifth Avenue, but on Fuller's $50 a week salary it was too costly for them to stay there.[35]

In a late November diary entry, Anne noted they needed to move to a less expensive place. A few days later the owner of the Virginia told Fuller about the Lake View Hotel as they discussed his bill. The Fullers immediately moved into the Lake View even though Anne lamented, "[I]t is a cheap, tiny place but clean so I think we can stand it for the sake of getting straightened out financially."[36] Three days later her attitude toward the new hotel improved a little when they moved into a sunnier room.

The Lake View, at 739 Belmont Avenue in the Lakeview District, was a new elevator building, completed in 1927. It was of fireproof construction, with brick walls and reinforced concrete frame, floors, and roof.[37] The neighborhood was zoned for apartments and businesses, with some industrial development to the south. To the east Belmont Avenue led directly to Lake Michigan and Lincoln Park. When the Fullers lived there, it was a fashionable, prosperous neighborhood. The Lake View was not as prestigious as his mother's building in Manhattan, but it was well situated with nearby shopping, movie theaters, a park, and a zoo[38] for outings with the baby (figure 2.3). It was also close enough to the Loop to allow Fuller to walk to work.

Like his contributions to his problems at Stockade, this is new information about Fuller's situation immediately after he left the company. The Muller job and a decent apartment in a respectable neighborhood are additions to his standard accounting of this period. Fuller considered adding the Muller job to the official version of his life story, but decided against it.[39] According to Fuller's official biography, after leaving Stockade he was broke, out of work, and forced to move his family into a tenement in a slum neighborhood on Chicago's North Side.[40] The documents reveal, however, Fuller was employed, even if his family may have found it difficult to live on his salary. In addition, the Lake View Hotel was not a tenement in a slum, but a new apartment hotel in a fashionable neighborhood. In 1939, before his life's story was codified, Fuller described this residence as "a small, clean, safe place . . . a one-room flat in a new fire-proof apartment building at Clark and Belmont, at $22 a month."[41] The notes for Hamilton's biography show that Fuller considered characterizing this apartment as "a one-room flat in a new fireproof apartment building,"[42] with no mention of the neighborhood. In his biography of Fuller, Hatch described their apartment as "one fair-sized room, with a sort of cubicle. . . . There was a small window in this storage space, so they fixed it up for Allegra. There was also an alcove with a stove and sink where Anne did the cooking."[43] In keeping with the established story of Fuller's life, Hatch portrayed the neighborhood as a slum. Fuller and his biographers misrepresented these facts because it allowed Fuller to misrepresent the beginnings of Fuller Houses, the project that ultimately became the Dymaxion House. As disclosed by the records but not his official biography, Fuller was already working on Fuller Houses in November 1927, when he was living in the Virginia Hotel and not yet employed by Muller.

Fuller worked diligently for his new employer even though he was more interested in his own projects than Muller flooring (figure 2.4). Fuller Houses was his most important new enterprise, although he explored other ideas. For example, "[a]fter much philosophical thought while walking about worked out theory of spheres" in early 1928.[44] He also contemplated patenting a cement mixer and a parking wheel, neither of which is described in the diary. He visited the annual automobile shows in January to see if any of the cars had a parking wheel like the one he devised; they did not. He must have discovered that another application for parking wheels existed because he abandoned this idea. He did, however, assist Chamberlain, a Stockade colleague, on a patent for an unknown type of wall system.

Chamberlain was employed by Stockade and, after Fuller was forced out, complained: "I will have to spend more time in Chicago now that you are away from the company, and I suppose they will run me ragged."[45] Fuller, despite Hopkins's wishes, did not disassociate himself from Stockade employees and projects. He continued to visit the Joliet factory, see former coworkers, and, as

STUCCO OF QUALITY

ASBESTONE

FRANKLYN R. MULLER, Inc.
Stucco and Flooring Manufacturers
Established 1906   WAUKEGAN, ILLINOIS
DISTRIBUTORS

2.4

F. R. Muller, Inc.,
Asbestone Catalogue,
ca. 1927.

late as January 1928, inspected a Stockade house under construction in Milwau-
kee. Whether surreptitiously or openly, Fuller remained involved with Stockade
until the discovery of his work on Chamberlain's patents and its conflict with
his legal obligations to the company.

Exactly when Fuller began to assist Chamberlain is unknown. The first reference to their collaboration is in November 1927. Chamberlain's name pops up
occasionally, and Fuller more or less kept him informed of his activities. Anne
recorded on November 23 that Chamberlain "was wild about the thought of
Celotex taking R.B.F. on very interested to know about RBF's 'Fuller Houses'
plan."[46] In late January there was a brief flurry of activity with Chamberlain.
Fuller met him in the Hotel La Salle where they "discussed patents and Stockade happenings. RBF advised MTC patenting new wall system."[47] Fuller's attitude toward Chamberlain soured within a month of that meeting: "M. T.
Chamberlain called to say he had finished Stockade & wanted RBF to meet him
at patent room of Library. RBF declined account cold. RBF does not want to
make further business deals with him."[48] The implication is that Chamberlain
willingly resigned from Stockade, although controversy about the patents was
the probable cause.

Developing new patents for products that could compete with Stockade's
constituted a conflict of interest for Chamberlain as a Stockade employee.
Fuller may not have considered his involvement with Chamberlain a conflict
since he was no longer employed by the company. Fuller, however, owned shares
in Stockade. Therefore, the company's board, including Hewlett, found his
work on Chamberlain's patents unacceptable.

Fuller worked with Chamberlain on at least two patents that conflicted with
Stockade's interests. One was the aforementioned, but undefined, new wall
system. The application for the other patent was included in a letter to Fuller.
Chamberlain described the device as "our joint invention covering the processes
and devices for mixing fibrous material and a binder cement"[49] into blocks for

constructing walls. This was suspiciously similar to producing blocks much like Stockade's by utilizing a method of manufacture much like Stockade's.

Although Fuller no longer worked for Stockade when Chamberlain sent him the application, they were both employed by the company when the potential patent was written. Chamberlain requested that Fuller "please attend to this at once and not delay it as you did before."[50] Out of naïveté or indifference, Chamberlain also instructed Fuller to immediately have the Stockade Midwest secretary verify their signatures: "I have signed one copy of each and will ask that you get in touch at once with Miss Feeney and have her acknowledge yours and mine, she of course knowing my signature. Keep the blank copy if you desire to and return the signed copy to me and I will get it into the hands of the patent attorney by next mail so there will be no further delays."[51] Chamberlain was in a hurry and may not have been thinking clearly when he directed Fuller to involve Miss Feeney because he "was informed yesterday that all employees of the company will have to sign an agreement to turn over all inventions to the company. This of course applies to future inventions applied for after the date of signing the agreement."[52] The patent for their joint invention was not filed, although nothing in Fuller's papers explains why. Fuller may have again hesitated to sign it or he may not have wanted to take it into the company's office, an undoubtedly hostile environment. It could have been signed and forwarded to Miss Feeney in the Stockade office where it was intercepted. The latter case is unlikely since Chamberlain continued to work at Stockade until the following February when hints of Fuller's legal problems appeared in the diary.

In October 1928, when Chamberlain and Fuller were no longer associated with Stockade, Chamberlain alluded to the problematic nature of their patent work. When he praised Fuller's patent application for the 4D House, Chamberlain remarked: "[T]his will be one patent which there will be no controversy about."[53] Fuller's willingness to assist Chamberlain in the development of one or both of his patents was controversial. Earlier in the year, Fuller was in very serious trouble because of it.

There are clues suggesting a conflict with Stockade and direct evidence confirming Fuller's complicity in his own problems. The first indication of trouble appeared in the diary on February 20, 1928, when Fuller recorded that Mr. Sweet, his patent lawyer, suggested he "at once place my Stockade matters in the hands of the best attorneys possible."[54] A couple of weeks later, Anne wrote that her husband "[c]alled on Lawyers Messrs. Tenney Harding Sherman & Rogers . . . discussed Stockade settlement."[55] On March 17, Fuller made the first of four diary entries regarding "serious trouble with Stockade."[56] The issue was resolved five days later when he "signed agreement with Hopkins relieving each other of all claims."[57] In the meantime, Fuller had some explaining to do and some ruffled feathers to smooth.

On March 18, Fuller sent an explanatory telegram about his new problems with Stockade to Hewlett:

> *Hopkins attorney advises former wrote you Saturday garbled facts serious accusation are not true but he has story which can hurt me terribly is willing to call off if I pay them money have some on hand and expect raise balance in time this seems only thing do stop not matter justice for moment but preservation decency you may have perfect faith me as have done nothing wrong and may count on my not letting it go further stop Hopkins attorney acknowledges I have done nothing wrong but am caught technically and advises settle quickly account Hopkins hatred of me.*[58]

Hewlett was not placated and his reply the following day was critical:

> *I received Hopkins' letter and your telegram and have talked with Hoffman. Your telegram is not at all a satisfactory explanation of the situation into which you have gotten yourself. Hoffman is certainly a good friend of yours and it seems perfectly evident to me that you have not merely done*

something absolutely improper but you have put him in the position of hav-

ing his loyalty to you endanger his position with Hopkins. If you need help

in straightening this matter out, (as far as it can be straightened out) let me

know and I will do what I can. . . . You should also write to me telling me

exactly what the situation is between you and Chamberlain in regard to

any patent rights having to do with Stockade or clips.[59]

Fuller assured his father-in-law the situation was resolved and assumed complete responsibility for his actions:

Any agreements between Chamberlain and myself are terminated. We have

no patents. I believe he has taken out patents, what they are I do not know,

he was never informative and I do not have any interest in them . . . I

merely know that I did something wrong, ill advisedly, but not morally

wrong. I feel frightfully about the many mistakes I have made. We have

been made to pay dearly for my mistakes.[60]

A week later, Hewlett's follow-up note was calmer and his attitude toward Fuller softer: "What annoyed me was that in letting that matter drift along you were stupidly encouraging F. H. to think and say that all that he inferred . . . was justified. . . . All I intended to infer was my impatience at you apparently supplying further ammunition to Hopkins which he might use against you."[61] Fuller managed to work through the problems resulting from his work on Chamberlain's patents with his father-in-law.

Hewlett was also concerned about how Fuller's actions might negatively affect others, especially Sam Hoffman. Hewlett expressed concern that Hoffman, who by this time was vice-president, might be compromised by his relationship to Fuller. Fuller was confused about Hoffman's participation and promised to exonerate him: "That Sam Hoffman is so loyal a friend . . . I appreciate. . . . I feel extremely sorry if I have put him in a bad position, I don't see how + why he is involved though as he was certainly not responsible for anything I have done. I will see Taber [Hopkins's lawyer] about it today and see that Hopkins realize it."[62] Fuller also apologized to Hoffman who reassured him: "Glad to note that the matter has been cleared up, and please don't worry about my getting in wrong with Hopkins over this. . . . For God's sake, Buck, keep out of jams from now on and if you do get into a hole don't keep it under cover for someone else to dig it up. Circumstantial evidence has ruined lots of people."[63] Hoffman was compassionate as he warned Fuller to be careful.

The warning arrived too late as the evidence of Fuller's wrongdoing, whether circumstantial or concrete, had already gotten him into serious trouble. On March 29, 1928, Fuller and Hopkins signed an agreement releasing each other of all claims, except for those regarding patents. The terms stipulated that each pay the other one dollar. In addition:

> *The Stockade Corporation hereby releases and discharges R. B. Fuller from all claims and demands (excepting those relating to inventions, patents, and licenses). . . . R. B. Fuller hereby releases and discharges The Stockade Corporation . . . from any and all claims and demands which he has against all or any of said companies. This release shall not be held to change or diminish any obligations of R. B. Fuller to The Stockade Corporation, its successors and assignees, with respect to inventions, United States Letters of Patent, licenses under United States Letters of Patent, and in the execution of papers and documents with respect to the prosecution of applications for United States Letters of Patent.*[64]

The agreement required Stockade to keep control of the patents and inventions Fuller developed for the company. The problem resulting from his work with

Chamberlain arose because Stockade either felt threatened by the potential patents or thought the company should own them.

The clause concerning patents and inventions must have referred to only those related to Stockade products. Fuller was granted many patents for later inventions, and there is no record of Stockade filing for rights against these. By the time the legal agreement was signed, Fuller had initiated patent proceedings on Fuller Houses. He obviously did not believe his problems with Stockade extended beyond the company's processes and products, a sentiment echoed by Chamberlain. Nothing in Fuller's papers indicates Stockade attempted to further exert any of the powers given to it by the legal agreement.

The agreement implies that Fuller surrendered some of his Stockade shares. Fuller's diary entries from this period also discuss the Stockade agreement, and Dave Taber, Hopkins's lawyer, told him Hopkins would accept stock in lieu of monetary payment.[65] The diary entries and legal agreement are in accord with Fuller's comment to Hewlett about having to pay dearly for his mistakes. This did not deplete Fuller's holdings of Stockade shares, nor did his association with the company end. In January 1929 he received notice from the current treasurer, his cousin Andy King: "We expect to get the final papers of dissolution of The Stockade Building System, Inc. very shortly. Will you kindly forward to this office your certificates of stock in that Corporation and we will return to you by registered mail your shares of stock in the Stockade Corporation. The basis of exchange is eight shares of Stockade Corporation stock for one share of Stockade Building System, Inc. stock."[66] The following month King asked Fuller to sign and return a proxy for the annual stockholders meeting, which he must have done because the form is missing. Fuller also sent in a certificate for 40 shares of the Stockade Building System requesting that they be reissued as 320 shares of The Stockade Corporation. Of these, 136 were to be in the name of his brother Wolcott and 184 in the name of Olive Cross, George Cross's wife.[67] Fuller still owned stock in the newly reorganized company even though he was no longer actively participating in its affairs.

Fuller was responsible for many of his problems with Stockade, but Hopkins's antagonistic attitude toward him exacerbated them. If the hostility Hopkins felt toward Fuller was as strong as Fuller's papers suggest, it is surprising that Fuller was not more cautious. It is unfortunate that Hopkins's papers have not been located as they would provide a different view of Fuller's problems with Stockade.

There is no mention of Hopkins or of the legal agreement in any of the published accounts of Fuller's problems with Stockade. Fuller may have alluded to the patent agreement or to being pushed out of the company when he wrote to George Buffington about "another enterprise, of which I lost control, in the bosom of an ethics fog"[68] while trying to convince Buffington to invest in the 4D House. It is impossible to determine to what he was specifically referring; it could have been the legal agreement, the hostile takeover of Stockade, or something else.

Fuller partially outlined the sequence of events in his letter to Mac:

> At a special meeting of the board of directors it was set forth that . . . if . . . additional territory could be secured from the parent company or other compensation . . . committee was appointed to negotiate with the parent co, which I was not on, due to the fact that Wayne Taylor and myself could not negotiate with Hopkins without a fight or disagreement, and from that time on politics ensued and I cannot tell you in a brief manner all that transpired except that I am now out and Hopkins is running things with my cousin Andy King and that they may make a go of it and that they will certainly try darned hard for Hopkins has a lot of money in it and is expecting to put in $200,000. more if necessary and that . . . should make everyone's chance of earning the better.[69]

The letter was written before the March 29 legal agreement and provides no insight into it. Other documents, especially the correspondence between Hewlett and Fuller, offer a better understanding of what gave Hopkins the power to force Fuller to sign the legal agreement.

Since Fuller readily admitted a hostile takeover forced him to resign from Stockade, it is curious that the legal agreement is omitted from his codified biography. He may have felt it unnecessary since he was no longer employed by the company when he signed it. Or, it may have too clearly revealed his problems were not always the result of his being misunderstood or abused as he and his biographers like to contend. The legal agreement and corresponding diary entries communicate how complicit Fuller could be in his own problems, an element of his personality he tended to exclude from his biography.

Characteristically, Fuller also never divulged his problems with Hopkins and the extent to which they contributed to the termination of his employment at Stockade. In the codified version of the Stockade story, he is presented as either collateral loss from the buyout or a victim of the new management. Fuller as a victim is a prevalent theme in his personal narrative. Karl Conrad first noted it in his dissertation "Buckminster Fuller and the Technocratic Persuasion" while discussing Fuller's description of the misfortunes of his youth: the death of his father on his fifteenth birthday (July 12, 1910)[70] and the high school injury that ended his hopes of a great football career. According to Conrad: "[T]he young boy as victim becomes the young man as victim; yet these are not unconventional examples of adolescent misfortune."[71] Conrad does not consider these calamities unusual nor does he discuss their potential for psychological devastation. Conrad does recognize Fuller's ability to exploit them to his best advantage by representing himself as a hapless, misunderstood casualty of events beyond his control. This is a thread Fuller further manipulated when recounting the Stockade story. In two collaborative autobiographies, *The Dymaxion World of Buckminster Fuller* (1960) and *Buckminster Fuller: An Autobiographical Monologue/Scenario* (1980), Fuller explained that when Hewlett had to sell his stock, the new management no longer required his services.[72] This is a very simplified version of the events, and Fuller did not identify the new management. Elsewhere he falsely identified the Celotex Corporation as the buyer that "voted him out of office."[73] Even though Celotex was one of Stockade's competitors, it played no part in Fuller's problems with the latter. Fuller unsuccessfully interviewed with Celotex in November 1927, but he was never employed by that company. Celotex, however, provided Fuller with a convenient veil for obscuring his own role in the loss of his Stockade job.

Another way this veil worked was to make Fuller appear as the vulnerable scapegoat of the hostile new management. One version was offered by Hatch when he explained that Fuller was fired from Stockade "with some justification, [since] the new regime did not appreciate his methods."[74] The unappreciated methods included poor business sense, out-of-tune singing in the office, and a fight about the Joliet plant. Hatch supplemented this with a quotation from Fuller: "I got pushed out . . . and the people who pushed me out were eager to be vindicated for doing so. They tried to make me out a bad man."[75] In sympathetic agreement with his subject, Hatch placed some blame on Fuller and then allowed his subject to present himself as innocently maligned.

Fuller was thus able to use his biographer to garner both sympathy for his maltreatment and criticism of those who betrayed him. He worked hard to ensure the company's success and later insisted the company had built 240 buildings before he was forced out.[76] His 1944 résumé claims he "[s]upervised 150 building operations at various points throughout the eastern half of the United States."[77] In its first five years, Stockade rapidly expanded beyond its humble beginnings and Fuller played a major role in its growth. Yet, instead of rewarding him, the new management rejected him. He complained that the new management then unjustifiably blamed him for his rejection. While Fuller's indignity at this mistreatment is understandable, it was not as unwarranted as he made it appear.

Fuller was partially responsible. The surviving documents illustrate his complicity and also show that Stockade's new president, Farley Hopkins, was hostile toward him. Fuller's actions, as Hewlett noted, often provided ammunition for Hopkins to use against him. Fuller's work on the patents with Chamberlain made him look like a "bad man," no matter how naïve his involvement may have been. There was no need for Hopkins and the new Stockade management to fabricate any justification for firing Fuller. Even if he later glossed over the sequence of events, he helped set them in motion.

But misrepresenting what happened to him at Stockade also allowed him to misrepresent the value of the experience. Fuller later claimed that he learned the folly of craft building, or using manual labor to construct individual houses, while working for the company.[78] He also credited Stockade with showing him how the financial structure of the construction industry inhibited the introduction of technological improvements.[79] These statements may well be true, yet, like his version of why he was fired from Stockade, they provide only one side of the story.

The other side of the story consists of positive lessons. Stockade taught him how to maneuver through the regulations and obstructions of the construction industry. It also taught him the wisdom of an organized plan and thought-out strategy. At Stockade, Fuller learned how to organize and operate a business from scratch. He learned how to market a new invention in an already established industry. Another valuable lesson was to take out patents on his inventions and maintain them to protect his interests. Even though Fuller never acknowledged that Stockade made these contributions to his development, they were potent lessons.

The knowledge and experience he gained at Stockade provided the background for his next project, Fuller Houses. In the development of this project, Fuller basically repeated the procedures used at Stockade. The first step was to determine a need and formulate a solution in the form of a marketable product. It was then necessary to protect one's interest and hard work with patents.

Next, a corporation to manufacture and distribute the product was needed, which required enlisting stockholders to help finance the venture. Concurrent with selling the idea to investors was to figure out how to actually manufacture the product. Once these steps were taken, it was simply a matter of marketing the product to the appropriate audience. After Stockade, Fuller was ready to follow his own footsteps to build another successful business based on his invention, Fuller Houses.

3

Fuller was positive the concept of Fuller Houses, a company to manufacture fully equipped houses, would translate into a lucrative business. The project first appeared in the diary in late November 1927. Building on this, Fuller and Anne chronicled the progress of Fuller Houses through a narrative of meetings, negotiations, sources, and confidants. This account is peppered with bits and pieces about their daily lives and complemented by other documents in Fuller's papers. Missing are discussions of the ideological foundation of the idea and the formal properties of Fuller Houses. Two essays, "Cosmopolitan Homes" and "Lightful Houses," contain the philosophical underpinnings and technical aspects of the project. Numerous sketches, a short essay "Fuller Houses," various notes, and the abandoned patent application reveal Fuller's struggle to find an appropriate formal expression for Fuller Houses. The diary discloses when the patent drawings were initiated without noting when Fuller began the project,

& volunteered help in statistics, etc."[2] Morgan was not mentioned again. Whatever potential Fuller saw in Morgan did not materialize, but the incident is indicative of Fuller's willingness to explore any possibility to help him realize Fuller Houses.

One of the tools Fuller considered useful was an office, a surprisingly ambitious goal given his $50 weekly salary from Muller. The couple did, however, have additional income. Their account at the F. M. Zeiller brokerage firm was active. Fuller purchased three shares of the Auburn Automobile Company for $128 in January 1928, which he sold in March for a ten-point gain.[3] He took advantage of the opportunity to speak about "Fuller Houses with Mr. Douglas . . . [who] said he would like to put money on it."[4] Anne and Fuller also received monetary gifts from friends and family that helped offset their expenses. According to Hatch, their financial situation was bolstered when "[o]ne or two people died and left them tiny legacies. A few old friends stopped by to pay forgotten debts."[5] Anne calculated their income as $1,153.41 with expenditures of $842.25.[6] She may have had her own money, which would have bolstered Fuller's salary. Before moving to Chicago, Anne confided to Fuller: "I guess after awhile I'll have my money which we won't use except in some great emergency."[7] With or without financial assistance from his wife, Fuller located an acceptable office space which he offered to "rent from [the Goodrich Company] for five years, commencing May the first 1928, the small office building formerly occupied by your company at the head of . . . Kinzid St. . . . for . . . $75.00 per month, to be used as a building material sales office."[8] Although Fuller rented this space, he never moved into it. He basically signed the lease and then did not honor the contract. Goodrich sent letters requesting payment and threatening to sue for noncompliance. He must have realized that he could not afford the office after he signed the lease. He may have tried to negotiate out of the contract, even though he apparently took no action to resolve the issue.[9] The office and its related problems eventually disappeared from his papers.

Another component of Fuller's life that faded away without explanation was the Muller job. He later claimed that he left the company for ethical reasons: "He worked for this firm for 3 months, but found that the time he should have been putting into the tile business he was using for thinking. His thoughts were coming too fast. As a matter of integrity, he resigned."[10] Even if he were suffering from a moral dilemma, one of his lawyers, Mr. Tenney, soundly advised him to keep his job until the new company became profitable. When he received his first Muller paycheck, Anne exclaimed Fuller was "very satisfied about his job"[11] and nothing indicates his attitude changed. He wisely used his sales position to network and test the viability of his idea. Fuller made the last direct reference to Muller in March, when he recorded that he "went to Kennedy . . . cork flooring contracts."[12] Almost two weeks later, he wrote he was offered a job offer through one of his lawyers, Mr. Harding.[13] No reason was given for this sudden interest in a new job, and no dissatisfaction with the Muller job cited. If his position at Muller had ended, it was not reported in the diary. Fuller's Muller job seems to have been a casualty of the accelerating work on Fuller Houses.

The buildup to the project's domination of Fuller's life was slow. The last diary entry, dated March 27, was written as if the chronicle would continue. The most logical conclusion is Fuller and Anne became too busy to maintain the daily record. The preparations for the patent application and the May meeting of the American Institute of Architects (AIA) must have prevented them from continuing to log the development of Fuller Houses.

Even with its abrupt end, lapses, and out-of-order entries, the diary provides a detailed accounting of how Fuller approached the project as well as with whom he worked. The genesis of Fuller Houses is not known. His idea of a factory-made, mass-produced house might have its origins in Stockade: in one sense, mass-producing an entire house is a logical step to follow mass-producing the blocks with which to build a house. Fuller might have taken the idea from contemporary trade journals or popular magazines. He could also have been influenced by the existing market in prefabricated wood-frame houses, like those sold by Sears. Whatever the origins of Fuller Houses, Fuller drew upon a variety of sources to help him solidify his version of an industrially reproduced, prefabricated dwelling.

His research included automobile shows, a food packers' exhibition, advertisements, boating magazines, as well as architectural and building trade journals. Fuller needed such a wide variety of research materials for Fuller Houses because his concept was comprehensive. He was not merely designing a house, a domestic shell, for industrial reproduction, he was attempting to create a system for manufacturing, servicing, and equipping a house, similar to the systems used by automobile manufacturers. At the Auburn exhibition, he "[l]ooked at body work with thought of its application to Fuller Houses . . . and how would apply to marketing."[14] He found "[e]xtremely interesting machinery for cleaning, preparing, and packing foods [and] useful mechanical ideas" during his visit to the American Food Packers exhibition.[15] A week later he "studied Motor Boat Magazine annual show number for relationship between boat construction & finish & accessories & operating plant as applied to Fuller Houses."[16] Double-page ads for Remington office machines offered models for service plans and policies. Trade journals and books helped Fuller identify architectural and building trends he could accept, reject, or adapt.

With the exception of *House Beautiful*, the magazines Fuller consulted were not named in the diary. Various trade journals, like *Architectural Forum*, *Architectural Record*, and *The Architect*, are in the "Reference List for *4D Timelock*."[17] On the other hand, Fuller was specific in the diary about the usefulness of these journals: "Hussey gave RBF number of copies of architecture and construction magazines to take home for search on relative matter to Fuller Houses. . . . He and Anne read these magazines all evening & clipped some remarkably pertinent articles & pictures."[18] The next day Fuller "read Sunday paper and wrote some notes for Fuller Houses . . . . Read construction method magazines. Made more notes for Fuller Houses and worked on files generally, straightening up."[19]

On another day he "[s]topped at Brentano's to look over building, arch. and business magazines."[20]

Fuller also studied recent developments in architecture. He may have purchased G. H. Edgell's *The American Architecture of Today* at Brentano's, but he did not state if he read it. He did read Le Corbusier's *Towards a New Architecture* "until very late at night"[21] on January 30, and almost a month later he again "[r]ead Corbusier."[22] He made notes to "get Le Corbusier's *Urbanisme* and *L'Art Decoratif d'Aujourd'hui*,"[23] but he did not indicate if he read them. *Towards a New Architecture* was the only one of the three books translated into English by 1927. Fuller studied French at his preparatory school, Milton Academy, and may have been able to read the language well enough to comprehend Le Corbusier's texts fifteen years after graduating.[24] While researching Fuller read widely, yet only English sources appear on the reference list.[25]

Fuller may have focused his research on texts in English, but he did not restrict the type of texts he read. On the same day he "re-read Corbusier," Fuller also "[r]ead diary of Timothy Fuller,"[26] one of his paternal ancestors. In addition, he studied the philosophy of Bertrand Russell after Bob Hussey bought "selections from B. Russell's writings for us."[27]

Discussions with friends, family members, business associates, lawyers, and architects — basically anyone who would speak with Fuller — played relevant roles in the development of Fuller Houses. He used these conversations to help formulate a business strategy and test his ideas. Some people were responsive, like Mr. Morgan who was "tremendously enthusiastic & volunteered help in statistics." Others were less enthusiastic, such as Ed Johnson of International Harvester who was "only mildly encouraging about Fuller Houses."[28] There were a few people, A. J. Sweet for one, who thought the idea sound yet felt Fuller would have problems working out some of the details. Anne recorded that after a "seven hour discussion Fuller Houses, Mr. Sweet, one of leading electric illumination engineers of U.S. . . . thought highly of plan. Approved except doubting ability to buck vested interests and public stubbornness. Discouraging experiences Gen'l Electric."[29] Sweet, Johnson, and Morgan were only three of the people who made minor contributions to the progress of Fuller Houses.

Fuller worked much more closely with other colleagues, like Bob Hussey, Cecil Cawthorne, and George Cross. Cawthorne and Cross worked passionately on the project, although not as intimately as Hussey. Cawthorne helped inspect potential office space, took dictation, and was transformed into the project's "confidential secretary"[30] the day after he informed Fuller he had "already sold some of the Fuller Houses."[31] Fuller was displeased with Cawthorne and he soon disappeared. The last recorded contacts are references to telephone conversations in early February.[32]

Fuller regularly telephoned George Cross, an investor in Stockade Midwest. He first appeared in the diary as an ally when Hopkins was orchestrating Fuller's ousting. He then resurfaced as an active participant in the development of Fuller Houses. Fuller trusted his judgment. He consulted Cross about the possibility of enlisting the aid of Mr. Woodlin, American Car and Foundry president, a contact from Fuller's Stockade days. Cross was not in favor of Woodlin because he felt Woodlin was "forced into things rather than choosing his own way."[33] Cross also accompanied Fuller to a meeting with "Foster Beamsley, banker from Duluth," who was "well impressed, felt RBF could tie up Fuller Houses from the insurance and loan end as he had already planned to do."[34] In addition, Cross presented Fuller's "ideas on furniture as related to Fuller Houses" to the Karpen company, which was "interested."[35] This furniture probably resembled two sketches for 4D furniture "much like acrobats [sic] equipment," an inflatable "air couch," and a suspended glass table and shelving (figure 3.1). Fuller described the table as "hoisted to the ceiling when desirable" with "neon tube lights along wires for illumination and warning against collision."[36] Like Anne, Cross's wife, Olive, engaged in the ongoing dialogue about the project. One evening, Fuller happily reported she "talked Fuller Houses" with them and as a "typical housewife, approved design."[37]

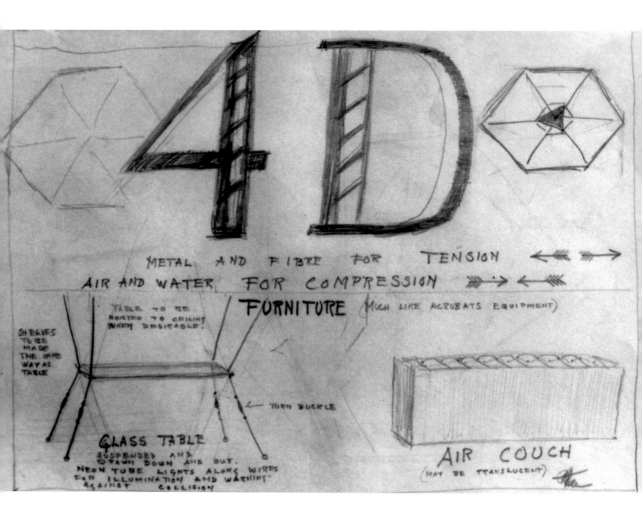

METAL AND FIBRE FOR TENSION ←———— ————→

AIR AND WATER FOR COMPRESSION ≫≫→ →← ←≪≪

FURNITURE (MUCH LIKE ACROBATS EQUIPMENT)

TABLE TO BE
HOISTED TO CEILING
WHEN DESIRABLE.

SHEAVES
TO BE
MADE
THE SAME
WAY AS
TABLE

← TURN BUCKLE

GLASS TABLE
SUSPENDED AND
DRAWN DOWN AND OUT.
NEON TUBE LIGHTS ALONG WIRES
FOR ILLUMINATION AND WARNING
AGAINST COLLISION

AIR COUCH
(MAY BE TRANSLUCENT)

3.1

Buckminster Fuller, sketches
for 4D furniture, 1928.

Fuller also solicited the opinion of Kay, Hussey's wife. Fuller described her as "an interior decorator of some moderate success much entranced with Fuller Houses."[38] He did not elaborate on what values Olive Cross and Kay Hussey found in the project, although they were probably influenced by their husbands' enthusiasm. The diary also details Hussey's collaboration with and influence on Fuller, information to which their wives would have been privy.

The Husseys first learned of Fuller Houses at dinner on January 10, 1928, and "Bob [was] tremendously interested."[39] Hussey helped Fuller inspect the office space in the Goodrich Building the following week. An evening of socializing concluded after "[m]uch discussion of Fuller Houses."[40] With the Husseys, as with many of his other friends, Fuller conflated the roles of friend and business associate.

The diary reveals Fuller felt comfortable enough with Hussey to discuss the various aspects of the unfolding project with him. In mid-January Anne wrote that Fuller had a "long & satisfying talk with Bob . . . during evening. He was particularly for all Bucky's ideas except the paying idea. The part he thought cleverest the marketing ideas & also referring to boat builders."[41] Fuller consulted Hussey the next day concerning "talk . . . heard around building circles suggesting leak on Fuller Houses."[42] Fuller's concern over a "leak" seems contradictory at best and paranoid at worst given the number of people with whom he discussed the project. For instance, while noting his concern over the "possible leak," he commented that "O'Neil Ryan . . . of Celotex . . . said still rather interested in Fuller Houses."[43] This is also where Cecil Cawthorne's appointment as "confidential secretary" is revealed. Fuller may not have been concerned if Ryan spoke about Fuller Houses with others because only he knew general details. On the other hand, Cawthorne and Hussey were involved with the project. Fuller might have feared that the details they could disclose would enable another entrepreneur to capitalize on his project before he could. Hussey obviously gave a reassuring response to Fuller's inquiry about the "possible leak" because his participation in the project grew.

Hussey and Fuller spent many hours discussing Fuller Houses, the direction of the project, and its corporate structure. Hussey helped Fuller's research by giving him construction and architecture magazines. On the same day Hussey gave Anne and Fuller the book of Bertrand Russell's writings, Fuller "discussed his first written outline of Fuller Houses" and "Anne's drawing" with him.[44] In addition, Hussey asked Fuller to send sketches to his office. These sketches presumably related to an earlier meeting about "writing up subject as an adv[ertising] and marketing man in form of quick brochure to present the subject to men when RBF wired to interest [them] in organization."[45] They also spent an "afternoon working on" the project even though Mr. Janey, the patent attorney, rescheduled "until February 8 . . . our meeting to discuss patent situation on Fuller Houses."[46]

Fuller initiated the Fuller Houses patent application in late January when he met with Mr. Janey about patents for the cement mixer and parking wheel. They "discussed Fuller Houses very briefly," and Janey "had [Fuller] meet the patent 'writer' in the afternoon to work up details."[47] A week later Fuller "wrote . . . an outline of Fuller Houses for Mr. Janey."[48] Janey then relegated the project to Mr. Sweet, who "instructed [Fuller] to make detailed drawings of the house and all its parts and methods of assembly."[49] He also requested that Fuller meet with him once the "drawings [were] ready when he is to immediately prepare patent claims and drawings."[50] Fuller enlisted a Mr. Hinkley in Russell Walcott's office to produce the drawings. Walcott, an established Chicago architect, "was very much impressed and favorably so. Going to help . . . as much as possible."[51] One way Walcott assisted Fuller was to permit Hinkley to make the detailed patent drawings without fear of compromising his job.

Fuller met with Hinkley and "outlined Fuller Houses to him. Hinkley agreed to start . . . Feb. 28th to make drawings, in minute details, which is necessary for patents and financing and budgeting. He was much taken with the spirit and bigness of the idea. Promises his earnest support."[52] After work on the drawings began, Fuller was at the "Wrigley Building designing Fuller Houses with

3.2

Buckminster Fuller, *4D Tower*, 1928.

Hinkley. Mrs. Hinkley present and criticizing from a housewife's stand point. Very helpful."[53] A few days later, Fuller and Hinkley were once again working "on drawings for Fuller Houses."[54] They were finished by the end of March, enabling Fuller to meet with Sweet to initiate writing the patent.

Neither Anne nor Fuller described the formal characteristics of the project in the patent application. Some sketches depict a round or hexagonal shape (figure 3.2) that differs from the orthogonal structure in the patent application drawings. Conservative, early sketches show a rectangular structure with a pitched roof and cross bracing (figures 3.3–3.9). Figures 3.3 and 3.4 reveal that Fuller considered setting the front entry between slightly projecting sides, referencing a Beaux Arts approach. Many sketches are of a two-story, rectangular house (figures 3.5–3.6). Masts at the corners or in the center provide structural support (figures 3.7 and 3.9). Figure 3.8 shows the first floor with a garage, office, storeroom, living room, and another room, probably a dining room. There is no indication of how the second floor, with bedrooms, dressing rooms and baths, was accessed.

The two-story concept is contradicted by the handwritten "Fuller Houses" essay: "Fuller Houses as isolated units are always one story or bungalo [*sic*] that is never excavate [*sic*]. build base up to the level of correct possible level connect unit with the ground on which it is built."[55] Fuller also described the lighting and heating systems, with the heating system doubling as a dust vacuum. The interior was divided by three types of partitions: blind, with a door, or with an insert. If the particular building was a "standardized house for a city lot . . . as much of the lot as is permissable [*sic*] . . . should come within the walls of the house . . . gardens . . . within walls of the house. Clothes drying etc. is done in the drying cabinets of the laundry unit."[56] The house was supported by reinforced concrete supports in compression and stabilized by piano wire which offered a degree of safety: "For fireproofing such construction and giving rigidity to it, use for down or tension member single ply (or multiples of this for required cross section) wire rope of piano wire."[57] Fuller included diagrams to

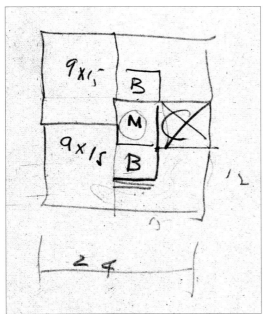

3·3

Buckminster Fuller, sketch
referencing Beaux Arts plan from
Fuller Houses, ca. 1928.

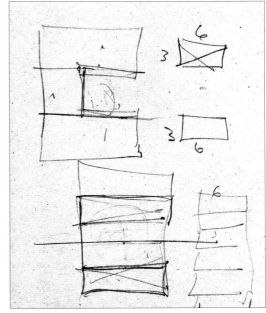

3·4

Buckminster Fuller, sketch
referencing Beaux Arts plan
from Fuller Houses, ca. 1928.

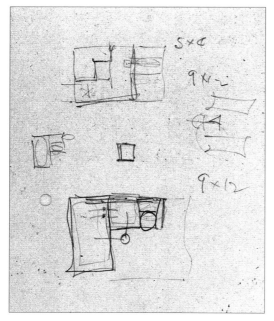

3.5

Buckminster Fuller, sketch
showing two-story house
from Fuller Houses, ca. 1928.

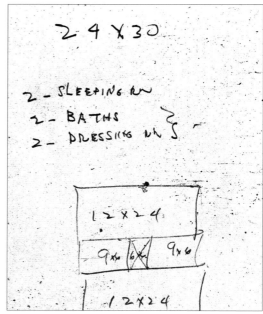

3.6

Buckminster Fuller, labeled
sketch showing two-story
house from Fuller Houses,
ca. 1928.

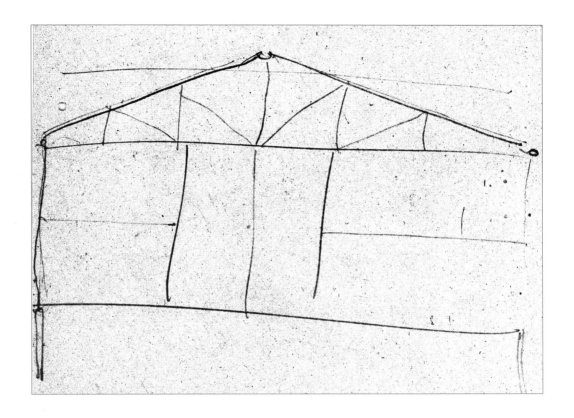

3·7

Buckminster Fuller, sketch with
mast supports at corners from
Fuller Houses, ca. 1928.

Buckminster Fuller,
sketch showing rooms
on first floor from Fuller
Houses, ca. 1928.

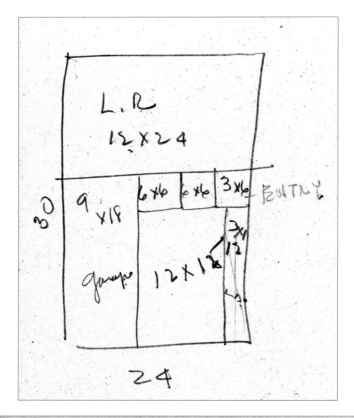

Buckminster Fuller,
annotated sketch from
Fuller Houses, ca. 1928.

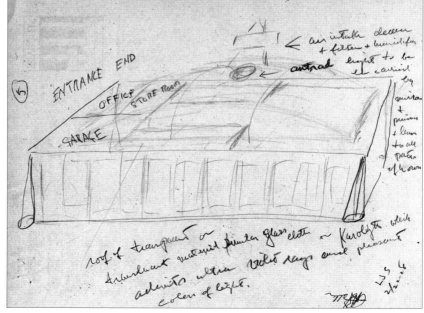

help explain the structural details. An annotated sketch combining material and technical explanations (figure 3.9) shows the entrance, garage, office, and storeroom to the left, taking up about a third of the space. The remainder of the interior is not labeled although divisions are lightly indicated. Cone-shaped supports are at each end of a long, fenestrated wall. Fuller noted a "roof of transparent or translucent material similar glass cloth or kerolyte which admits ultra violet rays and pleasant color of light."[58] Duraluminum, presumably for the walls and structural components, is stipulated. At the back of the drawing is a very minimal sketch of the "air intake cleaner + filter + humidifier."[59] Along the right margin, Fuller explained "light to be carried by mirrors + prism + beams to all parts of house."[60] Clearly, Fuller had specific ideas about the appearance and structure of Fuller Houses. It is impossible to determine how this essay relates to the various outlines mentioned in the diary, but it is a precursor to the abandoned patent application.

The patent application was by necessity longer and more detailed, with more accurate drawings than "Fuller Houses" and its hasty sketches. The formal properties and structural system described in the essay were significantly changed for the application. At some point in the process the name 4D was substituted for Fuller Houses. Anne explained the meaning and purpose of the new name to Fuller's brother Wolcott: "'4D' . . . does mean fourth dimension. It's more or less just a trade name for it. R. B. F. thought it was expressive of their aims and he wanted to get away from the personal element. - They were first called Fuller Houses."[61]

Fuller contemplated Lightful Houses or Cosmopolitan Houses as names for the project, but he chose 4D because it more accurately reflected his philosophy. On one level, Fuller considered the fourth dimension, time, to be the new economic standard: "Without legislation recognizing it, the world is now on a time standard instead of a gold standard in temporal things. Wasting time is exactly the same as throwing away gold used to be. Therefore we are forced to design and figure in the fourth dimension which is time."[62] Sydney Rosen, one of Fuller's biographers, gave a similar explanation of 4D: "[H]e was paying homage to [Albert] Einstein's theory of relativity. When we want to locate a point in space, we have to measure from some beginning point to three directions that are at right angles to each other. To these three *dimensions* of measuring, Einstein had added a fourth: *time*. Thus, 4-D represented the time dimension, the *new* dimension."[63] It was also meant to denote the industrial origins of the house: "Industry makes possible one more dimension in design, the fourth dimension."[64] Furthermore, as a play on Model-T, 4D referenced the efficiency of Henry Ford's automobile factories.[65]

Fifth, the time component alluded to the materials' life span: "When [a material] reaches its destiny, how long will it stay there? For the time limit of its existence. The fourth dimension is time. In the composition of synthetic materials, the fourth dimension is the most important . . . we must segregate [materials] for their usefulness . . . combining them with materials whose longetivity or fourth dimension is equal to their own."[66] In addition to the time element, there was a relationship to the spatial aspects of the fourth dimension. According to Linda Henderson: "Fuller used the term *4D* to signify efficiency. . . . Fuller also associated a circular shape with higher dimensional time and space. Building "from the inside out" in a circular shape would let the time dimension be incorporated as radial distance from the center, leaving behind traditional three-dimensional "cubistic" architecture in favor of trigonometry and spherical geometry."[67] There were also spiritual aspects connected to the "higher dimensional time and space" of 4D that would help "those who perceive the spheroidal progress . . . quickly [attain] the encompassing sphere of perfect light of truth."[68] Fuller made a color-coded watercolor (figure 3.10) to illustrate this progression, which he described as "an entirely symbolic study . . . to . . . present . . . the fourth dimensional progression of apparent color, starting with complete darkness at the center, progressing to complete lightness on the exterior, through the natural green or the mechanical red from the yellow of dawn to the exterior blue of the universe prior to the perfect light of eternity."[69] Finally,

3.10

Buckminster Fuller,
chart indicating 4D
color progression,
1928.

TIME INTERVAL 1 METER

Copyright 1928. 4D

CHART INDICATING 4D COLOR PROGRESSION
FROM DARKNESS THROUGH YELLOW OF DAWN (1ST LIGHT)
TROUGH NATURAL GREEN AND MECHANICAL RED TO

4D was a subtle homage to Fuller's introduction to the housing industry: Stockade Building System. Stockade's classification at the American Institute of Architects was 4-D-32 meaning concrete forms (4-D) used for solid walls (32).[70] Fuller never acknowledged this relationship to Stockade.

At Stockade Fuller learned to navigate the patent process—practical experience he found useful when preparing the 4D House patent. Therefore, Fuller's explanation of why he abandoned the 4D patent is suspect, a case of selective remembrance similar in purpose to his narrative about being pushed out of Stockade. In both stories he presented himself as naïve, too innocent to realize he was being mistreated by others until the damage was done. And, like the Stockade story, it has remained unquestioned. According to Fuller, the patent was abandoned because he did not understand how the process worked:

> In the case of my first two patents [for Stockade] . . . all the work was done
> by my attorney who did not consult with me after the first disclosure. It is
> the formal procedure of attorneys dealing with the U.S. patent office to file
> applications . . . that first make a philosophical disclosure of the state of the
> art in which the invention is operative, then carefully describe the inven-
> tion with accompanying drawings, then list a series of claims of what the
> inventor feels is the most economical statement of that which he feels is his
> unique invention . . . the patent office examiner sends back what is called
> the first rejection, rejecting a number of the claims but allowing one or two.
> The attorney and the inventor have the opportunity to . . . restate them. . . .
> [T]here are four such exchanges between the claiming inventor and the
> patent examiner. The patent attorney I had for the 4D House changed part-
> nership and moved out of town. He did not tell me that the first rejection
> by the patent office was anything but a rejection. I did not know that subse-

quent resubmission of the patent was possible; I just assumed it was a final

rejection and let it go.[71]

Yet he did not "let it go." Documents in Fuller's papers reveal that he not only knew the proper patenting procedure but also made at least one corrective response to the examiner's findings.

Sweet, Fuller's patent lawyer, informed him on November 1, 1928, they had until the following April to respond to the examiner's findings.[72] In January, Sweet sent Fuller notice of the amended filing canceling "claims 6 to 12, 23 to 25, 29, 30, 38, and 39."[73] Sweet next reported on the possibility of filing foreign patents on the 4D House.[74] In 1929 Sweet did leave the firm through which Fuller filed the patent application, but this did not end Fuller's work on it. Fuller's file was transferred to Roland Rehm, who notified him: "Since Mr. Sweet's withdrawal from this organization prosecution of your pending application (file 1793) has been turned over to me."[75] In addition, there is a $75 invoice from one of the firm's principals for "conference with Mr. Fuller re his applications and new developments . . . on his dymaxion [4D] house. Study of foreign patent laws with reference to the filing of foreign applications."[76] This invoice was followed by a larger one, for $342.20, for services in 1928 and 1929.[77] In October 1930, Rehm sent Fuller an overdue notice and complained about his client's vanishing act: "For about a year I have been wholly unable to reach you by letter. . . . I desire to call to your attention to the importance of keeping us advised of your whereabouts. It is absolutely impossible to prosecute your applications unless you cooperate with us."[78] The invoice was for "preparing amendment and argument in your application for Building and Method of Constructing the Same, Serial no. 275,840, File no. 1793."[79]

As the correspondence makes clear, Fuller was not naïve about the patent process. If four exchanges are common between the inventor, patent attorney, and patent examiner, the Stockade patents would have gone through a similar process. Similar because the process was more demanding when Fuller filed the

4D patent, as he explained to Hewlett: "You must realize that to draw a really good patent today, that will 'Hold water', the <u>actual complete working details</u> must be indicated in the drawings, or verbally specified. They must be so shown as to make possible their easy interpretation by any ordinary mechanic (I mention all this as you will find a divergence from the former patent practice with which we are mutually familiar)."[80] Obviously, Fuller knew what was required to secure a patent. He pursued the 4D patent for more than a year before abandoning it. He later claimed he let it lapse because the AIA refused to assume responsibility for it. Fuller knew of the AIA's decision in mid-1928; it did not factor into the application's abandonment. Fuller was more likely motivated by the results of the search for related patents, a requirement of the application process meant to verify the originality of the pending invention. This revealed that the 4D House was not as unique as claimed.

The concept for the 4D House included integration of structural and mechanical systems, and the originality of each required verification. In the case of the 4D House, the related patent search disclosed nine related patents, dating between 1881 and 1928.[81] They also established prior claims on different aspects of the house. William Beecher had been granted a patent for a heating and ventilating system similar to the one Fuller described in his design.[82] Charles Nichols had been awarded a patent for the "Arrangement for Inclosing Vacuum Conduit Systems," which functioned much like Fuller's dust removal system.[83] Another of Fuller's ideas, a transparent or translucent roof, had been included in the patent for the "Sanitary House" assigned to William van der Heyden.[84] As Fuller worked on his application and negotiated with the patent examiner, Paul Liege was granted a patent for "Translucent Wall, Ceiling, and Floor Structure."[85] Ironically, the details of Liege's patent were not identical to those of the 4D House, but they were similar enough to some of his specifications to make Fuller's concept seem unoriginal.

One of the more unusual qualities of the 4D House, its ability to withstand storms, especially tornadoes, was preempted by two earlier patents.

Dudley Blanchard received a patent for his rotating "Tornado-Proof Building
. . . an elongated and sharpened form . . . to part the current air like the bow of
a vessel."[86] In his successful application, Allan Rush described "a new and useful Observation, Amusement, and Utility Tower . . . to be free from liability of
destruction from wind pressure or storm."[87] Neither of these structures relied
upon construction methods or structural systems similar to those of the 4D
House, but they made the claim it was storm-proof seem redundant.

There were, however, three patents for construction methods and structural support akin to those Fuller designed for the 4D House. The first had
been granted to Alexander Thorne for "Cantilever Building Construction."[88]
Thorne's method used horizontal beams cantilevered from internal supports
to sustain the building. The exterior walls were nonbearing. The exterior walls
of the 4D House were also curtain walls since the building was supported by
an internal frame of vertical and horizontal members. Libanus Todd had been
given a patent for a round, low-cost shelter supported by a central column,[89] in
a manner much like the central support Fuller described for the rectangular 4D
House in his patent application.

The patent most closely approximating Fuller's ideas for the structural system of the 4D House was awarded to Archibald Black for "Building Construction."[90] Black's procedure was "manufacturing buildings in substantially
complete units and the assembling of said units to form the building . . . the labor required for erection of the building can be almost entirely confined to that
required for the assembling of the completed units."[91] This method was almost
identical to Fuller's idea of manufacturing the components of the 4D House,
shipping them to the site, and then using manual labor to assemble the house.

Black's patent was assigned in September 1928, four months after the 4D
House patent application was filed. Fuller implied that he abandoned the patent very quickly after his initial filing. No date is given, although some point
in mid-1928 is generally accepted. The presence of Black's successful patent in
Fuller's papers as well as the late 1928 and early 1929 correspondence from Sweet

and Rehm contradict the notion of an immediate abandonment. Exactly why and when Fuller abandoned the patent are not known. The best explanation is that when he learned each of his forty-three claims were included in previous patents, he knew it was useless to continue.[92]

Fuller also maintained that abandoning the patent application meant abandoning the specifications letter and original artwork as well.[93] This may be so, but he kept copies. The specifications letter and accompanying drawings are reproduced in varying formats[94] without the list of claims that summarize the originality of the invention.[95] Fuller was wise enough to stop pursuing the patent at a prudent point without foolishly forsaking the physical representations of his idea.

Writing the patent application allowed him to pull his ideas together in an organized manner and served as a precursor to the better-known Dymaxion House. His premise was as follows: "My invention relates to buildings and the erection thereof and includes among its objects and advantages the application of mass production methods facilitated by changes in the building itself of such a nature as to make its completed parts capable of convenient transportation."[96] In other words, Fuller created a new kind of building and new method of construction by using industrial methods to fabricate the structure's components that could be easily shipped, presumably from the place of production to the construction site. The stage was set for the accompanying illustrations. The drawings are mechanical and the majority delineate technical details as seen in figure 3.11. The front elevation in the patent application (figure 3.12) is the first-known presentation drawing of the 4D House. It shows an asymmetrical façade divided into three unequal bays and a symmetrical roof capped by a triangular ventilator hood. The bungalow-type design is banal and only distinguished by the substitution of the triangular ventilator hood for a traditional chimney. Fuller later credited its rectangular shape to his patent lawyer who argued it would be more acceptable to the examiner.[97] This, of course, contradicts the fact that early sketches for the house were rectangular in plan (see figures

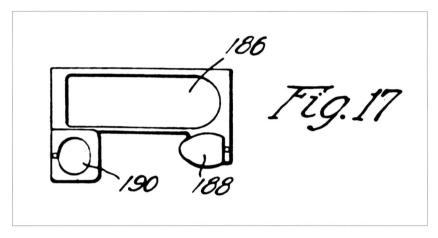

3.11

Buckminster Fuller, fig. 17 of patent application, 1928.

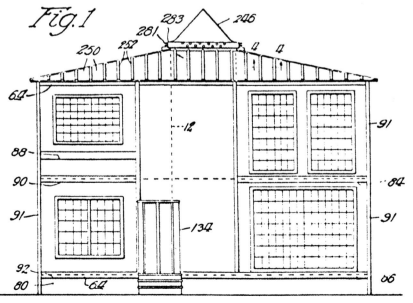

3.12

Buckminster Fuller, patent application front elevation of 4D house, 1928.

3.3–3.7). Fuller preferred a circular footprint as he explained in his attempt to win Hewlett's support. Fuller attached to his letter "a copy of the patent specifications and drawings minus the claims, as they are being kept by the patent attorneys only, and are not for the present to be revealed. The drawings don't look at all like the harmonious 4D House, and the cubicle termination of the design is only shown to indicate its possibility from the central rounding plan. They look like pictures of a man with but one foot and one toe on that foot."[98] The attorney's supposed insistence upon a rectangular design seems strange since Blanchard's "Tornado-Proof Building" and Todd's "Shelter" were patented and neither had orthogonal footprints. Whether it was Fuller or the patent lawyer who decided upon a rectangular shape for the patent drawings, the problems with the application were in the claims, not the drawings. The claims were to demonstrate the new and innovative aspects of the 4D House. The patent drawings were to illustrate the different components and "to make possible their easy interpretation by any ordinary mechanic."[99]

Within the patent drawings are numbered elements to help an average mechanic correlate them to the detailed written description. Fuller began by describing the laying of the foundation. First, it is necessary to dig a shallow hole where the center of the building would be. The foundation is made by pouring a concrete caisson into the hole. The caisson will support a mast running through the house and exiting at the roof. At each story, load-bearing beams radiate from the mast, providing a framework for the floors. At the outer ends, the beams attach to an exterior frame or tube for stabilization. The weight of the structure is transferred from the radiating beams to the central caisson. The non-bearing exterior walls host fenestration and doors, either framed in metal or inflatable tubes in fabric. Like the exterior walls, the interior partitions are nonstructural and either pneumatic or metal framed. The floors are a series of wires on top of the radiating beams. A strong canvas or tarpaulin is laid on the wires and in turn covered by pneumatic mats. This material constitutes the first five sections of the patent application.

The following sections are concerned with interior organization, utilities, and services. The first floor is entered through revolving doors or via the garage and holds the more public rooms: entrance hall, a combined living/recreational room, kitchen unit, and a garage with a false door over a storage room. The second floor is reached by two semi-circular stairways — one in the entrance hall, the other in the garage. Curiously, the bathrooms are located on the second floor and set into the central mast, which goes from a box- to an H-section at the second floor. There are four bedrooms on the second floor with their furniture attached to and supported by the structural frame. Hallways connect the bedrooms along the width of the house and utility rooms connect them along the length. The utility rooms contain a laundry and hobby room if one family occupies the house and two laundry units if two families live in it. Fuller made no mention of how the first floor would be divided if two families lived in the house. He also did not discuss how the rooms on the first floor would be separated from one another although he specifically designated sliding doors or overhead rolling doors on the second floor. With the exception of natural light, the central mast provides utilities and services for both floors.

Natural light enters the house through the ceiling, windows, and the triangular ventilator hood. A lens in the ventilator transmits natural light to reflectors that send it into the interior. Shutters and stained glass help control the intensity of the natural light that is augmented by artificial light. The artificial lighting can also be used to help heat the house. An electric fan near the top of the central mast circulates air. The air cools the lights by drawing heat from them; this heated air could then be used to warm the interior. In cold weather, heating coils along the outer sides of the mast and right below the triangular ventilator hood supplement the circulating warm air.

In addition to the heating coils, the mast holds an oil tank, septic tank, water pipes, and an electric generator. The plumbing could be connected to a municipal source or a well. Furthermore, the electric fan at the base of the hood assists the exchange of interior and exterior air. Tubes placed along the exterior of the mast at the roof level expel interior air and replace it with exterior air. The exterior air is filtered and cleaned. Dust and other solid particles are collected in a dustbin or baffle and flushed out through internal gutters running the length of the mast. In dry weather, the spray that flushed the gutters could also add moisture to the air.

The air filtration system helps keep the interior clean and dust-free. Fuller described a network of attachments or coupling units throughout the house for detachable hoses. The hoses use forced air to push dirt and dust into bins. These are the same bins into which the solid particles removed from the incoming air are collected. While Fuller's concern with the housewife's ability to clean her home was one of the more novel elements of the patent application, the wisdom of using forced air to clean an interior is questionable. The forced air system was probably inspired by the water hoses used to wash off ships' decks, a more practical application of such a method. Fuller's system was also similar to central vacuums with their portable hoses, refuse bags, and nozzles strategically located throughout the house. The vacuum, of course, sucked the dirt into a hose and then fed it into the collector; it did not use pressurized air to drive the dust into the apertures. Central vacuums may have been installed in the hotels where Fuller and his family lived during the project's development, giving Fuller firsthand experience with them. He may also have been encouraged to include mechanical cleaning equipment in the house by Kay Hussey, Olive Cross, and Mrs. Hinkley, the wives of his collaborators, and by his own wife, Anne.

While Fuller worked closely with his wife and many associates, Fuller Houses was clearly his project, his idea. He was wise enough to consult others when he needed help, but was also leery of losing control after his Stockade experience. Therefore, of the people who contributed to Fuller Houses, Anne was the most informed because Fuller freely discussed the project with her. On February 23, Fuller noted that he "worked on Fuller Houses corporation book and chart all evening working out fields of utility and procedure of various departments. Worked out architectural dept. Had long discussion with Anne on the philosophy of the business end, the business side."[100] In addition, by living with Fuller in the small Lake View apartment, she was privy to his telephone conversations and knew what he was working on as he worked.

And Fuller worked doggedly to ensure the project's rapid progress from the idea and outline of November 1927 to the patent drawings of March 1928. He spent many late nights figuring out its diverse details. Sometimes he had help, for instance when he "worked till midnight on write up of Fuller Houses, making up organization book and devising a system of digits for filing reference, etc."[101] with L. J. Stoddard. On other nights Fuller was alone, as Anne noted when he "marketed in evening & got . . . drawing board & materials & about midnight closeted himself in the kitchenette & worked until 5:30 am on Fuller Houses plan."[102] The first weekend in February he was up until 2:00 a.m. both nights. On Friday he studied connections between boat construction and the project. The next night he and Anne searched magazines for relevant material.[103] These late nights were on weekends since he had to juggle working on the project with earning a living. In March, the Stockade problems were added to the mix. He worked his way through these and remained focused. The Muller job and Stockade negotiations presented different degrees of distraction, yet neither slowed the development of Fuller/4D Houses.

4

TRIAL OFFER

Fuller rushed the 4D House project because he planned to present it at the up-coming AIA convention. He hoped that acceptance by the organization would provide a seal of approval. The institute might also be persuaded to assist in the project's realization. As noted previously, the AIA used a building materials clas-sification system; Fuller used 4D to refer to its classification of Stockade blocks, 4-D-32. Perhaps he thought the name would help AIA members understand his newly developed contribution to the evolution of mass production: from build-ing blocks to the entire house. He also knew AIA members would be more criti-cal of his idea than business associates. The convention would open on May 16, which left Fuller little time to prepare for his toughest audience.

The patent application was a large part of his preparations. Another was the first version of his combined business prospectus and architectural manifesto, *4D Timelock*. In addition to the written supplements, Fuller might have made a model for the patent application and exhibited it at the convention[1] although the only reference to a model is by Earl Reed, a Chicago architect, in 1940: "Re-member way back, if you can, to the old St. Louis days — little hotel room, two architects and a delightful enthusiast with model of Dymaxion House, then perhaps you will also remember Earl Reed."[2] In his enthusiasm, Reed undoubt-edly misremembered what happened twelve years earlier. Fuller never referred to the use of a model at the 1928 convention, although he cited a hastily writ-ten essay he gave to interested parties.[3] Fuller related this essay to neither the different preconvention outlines nor the patent application even if he did use some of the latter's drawings and technical information to supplement it.

Fuller also drafted a speech for the convention, but if he delivered it, it was not to an assembly. Fuller is not listed in the schedule or in the proceedings.[4] Immediately after the convention he wrote a response in which he intimated that he had not been permitted to deliver his speech because it had not been arranged in advance.[5] In another context Fuller described the presentation in St. Louis as private, although whether private meant one-on-one or an unofficial closed-door session is not noted.[6] In addition, after the conference he informed

Tomlinson that he "was asked to attend the convention by several of the Chicago delegates."[7] This was simply an attempt to impress Tomlinson. Nothing in the archives of the Chicago Chapter, St. Louis Chapter, and national AIA office supports Fuller's remark.[8] If delegates from Chicago had asked Fuller to attend the convention, they would likely have covered his expenses. Yet Fuller paid for the trip as he confided to Hewlett: "About our last pennies were spent in getting the booklet together, in mailing it out, and in making the trip to St. Louis."[9] Fuller sent Tomlinson a "write up of my house" that was "presented . . . at St. Louis" in an "official though private presentation,"[10] implying the AIA had sanctioned it.

Fuller may have expected he would be given an opportunity to present the project by one of the organization's members who supported him. Or he may have simply gone to seek out members who would be supportive of the 4D House and whom he could enlist in its further development. In either case, Fuller knew he needed to be exceptionally persuasive. Therefore, in the draft of his speech he relied upon a combination of prayer, criticism, and recent events:

> *In the name of Christ (and in twenty centuries this name has not been invoked more reverentially) let us cease distrusting others in our selfish way. . . .*
>
> *Architects of the American Institute let this new spirit of St. Louis, break down forever this wall of distrust of others which must ever make you distrust yourselves, God make . . . you unselfishly recognize the artistry in your fellows that you may free it in yourself. All must balance.*
>
> *Recognize then your . . . unborn, artistry . . . the new story of the architecture in . . . individualism with its scale of the universe, with a million editions. Let this be the temporal . . . harmonious . . . manifestation of your art in the everlasting monument to the new spirit of St. Louis. Amen.*[11]

Fuller cleverly referred to the plane, *Spirit of St. Louis*, in which Charles Lindbergh had made the first solo, nonstop flight from New York to Paris in May of the previous year. Technology made such an astounding feat possible. Fuller used the analogy to emphasize that through technology improvements in house construction could also be achieved.

If Fuller delivered his clever analogy, it garnered less support than he expected. In retaliation he wrote a lengthy rejoinder about his convention experience that immediately follows the draft of the speech in his papers. The complex response praised the members who accepted Fuller's idea. It was also strongly critical of those who did not because of their backward attitudes:

> *Upon completion of this paper it was rushed to St. Louis . . . for the . . . 61st . . . Annual convention of the American Institute of Architects . . .*
>
> *Despite a benevolent reception on the part of almost all with whom contact was made . . . Said many members approached, "Yes, this seems very important, I will study it after the convention." (Not explaining that the two hours necessary to its study during the convention was elusive for a little convention drinking, golf, etc. For such is the standard value of conventions.)*
>
> *Everything that is to occur is taken up weeks and months in advance by steering committees . . . [a] question at a convention brooks no answers. Except for . . . predetermined measures there would be no necessity of convention. . . . The artful guise of feudalistic . . . or basic material lobbying . . . parading as artistic and dignified patronage at the architect's convention which seeks to keep the histrionic, inimitable glory . . . over architecture . . . in ancient and . . . otherwise obsolete methods on the part of the producers, is heart rendering to the . . . champion of individualism. No where else has*

feudalism . . . such a rotten hold as on this most important of . . . industries, that of home building. . . . The new patron of art is the great individualism of democracy which will lavish the artist with economic sustenance . . . if he will but create for them living enjoyment through mass reproduction (the creative step up, of truth, economics, standardization love & life.)

(The very secret of nature is reproduction . . . in the most standard undeformed manner . . . ten fingers & ten toes.) Here stands feudalism between the permanent competence of individual man through . . . the house. So long as homes can be kept stylistically deferred will selfish feudalism be able to bully its way along, without having to lift a finger or . . . install a machine to relieve back breaking labor, to compete with progress. . . .

To stoically, with this knowledge established permanently in other industries, & with the nauseating mawkish clutch of the ancient stone and other feudal holdings upon this convention of architects . . . who . . . would if . . . intelligent at all, be the first to release the hold, are complacently befuddled with liquor every time they approach an economic question . . . & aesthetic drivel supplants enlightening argument. . . .

With the aid of stalwart friends amongst these architects, given prior to this convention, a careful survey was made of how who might be approached and at the same time be helpful if approached . . . the charming but . . . standard ineffectiveness of the meeting . . . [the] spread of criticism designed to bring forth enlightenment was written down, when it was realized that a personal delivery of it to as many as possible would be a thousand times surer . . . than the possible blundering loss of all interest due to the personal equation in a general address. This proved to be a wiser course

and . . . an effective number of the convention's most worthwhile members
went forth from this convention imbued with the new spirit. This in effect
was the speech as . . . composed and generally given.[12]

The excerpt illustrates the disparate reactions by AIA members to Fuller's
proposal. It also accentuates Fuller's conflicting attitude toward the organization: he wants its approval even as he dismisses its policies. In it he complains
about the rigidity of conference planners and domestic design. Fuller points to
flaws in the architectural system that render the architect subservient to the
client and to economics. His project for an industrially reproduced house, the
4D House, would free the architect from both. Hope for the future of domestic design existed in the form of architects who understood and embraced his
message. Fuller received enough encouragement to believe his "new spirit of St.
Louis" was sturdy enough to carry him to success.

Whatever his original plan for the convention, Fuller presented the 4D
House to only a few conference attendees. He admitted that he carefully studied AIA members to determine who would be receptive. His choices were so
accurate his idea was given a "benevolent reception" by "almost all with whom
contact was made." In his postconvention letter to Tomlinson, Fuller happily
reported his house "was presented to 18 members of the American Institute at
St. Louis, who were picked out as being broad and unselfish thinkers and with
more than satisfactory results."[13]

Fuller wanted his associates to believe he officially introduced the project
to a select group. He implied a formal presentation, perhaps with a speech and
a model. Yet many of the solicitation letters Fuller sent to AIA members he
met in St. Louis noted a more casual approach.[14] He sent A. P. Herman of the
University of Washington "the paper which I spoke of to you in the bus at St.
Louis."[15] He reminded T. R. Kimball, a former president of the AIA, that his
father-in-law "was kind enough to introduce [us] at the convention. Attached

is the paper which you asked that I send to you."[16] None of the correspondence hinted at a presentation, a speech, or a model in a "little hotel room."

Nor did any of the responses. Hewlett, who certainly would have attended any presentation, made no comment about it although he carefully assured his anxious son-in-law he had "read your pamphlet very carefully."[17] About a month after the convention, Allen Erickson, the head of the Architects Small House Bureau in Chicago, informed Fuller, "[I] read your discourse on the industrialized home which you gave me at St. Louis, but I have not studied it."[18] Two of Fuller's early supporters, John Boyd Jr. and Arthur Holden, both Manhattan-based architects, also failed to comment on any presentation even though they were quite excited about the project.[19] The correspondence convincingly demonstrates that Fuller gained support for the project from AIA members who were willing to learn about it despite the organization's stance against standardization of design.

Fuller later claimed that his presentation of the 4D House compelled the AIA to pass a resolution declaring it was "inherently opposed to any peas-in-a-pod-like reproducible designs."[20] This is an incredible boast and another misrepresentation of events Fuller exploited to his advantage. Even if Fuller had made a formal presentation to the entire convention, it is difficult to accept the AIA would have been so threatened by the 4D House it would have immediately pushed through such a resolution. Large member- and committee-driven organizations like the AIA simply do not react so quickly; issues need to be tabled, debated, and voted. There was no reason for it to be threatened and attempt to nip a potentially dangerous competitor in the bud since various types of mass-produced houses were already on the market. The AIA could not have been motivated by the 4D House to take a stance against industrially reproduced houses because opposition to standardization of design in architecture was a conference theme.

The *St. Louis Star* reported "[c]riticism of a growing tendency to standardize architectural design throughout the country was placed before the American

Institute of Architects by its board of directors."[21] The board accepted "certain functions of the architect may well become standardized" and expressed concern for "the art of design."[22] The AIA was concerned because standardization of architectural design produced "a universal product made to sell"[23] whose appearance was determined more by profit margins than by aesthetics. The detrimental effects of standardization of design included the disappearance of what Kenneth Frampton would later refer to as critical regionalism[24] and what the AIA board described as local architectural character: "Local characteristics are fast disappearing in this era of common thought and mechanical advancement. Communities are coming to look more and more like peas of one pod. A certain commercialism is making itself more and more evident in the type of architecture employed throughout the country."[25] The prevalence of commercialism and poor design quality could not "be attributed alone to the efforts of the uneducated or inefficient architect."[26] Even architects of high repute and strong ability were losing sight of the "Character of Design" and falling "under the influence of a cosmopolitan and general type of architecture."[27] This trend could be reversed if architects would imbue their designs with character "whose importance cannot be overlooked or neglected without a marked deterioration, rather than an advancement in our work. Character of Design is the spirit, the soul, and the life of any architectural achievement, something deeper by far than style, expression of usage, or choice of materials."[28] Ironically, this essay also called for a "new spirit" in architecture responding to local conditions and exhibiting quality in design. Obviously, Fuller and the AIA were describing different types of spirit: the AIA drew upon its connotation as essence while Fuller used it as a sense of adventure, a form of individualism. The problem of standardization in architectural design was addressed at the convention in order to "plant a seed that during the coming year may grow to larger and possibly unexpected proportions."[29]

Milton Medary, the AIA president, criticized the monotony of modern, standardized buildings that fail to respond to local traditions:

*Cities once typical of the geographical, historical, and climatic conditions
out of which a definite character was established, today exhibit a clearly
marked line between that original character and the standardized type. . . .
Side by side with the old . . . is the modern bank, hotel, and high school,
alike throughout the United States, while . . . "Main Street" is lighted by
a row of typical standards, cast in the same foundry, and is lined with the
standardized contribution of chain store organizations.*[30]

He criticized standardization and mass production when they contributed to
the abandonment of distinctive, local traditions to produce uniformity. He was
dismayed by the role standardization played in the growing homogeneity of architecture, design, and taste.

Standardization of design, not standardization of production methods, was
clearly the problematic issue. Medary's comment about street lamps being
made by one manufacturer disparaged the resultant similarity of city streets,
not how they were made. He was opposed to standardization when it limited
design options. After all, brick making had long been standardized and the mass
production of standard-sized nails was welcomed. Bricks and nails are tools
used to realize architectural designs, yet the buildings made with them are not
uniform in appearance. To the AIA standardization as a tool for production was
not detrimental to architectural character, but standardization as a method of
design was.

Fuller advocated the use of standardization in both applications for the
4D House, an unfortunate proposal given the AIA's position. The patent application included standardized, mass-produced building components. These
would be assembled into identical 4D Houses without concession to regional
differences. Theoretically, different versions of the 4D House could be developed. Sears, Hodgson, and Gordon-Van Tine sold many different models of
their mass-produced houses, some with regional features. Diversity did not

figure into Fuller's plans because he felt one design best represented the ideology behind the house. He believed deference to style and the search for individuality inhibited the appreciation of the industrially reproduced house.[31] While trying to promote a new version of Fuller Houses in the 1940s, he explained how individuality in mass-produced houses could be "achieved in the setting of a house, by planting . . . by the way the walk is laid out, through use of a terrace" and selective application of paint.[32] Formal (and name) changes to the 4D House occurred over time with each new design superseding the previous.[33] Fuller considered no historical designs, no Colonial, no Tudor, no California Mission options. To Fuller, standardized methods of production meant a single standardized design.

Standardized design, Fuller argued, was normal and desirable. He posited that uniformity of appearance was the norm: "The very secret of nature is reproduction of its own form in the most standard undeformed manner."[34] Fuller drew upon the criteria of human beauty: "The most beautiful . . . child is the one with the least . . . ataxia, who . . . has . . . ten fingers and ten toes."[35] He found a certain freedom, a certain confidence in standardized appearance: "Is not the public intuitively aware that the very beauty of a child lies in the . . . most regular of material features, unharassed into unbecoming self-consciousness, by the least unstandard deformity? Is it not the truth of standardization that ever pours more individual freedom and happiness into life?"[36] Fuller presented a logical if one-sided argument. By focusing on typical human features and the predilection that like produces like, he was overlooking the differences between individuals that make one more attractive than another.

He also overlooked the differences in the use of spoken and written language, "standardized symbols,"[37] that created personal expression. Even though the spoken and written word have standard formats, the way they are used enriches their meaning and their presentation. It also reflects the individuality of the person using them. In effect, by asserting conformity to the norm allowed for unconscious individuality, Fuller was discounting how variations of the human body and personal expression denote individuality.

It was this second type of individuality, singularity in appearance and personal expression, the AIA found lacking in standardized design. The AIA felt standardized design exhibited no character and was artless in its uniformity. Fuller thought the interest in art and insistence upon character of design was pandering to tradition and patronage. He contended that it took a strong individual to oppose this entrenched position: "It takes a real character to about face weeding up all the old fallacies of custom, deep rooted prior to personal responsibilities."[38] The personal responsibility was to design houses to be built with the most modern means available: mass production and industrial methods. Fuller believed standardized design would free architects from eking out a living as they catered to their clients' whims.

Given the polarity of their attitudes toward the use of standardization, Fuller's decision to use the AIA membership as his test audience was ill-conceived. He most likely did not know the organization was planning to announce its firm opposition to standardized design. The "suggested theme" of the convention was "The Mobilization of the Forces which make for better architecture."[39] These forces included collaboration in the arts of design and excluded standardization. Even if he had been forewarned about the organization's dismissal of standardized design, Fuller may have believed his idea was compelling enough to overcome any opposition. He ripped the printed version of Medary's speech out of the board's report and wrote along its margins: "On the basis of this question propounded by the Institute President to which many answers are given in our essay. The question can be materially presented to the convention in the form of the essay."[40]

Two articles from the February issue of the *Journal of the American Institute of Architects* may have bolstered Fuller's confidence that the 4D House and its corresponding essay would overcome opposition at the convention. These were "Collaboration in Art Education" by Everett V. Meeks and "Our Industrial Arts:

Reflections on the State of Design" by Richard F. Bach.[41] Fuller sent each a copy of *4D Timelock*. He informed Meeks, dean of the School of Fine Arts and director of the Department of Architecture at Yale University, that his article and the "striking design now coming from your school, encouraged us to hope that you may find time to read and comment on this paper."[42] Fuller did not communicate which parts of the article appealed to him. Meeks's premise was that collaboration between different "specialists" should be taught to art and architecture students "if we are to carry on the torch of veritable and living art, it is by giving the fullest training possible . . . together with the fullest possible advantages of technical instruction. . . . This the university can do if it will plan for and develop the dual program of both academic and technical curricula."[43] Fuller may have misinterpreted Meeks's call for "technical instruction" and "technical curricula" as meaning industrial techniques. This was not Meeks's intent; he was referring to technical proficiency within an art student's discipline. If Meeks responded, his answer is lost.

There is also no record of a reply from Richard Bach, associate in Industrial Design at the Metropolitan Museum of Art. Fuller explained that he was sending the essay because certain phrases in Bach's text "seem almost to relate us mentally."[44] Bach ruminated on the current state of industrial design and the dearth of designers capable of producing quality objects via machine or traditional methods. One way to ensure quality was "adherence to principle and a study of practical requirements which together aid in designing from the inside out."[45] Bach also proclaimed that it was best to analyze a problem by "seeing it in the round, so that various aspects here barely mentioned may be seen at closer range."[46] The phrases that caught Fuller's attention were "designing from the inside out" and "in the round."[47] Fuller felt affinity toward these because they were the same criteria he employed. Fuller had already analyzed the problem of housing from these angles as Bach suggested; the end result was the innovative 4D House.

In Fuller's mind, Bach's and Meeks's articles confirmed that he and others thought along similar lines. Surprisingly, neither article is in the *4D Timelock* reference list. Their ideas may have played only secondary roles in the development of Fuller's thinking, yet they were AIA members whose support Fuller wanted. In writing directly to them, Fuller utilized the same strategy he used in St. Louis: sell the project to AIA members one at a time. This may seem an odd objective given the organization's opposition to standardized design. Fuller's experience in St. Louis demonstrated, however, that some AIA members did not accept the organization's opposition to standardized design.

To persuade these potential supporters, Fuller argued that the AIA was opposed to the use of standardization when it was applied to objects as if it were surface decoration. In a letter to his father-in-law, Fuller reminded Hewlett that they agreed on this: "[A]s we discussed . . . the standardization referred to was that, attempted . . . by manufacturers of . . . confined exterior limitations, of a method of design that starts on the outside."[48] Some of Fuller's supporters accepted his spin on the AIA's stance, such as John Boyd who wrote: "Regarding the matter of standardization at the A.I.A. Convention, under present conditions the type of standardization which the directors of the Institute warned against is entirely different from what you have in mind."[49] Fuller was emphasizing the distinction between his interest in standardization and what the AIA rejected because he wanted the organization to assume trusteeship of the 4D project.

Fuller did not broach this subject in St. Louis; he first suggested it in his June 8 letter to Hewlett: "This is an official offer to you in your capacity of first Vice-President of the American Institute of Architects. . . . I thereby offer to the Institute, prior to its becoming in anyway commercialized, an eleven months option to acquire the controlling interest of the 4D patents."[50] Fuller was only offering the AIA a controlling interest, not ownership. Basically, he wanted the organization to assume responsibility for protecting and developing the 4D House, perhaps to help ease the financial responsibility of his two committed investors, Russell Walcott and John Douglas.[51] He explained to Hewlett: "If [my offer is] taken up by the Institute the two main requirements will be that an international contest of design be worked out . . . with a contractual obligation of the contestants that all title to ownership of . . . design automatically accrue to the AIA; the second is that the Institute place and carry adequate patent insurance of the 4D letters patent."[52] Fuller also requested the AIA work in tandem with the Harvard Business School: "a portion of the patent interest . . . deeded to the Harvard School of Business Administration, in turn for its services in the evolution of . . . administration and stock ownership distribution that will make 4D most widely participated in and beneficial to, the permanent competence of mankind."[53] He abandoned the idea of contacting the Harvard Business School by mid-August because he realized it was a bad idea. Fuller did not explain what his own role in this three-way partnership would be.

Fuller was clear all involved parties would benefit financially. He emphasized that the AIA would gain from the collaboration since he was rather audaciously asking it to help develop the project. In return for its assistance, the organization would earn income and maintain its significance within architectural culture. He worried about the AIA's solvency as "the treasurer's statement . . . reveals a trying financial condition."[54] Fuller focused on the benefits the AIA would reap because he wanted his father-in-law to act as his representative in the negotiations.

Hewlett was skeptical of Fuller's proposal on a number of levels. He thought the project was sound, but needed to be more thoroughly developed: "Granting the economical soundness of the basic idea — which I certainly do grant — I am rather appalled by the number of supplementary matters in regard to which some solution will be necessary before making an actual plunge into production but that of course is a matter that you have been giving constant thought to."[55] Hewlett also informed Fuller that he was returning some materials because he was too busy to give them the attention they required:

I am returning herewith the information you sent me in regard to the patents, applications, etc., as I do not think there is any likelihood that I can contribute any useful ideas unless I get a great deal more time than at present seems to be available to think over the matter. . . . I shall be interested to hear further of your plans as they develop and, also, whether the backing that you are relying upon is in your judgement sufficient to tide you over what must necessarily . . . be a long period of experimentation and promotion.[56]

He encouraged his son-in-law to pursue the project without losing sight of his financial considerations.

This kindly letter was sent a little over a month after Fuller initially offered controlling interest of the 4D letters patent to the AIA through Hewlett. His father-in-law did not respond to that proposal, and Fuller apprehensively awaited Hewlett's reaction:

Anne has written you that I am extremely anxious to hear from you in reply to my letter of June 8th. . . . A number of the architects out here know of my proposal and are anxious to know what your action will be. Those who are interested in the Institute would like to see them take it provided it was assured of a progressive management, but they are all fearful that there are too many habitual worshipers of "good old times" to permit its acceptance.[57]

Fuller was pressuring Hewlett for an answer his father-in-law may have wanted to avoid giving.

Hewlett's response arrived on July 12. He reminded Fuller that a mass-produced, standardized house went against the AIA's position of promoting the art of architecture:

> *Under the constitution of the Institute I do not see how it would be pos-*
> *sible . . . to accept such a position in relation to any proposed program of*
> *procedure. The basic principle of such an organization is the encouragement*
> *of proper individual effort in the practice of the art of architecture. . . .*
> *Whether you like it or not and whether you think this attitude is progres-*
> *sive or not, the fact remains that it is the prevailing sentiment of the Ameri-*
> *can Institute of Architects . . . that the sort of standardization now going*
> *on in many branches of industry is definitely hurtful to the development of*
> *architecture as an art.*[58]

Even though he was losing patience with his persistent son-in-law and was not willing to act as Fuller's emissary, Hewlett explained the correct procedure for approaching the AIA:

> *The proper way for you to handle this matter is . . . to address a communi-*
> *cation to the American Institute of Architects describing . . . the fundamen-*
> *tal ideas . . . and expressing the desire that the patents covering these ideas*
> *should be placed under the control of a body of men or a board of trustees*
> *selected with the sole view of utilizing those patents for the benefit of the*
> *art of architecture in general. My expectation would be that if the matter*
> *was presented to the Board of Directors . . . in that form, the whole matter*
> *would be referred to the Structural Service Committee of which Mr. Max*
> *Dunning of Chicago is the Chairman, and any subsequent action on the*
> *matter by the Board would be dependent on the report of the Structural*
> *Service Committee. . . . You understand that this is entirely a personal let-*
> *ter and not in any way a reply to any formal proposition on your part to the*
> *Institute. If and when such formal proposal is made, it will have to come*

*through the regular channels as I have outlined above but my advice to you
would be to see Max Dunning and explain the matter personally and fully
to him, showing him, if you like this letter and see what he says.*[59]

Hewlett wanted to dissuade Fuller from continuing with his offer. But, if Fuller
were going to proceed, he would shift responsibility for its probable rejection
to Dunning.

As instructed Fuller sent the material to Dunning, and a bit later lamented:
"Have not as yet heard from Dunning!"[60] By the end of July, Fuller knew the
AIA was not interested in his offer. He sent letters to Raymond Hood and Mr.
Sternfeld conceding that his plans for the AIA's participation were not going to
materialize: "The possibility of the acceptance by the Institute of the proposition referred to in the letter seems, at this time, to be improbable. . . . It would
be feasible, but the mental reorganization of so large a group, fixed in habit,
would seem too great an undertaking within the specified time."[61] Dunning and
Hewlett may have stalled on accepting the 4D patent instead of rejecting it.
Fuller insinuated as much to George Buffington, a banker he tried to interest in
the project:

*You undoubtedly are wondering about the outcome of the offer to the
AIA. . . . Following Mr. Hewlett's suggestion I submitted it to Mr. Max
Dunning. . . . Mr. Dunning said that the Institute would need 3 or 4 years
to even bring about its submission as a question. . . . This of course precludes
the possibility of its being accepted by them, though Mr. Dunning, as also
suggested by other architects who are interested, advised leaving the offer
as a tantalizer for . . . 8 months.*[62]

Hewlett and Dunning succeeded in convincing Fuller to abandon his efforts
to enlist the AIA as a partner in the 4D House project. The events at the

convention should have forewarned him of this outcome. At the convention he did convince a few members of the soundness of his idea. He also realized that successful promotion of the project did not require sanction by the organization, although it might have helped to put the 4D House into production.

The AIA's opposition to standardized design, and therefore to the 4D House, did give Fuller an unusual opportunity to transform a potential ally into a foe. Since the organization felt standardization was detrimental to the art of architecture and to character of design, Fuller was able to infer that its insistence on traditional qualities meant reliance upon traditional methods. He was then able to portray the AIA as a backward group "fixed in habit." The fixed habit was traditional custom design built by traditional construction methods. Thus, Fuller was able to use the AIA's opposition to standardization of design as a powerful tool in the engineering of the platform from which he advocated the advantages of the 4D House, his ideal, industrially reproduced dwelling.

5

SUPPORTING DOCUMENTS

Of course, when Fuller went to St. Louis, he had a strategy for promoting the 4D House. He was prepared to persuade the AIA to accept the part he wrote for it. His strategy involved speaking to as many members as possible to gauge from whom he might gain support. This meant he could put his essay into sympathetic hands and avoid giving it to people who might discard it as extraneous material picked up at the convention.

The text was most likely the first eighteen chapters of *4D Timelock*. It is highly unlikely he would have shared the patent application since it had not yet been granted. The "Fuller Houses" essay was too technical and not developed enough to circulate. Since *4D Timelock* was a compilation and refinement of Fuller's other writings on the industrially reproduced house, it is logical that he would give this more polished essay to his most important audience.

Among the texts assimilated into *4D Timelock* are a three-part, short document written under the aegis of the Cosmopolitan Homes Corporation (CHC) and a lengthy essay entitled "Lightful Houses." CHC is only used in this context and may have been the first name change for Fuller Houses, which became 4D in the patent application. The CHC essay is probably related to, if not the same, as the outline Fuller distributed at various times during the project's development. It is a short, concise text proposing the establishment of a company to manufacture a new, industrially reproduced house. Fuller was very clear that the subject under consideration was an innovative idea, worthy of attention.

The CHC essay describes the characteristics of Fuller's project, outlines the advantages of the proposed house, and unabashedly solicits comments from its readers. Fuller drew upon his Stockade experience by petitioning testimonials. To help the reader comprehend its message, the CHC essay is divided into three clearly delineated sections: cover letter, "Cosmopolitan Homes Corporation Lightful Products" ("CHC/LP"), and "Cosmopolitan Homes Corporation Lightful Products Trademark" ("CHC/LTM"). This organization introduces the reader to the ideological basis of the house before presenting its formal properties and accessories. Fuller may have thought the reader would be intrigued enough by the ideas expressed in "CHC/LP" to accept the novel structure described in "CHC/LTM."

"CHC/LP" begins with a distinction between stoutness and weight, as demonstrated by a character in *Beau Geste* called Stout Fella. Fuller used Stout Fella's strong body to segue into the abstract notion of stoutness that he defined as "great power, but no weight—courage, love, truth, faith, all things which are of God."[1] As he informed Larry Stoddard, God was the foundation of his idea. Through the combination of God, spirituality, and commercial enterprise, Fuller was positioning himself, in Karl Conrad's words, as an "evangelistic businessman."[2] Industry was the vehicle through which Fuller intended to transform himself into an agent of benevolence and to realize his ideal of the spiritual obtaining the material: "[W]e have researched, analyzed, and designed a proper HOME for industrialized production and distribution, for the individual promotion of mankind. This is our religious practice, our complete faith is in God who is love."[3]

Direct reference to God would quickly disappear from Fuller's writings. Perhaps he realized how unfashionable religion was in an industrial world that praised machines, efficiency, and geometry as if they were divine. Fuller believed technology could only make a house that would be transformed into a home through the presence of God and spirituality.[4]

Fuller believed the spiritual and industrial needed to be employed in tandem because sole reliance upon the technological resulted in debased materialism. He thought some industrialists, like Henry Ford, were advocating this type of dangerous philosophy. Fuller criticized Ford's glorification of industry and its machines. He felt Ford attached too much importance to materialism as evidenced by the titles Ford gave to some articles, especially "Machinery and the New Messiah."[5] He generally considered Ford and his assembly line method of production models to emulate but did not accept Ford's attitude toward machinery. Furthermore, since Ford was primarily working for his own benefit, Fuller found him selfish.

Unselfishness to Fuller meant working for the benefit of others without compromising one's well-being. For example, when possible Fuller patented his ideas and maintained control of the patents, which allowed him to collect licensing fees. Collecting fees was not a selfish act to Fuller since they provided him with the means to continue to work for the benefit of humankind.

Selflessness and working for the benefit of others would become mantras in Fuller's discourse unlike spirituality and God. One other theme in "CHC/LP," lightweight materials, would continue to figure prominently in Fuller's rhetoric. And, like spirituality and God, other themes would be pushed into the background. These included the fourth dimension, the gold standard being replaced by the time standard, and the drudgery-free house.[6] Even though he would personally benefit from the design, manufacture, and marketing of the drudgery-free house, Fuller believed that his willingness to produce such a house to make life better for others exemplified his selflessness.

Of course, the purpose of "CHC/LP" was to persuade readers to invest in the start-up company that would manufacture the ultimate drudgery-proof house. Fuller was subtle and did not explicitly ask for financial commitment even though he was specific about his goal to put such a house into production. He was able to focus so clearly on the project because he had developed it "through systematic PRACTICE of RESEARCH * ANALYSIS * DESIGN * AND PRACTICE,"[7] just as Richard Bach advised. The results of this methodical approach were not divulged in "CHC/LP"; rather, they were presented in "CHC/LTM."

"CHC/LTM" is similar to the patent application in that they both describe the house using technical details. In the patent application, Fuller could only discuss what he created, but in "CHC/LTM" he could also include commercially available products. "CHC/LTM," therefore, is the first in-depth description of the house and its accessories. Fuller estimated his ultimate drudgery-proof house with its complement of mechanical systems and appliances would soon be in production. With characteristic confidence he explained to his mother in the summer of 1928: "In a year or so when my . . . houses are ready we will be able to put them up . . . in one day with every facility of modern city luxury built in, quite as comfortable in winter as any other time."[8] Fuller obviously intended to put the house into production as quickly as possible. It was designed neither as something to be realized in the future nor as something beyond the reach of contemporary technology, which was also true for the final version, Dymaxion House. Fuller began to present the project as futuristic once it became clear the house would not be realized. By turning the house into something to be desired, something unattainable in the present, Fuller was able to keep it in the public arena and give the project much more power than it would otherwise have had. It was a brilliant strategy. It is important, however, to remember that he intended for the house and its accessories to be produced with technology available in 1928, even if the technology would require a little fine-tuning to meet his specifications.

Fuller, after all, was not trying to interest potential investors in a futuristic design, but in a new company eager to manufacture its innovative product. CHC was more than a design-research company; it was a company in search of capital that would allow it to produce a house reflecting its research. Research indicated the public was ready for an affordable house, full of mechanical conveniences to make life easier, just like the one described in the text.

The house promoted in "CHC/LTM" combines new components with elements from the houses diagrammed in "Fuller Houses" and the patent application. It would have two bathrooms, a grill or kitchen, laundry, garage, living room, and presumably sleeping quarters although none are mentioned. Each room would be full of life-improving accessories. The bathrooms would be for personal hygiene and exercise with shower, tub, scales, vacuum-electric hair clippers, vacuum toothbrush, and chinning bar. The grill would have glass-doored cabinets, a formal table, a counter, and numerous appliances such as an electric cooker, electric refrigerator, and dishwashing machine. The laundry would contain a cornucopia of labor-saving instruments: electric washer, centrifugal wringer, hot air dryer, electric ironing equipment — all reduced from industrial scale for home use. In addition, there would be a special tub for fine laundry that would mechanically wash the linens and place them in the hot air dryer until they were to be ironed. While everyone living in the house would benefit, the grill and laundry room appliances were specifically intended to ease the drudgery of women.

The rooms for traditional women's work were balanced by a place for traditional men's work: the garage. It was designed as a workroom, storeroom, and service area. Among the items Fuller thought necessary for a properly arrayed workplace were a compressed air pump, lathe, tools, vice, machine shop, and laboratory. Some of these were geared toward easing work, while others straddled the boundaries between work and play.

This is also true of some of the devices intended for the living room. Fuller outfitted this room as a combination entertainment center and office with a "desk, filing cabinet, typewriter, calculating machine, telephone/radio-television receiver, dictaphone, stationary . . . and a valuable safe."[9] Obviously, the various items Fuller specified for this room, and the house in general, were the things that he thought were needed in a home. Some people might prefer their living room to be more a place for relaxation and less a place for work.

Fuller believed instruments for work and play were required to balance those necessary for meeting people's basic needs: eating, sleeping, and keeping clean. Utilizing machines to deal with these necessities would lead to unprecedented creativity and personal growth. To Fuller appliances were not simply labor-saving devices; they were a means to a better, more meaningful life.

The life-enriching and protective house Fuller proposed in "CHC/LTM" consists of mechanical systems, enclosing walls, and structural supports very similar to those detailed in the patent application. It would have unbreakable windows that would let in healthy light but keep out bothersome noise and heat. In addition, an automatic ventilation system would regulate temperature and humidity levels while removing dust and odors. Fuller planned to optimize materials and equipment to provide a clean, healthy environment in which individuals could pursue their interests. Therefore, lighting would be flexible, indirect, of varying intensity, and of any color desired. It would also provide heating. Light-radiated heat would enter rooms via ceiling ducts and be expelled at floor level. This is another feature shared with the house in the patent application.

Like the patent application house, the "CHC/LTM" house would also be supported by a central caisson mast "similar to cage mast of battleship, or lighthouse or airship tower."[10] The house's position on the caisson mast depended upon its location; it would be higher in regions prone to flooding and near the ground in dry areas. The caisson mast contributed greatly to the extraordinary soundness of the house since it would be sturdy, clean, able to withstand natural disasters, and equipped with alarms to ward off burglars. It would also hold the septic tanks, oil storage, air filters, electric generator, batteries, motors, and water treatment facilities. In other words, it would be a service space that also acted like a supporting skeleton.

Fuller was clear that the design of the house was related to that of the human body. He categorized the "arterial pumping and filtering units" as a "nervous system (similar to human body)" with each function "segregated (as in the human body)."[11] The two-story body of the house would be stabilized by steel piano wire in tension, attached to the caisson mast in a manner reminiscent of the way human ribs attach to the backbone.

Like those in a human body, the nervous system and skeleton of the house would be encased within protective coverings. All materials would be noncombustible and all metals rust-proof. The windows would be of safety glass in varying degrees of transparency. Floors would be covered with a football-like fabric. In contrast to the human body where the hard skeleton is inside the body, the harder, more protective materials were intended for the house's exterior.

Fuller thought of the human body as an appropriate analogy for the house since each was an optimal design. According to Fuller, God "solved every mechanical problem and completely segregated every function and material in the

construction of the human being."[12] He was following God's example in his reliance upon standardization since God designed humans to be as "alike as two
peas, none with noses in the middle of the back."[13] He also found a model in
nature because "slowly nature has centralized production through industry and
taken the one best mechanical way of doing something."[14] Fuller would utilize
standardization and mechanics because the "house and its functions are material and therefore solvable in but one best way."[15] That "one best way" was a
house unencumbered by foolish dependence upon style and designed to function with utmost efficiency, like the human body.

On the other hand, Fuller grudgingly conceded that issues of style could not
be dismissed so easily since people were often slow to accept change. Therefore, a stylistic overcoat might need to be applied to the industrially reproduced house. He described the structural system as a standardized, reinforced
concrete or fireproof steel chassis with 9' bays. Chassis referred to the frame
created when the different structural components, such as floor wires, were
connected to the caisson mast. Fuller was specific that the stylistic overcoat
would be affixed to the chassis and not be an integral part of it.

The chassis would significantly reduce the amount of time and the labor
needed to construct the "CHC/LTM" house. Contradicting the statement to
his mother that the house could be erected in one day, Fuller here estimated a
few days would be needed to assemble the standardized chassis and roof. He
promised even more savings would be realized as the business became profitable
and more parts of the house were standardized, such as the plumbing and utility units. When most of the house was standardized, architects would become
interested in it and would recommend it to their clients. This would happen because architecture is the "most altruistic of professions" and architects are willing "to lend themselves to progress and its harmonization."[16] Architects would
embrace the standardized house and its components without being threatened
since they "are responsible for but 5% of the home building and . . . will always
have their monumental and tailor made jobs."[17] The standardized "CHC/LTM"

houses would not replace custom houses; they would make it possible for architects to devote more time and energy to the latter.

Architects would have access to products manufactured by CHC through licensing contracts granted by vested interests. Fuller acknowledged a need for patience until business picked up. He cleverly extolled the rewards interested parties would reap as he slyly solicited their monetary contributions.

Fuller was very clear "CHC/LTM" was a business prospectus intended to attract capital. He outlined the company's status and explained what steps needed to be taken to ensure its success. He claimed almost all the necessary capital was invested, and just a bit more was needed to protect the patent and hire certain specialists. He was carefully reassuring interested parties their monies would be properly utilized while subtly hinting investment opportunities in the attractive new business could quickly disappear. After all, almost all the required funds were secured.

This was a slight exaggeration albeit a shrewd sales technique. Only two investors, Russell Walcott and John Douglas, had signed contracts and contributed funds to the project. Fuller knew people were willing to invest in a company that appeared financially sound. Therefore, he ended "CHC/LTM" on as strong a note as possible, even if it meant making the company seem a little sounder and more structured than it actually was.

"CHC/LP" and "CHC/LTM" are compact and straightforward compositions cataloguing the purpose of CHC, where the company stood in terms of development, and what remained to be done. Given their factual, businesslike nature, it is easy to consider them as outlines or brief explanations of Fuller's project. This may be one reason he either wrote or polished the more poetic treatise "Lightful Houses" during "holly [*sic*] week" in April 1928.[18] A couple of months earlier he noted that he "worked on Fuller Houses . . . all evening working out fields of utility and procedure of various departments. Worked out architectural dept."[19] These are components of "Lightful Houses," not the

CHC texts; Fuller must have realized he needed lengthier, more philosophical descriptions of his purpose and his project.

Fuller wrote "Lightful Houses" as if he were telling a story, recounting to the reader his journey of discovering the benefits of this type of house. As a combination of biography, manifesto, sermon, and predictions for the future, "Lightful Houses" established the format Fuller would follow in the majority of his later writings. Because it was part of a corporate prospectus, "Lightful Houses" also includes an outline of the company's activities, departments, and "Objects of Corporate Activity."

Fuller arranged the four corporate activities—research, analysis, design, and practice—in order of importance. He translated his principles for designing from the inside out into business activities. The company would have twelve equal departments: Administration, Advertising, Architecture, Engineering, Fabrication, Financial, Information, Legal, Service, Personnel, Selling, Transportation. The relationships between the activities and departments are not elucidated, perhaps because each department would be involved with every activity at some level. He itemized the fields of activity for only two departments, Architecture and Administration; the other departments he viewed as standard business divisions that did not require definition. In addition, he wrote a definition only for Architecture: "[A]rchitecture is the harmonious expression of character in building, within any or all of the media of conscious expression."[20] The twelve departments would periodically revisit the corporate activities in order to achieve the corporate objectives.

Fuller next described six Objects of Corporate Activity geared toward establishing a monopoly over all stages of production of the house and its components. He was careful not to use the word monopoly, preferring the more subtle "exclusive."[21] He intended to maintain control over the manufacture, assembly, and marketing of Lightful products by restricting the allied industrial companies to exclusive contracts. Perhaps memories of his Stockade difficulties influenced the structure of the corporate activities. As at Stockade, Fuller was attempting to fit a new product into an existing network of financiers, manufacturers, and distributors.

This was to be a temporary situation since he planned to acquire ownership of all related industries. Fuller used Ford and General Motors as business models. His corporation would mimic their development by centralizing production through the acquisition of related industries. Fuller considered centralized organization essential to efficiency and the end of exploitation by competing interests. Competitors were able to promote their own products because house building was not an organized industry. Fuller acknowledged that he was not the only one to recognize this situation, but he claimed to be the only one poised to act by establishing the Lightful Corporation.

Lightful Corporation was one of the various names, like Fuller Houses and Cosmopolitan Homes Corporation, Fuller considered before temporarily settling on 4D. It is clear that Fuller Houses was the first name of the company. Whether Cosmopolitan Homes Corporation preceded Lightful Corporation or was a short-lived alternative to it is uncertain. During the preparation of the *4D Timelock* manuscript, "Lightful" was replaced by "4D," a change precipitated by the patent application.[22] Fuller did not discuss why he changed Lightful to 4D, unlike his explanation of why 4D became "Dymaxion," the final name of the project.

The meaning of Lightful is obscure unlike that of 4D and Dymaxion. 4D, as noted, refers primarily to the fourth dimension. Dymaxion was fabricated out of three words: dynamic, maximum, and ion.[23] Fuller gave no clear-cut definition for Lightful. Joachim Krausse and Claude Lichtenstein argued in *Your Private Sky* that Lightful denoted "'full of light,' 'lightweight,' 'delightful,' 'light-Fuller.'"[24] Y. C. Wong felt it was a "double-coded semantic contrasting the significance of lightness as opposed to weight and substance on one hand; and light as opposed to darkness on the other hand."[25] Christian Øverland understood Lightful as "meaning most efficient in terms of the available technology. In essence, Lightful means doing more with less."[26] Given Fuller's proclivity for word games, it is conceivable that each interpretation is correct, but they do not exhaust the possibilities.

Lightful also indicated the house was a healthy environment filled with the presence of God. God, spirituality, and religion were not academic exercises to Fuller; they were living presences in his life. He regularly attended St. Chrysostom's Episcopal Church in Chicago during the project's development. Undoubtedly, Fuller knew the association between God and light in Christian theology: God is light. Therefore, the Lightful House would be a Godful house.

God was, as noted earlier, "the basis of the plan." The plan was to establish a corporation to design, manufacture, market, and service an industrially reproduced house. Fuller thought the corporate structure should be reflected in the house: "The home is a corporate soul and corporate life in a house."[27] It seems likely that in Fuller's corporate home God's significance positioned him at the head of the corporate household—God was president of the corporate house. The corporate house, like the corporate business, was divided into different types of activities. The activities described in "Lightful Houses" are similar to those outlined in "CHC/LTM" and are divided into what one does out of necessity and what one does by choice. Fuller did not include religious worship in either category. He may have believed God's presence would be understood since the house was called Lightful.

The Lightful (Corporate) House would be independent and self-supporting like a corporate business. Fuller knew corporations have hierarchical structures and issue different types of stocks. He may have been willing to let investors participate in his new venture, although he was not going to relinquish too much power. His position would be strong enough to allow him to be altruistic without fear of losing control of the project or the company. Fuller learned at Stockade not to lose control of either. God may be the head of the corporate household, but Fuller would be the head of the corporate business. His determination to secure patents and the Objects of Corporate Activity demonstrate his desire to control all aspects of the business.

Two very important components of the Lightful Corporation would be sales and customer relations. The general public would contribute to the company's success through these. Its roles would be limited to consumer and critic, much like the roles minor stockholders play in large corporations. Feedback via purchases, complaints, and compliments would help the board of directors make decisions. The board would function as a benevolent guardian responding to the appeals of its wards. The public's input might influence the board and might prompt it to act, but it would not share equally in decision making.

The board would primarily oversee the corporate activities in order to make the standardized, industrially reproduced house available. Even though he believed prejudice and misunderstanding created resistance to it, Fuller felt the public could adjust to this type of house because it was already used to mass-produce amenities, such as fabrics, prints, books, and automobiles. The standardized house need not suffer from a lack of aesthetics just as the standardized automobile did not.

In "Lightful Houses," Fuller used the analogy of the custom car to the custom house for the first time:

> If . . . a man wished to acquire an automobile, he were to . . . visit one of two thousand automobile designers in the city and they were together to pick and choose from the automobile accessory catalogs motors, fly wheels, electric wires, wheels, fenders, frame pieces, etc. and succeeded in designing an automobile somewhat after the style of some other fellow, and were then to have the design bid upon by five local garages . . . picking one of the bidders for his ability and price and the successful bidder were to insist on the use of some other wheels, etc. than were specified and the local bank in loaning the money to the prospective owner to help finance, were to insist on the replacement of some other units of the design . . . then the insurance

company were to condemn a number of the units used and others were to be substituted and finally, the local town council had to approve of the design and give permit, it is questionable whether anyone would go through with the building of the automobile, and should he . . . the automobile would finally cost him somewhere in the vicinity of 50,000 . . . completely without service when finished . . . in the building of the automobile there undoubtedly would be strikes by the plumbers . . . who would insist on the design being changed to conform to their rules.[28]

One problem with this story is that automobiles are manufactured products. Houses, however, have a long history of custom construction. In attempting to manufacture houses in the manner of automobiles, Fuller was attempting to launch a new product into an already established market. Some people were receptive and some were not.

Fuller was familiar with the problem of overcoming resistance to a new product from his Stockade years as he explained: "In introducing . . . an extremely advantageous and improved method of building . . . the writer ran up against . . . many conditions. He . . . exhibited his material . . . at Own Your Home Shows in New York and Chicago. . . . Literally thousands of enthusiastic prospective owners . . . had every intention . . . of building with the new system . . . the many obstacles such as building departments, etc., finally prohibited it."[29] In "Lightful Houses," he set the pattern for how he would manipulate this story to reinforce his own tale of struggle and travail. Fuller's audience would only have access to the version he was currently telling with its particular emphasis on how his innovation was repressed by the status quo. Fuller could thus present himself as a misunderstood underdog struggling to succeed against powerful odds. He often obscured his ambition by claiming that he was only trying to benefit others. Fuller wanted to be successful, to make money. One can only wonder

PLATE I

Anne Hewlett Fuller,
Tribune Tower, 1927.

PLATE 2

Buckminster Fuller,
4D Tower, 1928.

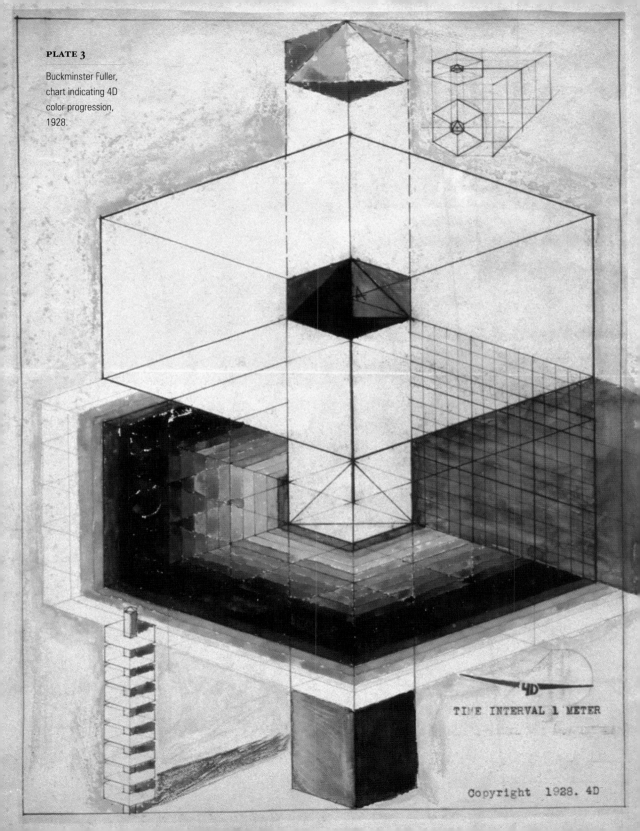

TIME INTERVAL 1 METER

Copyright 1928. 4D

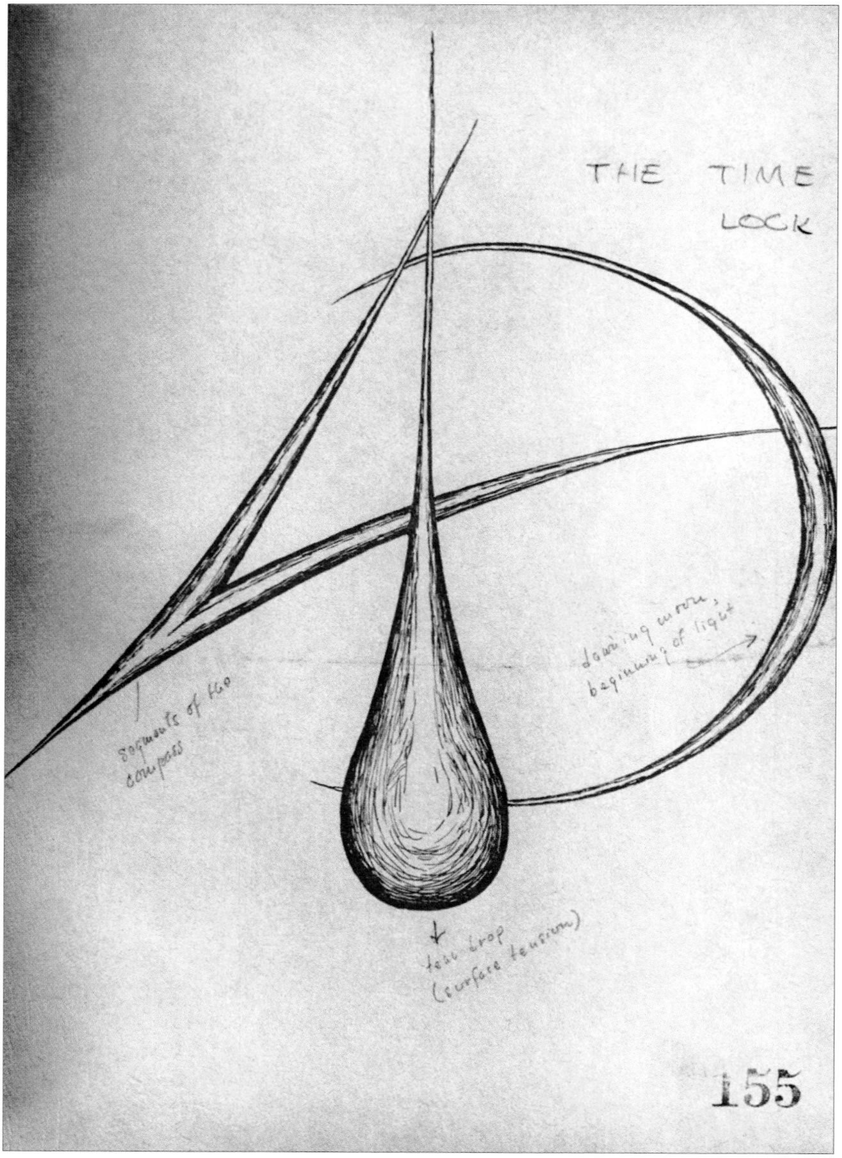
THE TIME LOCK
segments of the compass
dawning moon, beginning of light
tear drop (surface tension)
155

PLATE 4

Buckminster Fuller and unknown person, annotated cover of *4D Timelock,* copy #155, with symbolic 4D logo, ca. 1927.

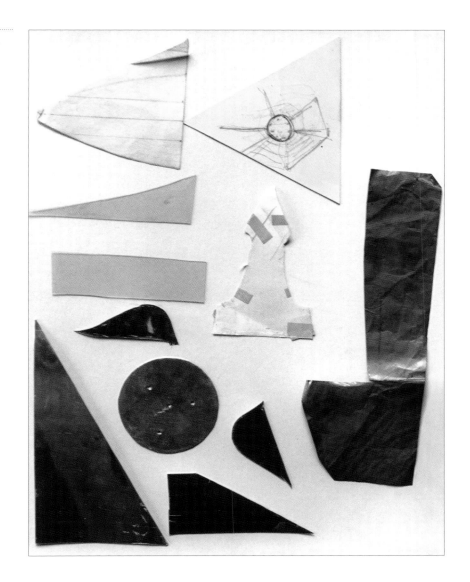

PLATE 5

Sample materials
used in first
Dymaxion House
model, 1928.

PLATE 6

Anne Hewlett Fuller,
third Dymaxion House
model, after 1932.

PLATE 7

Lee Atwood,
watercolor of
Dymaxion House
interior, 1929.

if his personality and drive thwarted his ambitions in this venture as it did at Stockade.

"Lightful Houses" is the first text in which he combined the personal, biographical, and industrial elements of his program. He did not cast himself as a misunderstood prophet of mass-produced houses; such characterization would come later. He had not yet failed, so he could not turn that to his advantage. The CHC texts and "Lightful Houses" are very much about business promotion, the primary theme of *4D Timelock*.

4D Timelock was a significant development in Fuller's ability to express his intentions in writing. It served as his business prospectus as well as his treatise on the philosophical underpinnings and formal properties of the industrially reproduced house. He must have believed it was the best representation of his work between 1927 and 1928 because it was the only text he reprinted. In it the intensive thought, thorough canvassing, and diligent research expressed in the other texts were synthesized into a single composition.

4D Timelock is a manifesto on the benefits of industrially reproduced houses, a set of guidelines for organizing a corporation to manufacture them, and a business proposal seeking investment capital. The somewhat unruly, rambling text is a thorough explanation of the philosophical foundations of Fuller's program. He treated many of the same issues, such as metal, standardization, time saving, style, and designing from the inside out, addressed in the earlier texts. Yet he did not carry all of the components of the earlier writings into *4D Timelock*. The references to personal elements are gone, a calculated decision on his part. Fuller may have thought the personal components would detract from the professional tone he was trying to convey. A note in the manuscript files reminded him to keep away from it: "Fuller Homes corporate activities and scope. Covers only what you will show to prospective interested parties. Therefore do not put in any RBF personal stuff."[30] Eliminating the personal would help the reader understand the text as a company's prospectus, not as a private project.

Fuller cleverly did not begin *4D Timelock* by jumping into the subject, but used a series of lead-ins to instill the urgency of his treatise upon the reader. To arouse curiosity, Fuller designed an attractive cover with a symbolic 4D logo (figure 5.1). The hook shape represents "segments of the compass"; the "curved shape" stands for the "dawning moon, beginning of light"; and, finally, the "teardrop" designates "surface tension."[31] This attractive, albeit enigmatic, cover was intended to entice the reader to open the book where the mystery continued for a few pages. Fuller warned readers that the contents were "STRICTLY CONFIDENTIAL" and "PROPERTY OF 4D" and then clumsily described the book as "[a]n Aphoristic essay of research and analysis of the past and present creation methods of man's living abodes. . . . Analysis by abstract and material comparisons to the activities of other industries. A wide discourse on the artistic and practical considerations surrounding the proper design of the new home. The birth of industrially reproduced housing . . . and individual duties."[32] Fuller further enticed the reader by stating the problem the text addresses. This was the house, and the solution was disclosed in the ensuing chapters.

The specific problem with the house, as Fuller defined it in chapter 1, was economic. The solution was to industrially reproduce, or mass-produce, houses. Not only had he figured out the problem and how to correct it, he had already organized a paper corporation to eradicate the problem. It was now up to the reader to act by investing in this fledgling industry and help make it a reality. *4D Timelock* is not simply a book about the benefits of industrially reproduced houses; it is also about the benefits of setting up a corporation to manufacture them. This does not invalidate Fuller's insistence upon selflessness: he would selflessly work to improve the lot of others while consequently improving his own. The vehicle to this improvement was the industrially reproduced house.

In chapter 1, *The great economic problem of this age, and all ages, the HOME,* Fuller explained that he was going to solve the small house problem by updating the housing industry. This meant founding a company to manufacture houses. Fuller's diverse background and Stockade experiences qualified him for this

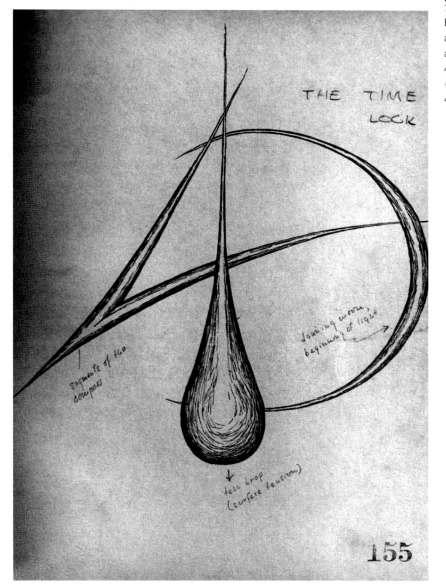

5.1

Buckminster Fuller
and unknown person,
annotated cover of
4D Timelock, copy
#155, with symbolic
4D logo, ca. 1927.

task. Using the statistics of the economist Roger Babson, Fuller pointed out that profits from the present housing industry were low. The way to improve the economics of the home-building field was to industrialize, or modernize, it.

Fuller demonstrated his understanding of the relationship between money, profit, and development in chapter 2: *The new generation and the revolution of truth*. Fuller believed children would reject their parents' houses in favor of the new mass-produced house. This new house would bring economic prosperity through its great potential for unlimited production. The industrially reproduced house could only ensure economic prosperity if organization, design, and promotion were used competently.

Fuller touched upon design issues in chapter 2 and focused on *The waste of Stylism, v's the worth of Character* in chapter 3. He advocated that a properly designed, industrially reproduced house would be functional, proportionate, and agreeable. He took a cue from his Stockade experiences and called for the use of scientific materials to make the house lightweight. Acceptance of the industrially reproduced house, he lamented, was inhibited by the problem of style since individuality and character are mistakenly attributed to material expression. The character of a house was not derived from its architectural style, especially any historicism that precluded designing from the inside out. To Fuller, character in a house resulted from a design based in the present. To design for the present was to design from the inside out for industrial production.

Industrial production, Fuller proposed in chapter 4, *Present chaotic picture of home building materials, methods, planning, and finance*, literally meant taking architecture out of the stone age through the use of metal. The time had come to use metal in houses for more than nails. Although he praised the virtues of metal, Fuller did not specifically state that industrially reproduced houses should be made of it. Instead, he switched to time saving and the economic benefits of mass production. To support his thesis, Fuller reused the story from "Lightful Houses," detailing the trials and tribulations one would encounter when ordering a custom car in a historic style. The slightly altered story was used to reiterate the need to organize the home-building field. Its disorganization allowed special-interest groups to dominate and prevented centralized quality control. This was probably a reference to the various regional certification tests Stockade had to pass when expanding into a new territory. Many of these tests were repetitious, and Fuller may have proposed this system to establish a central standard. He must have realized that not all regional tests could be eliminated since different areas have specific climatic conditions, such as excessive precipitation, and hazards, like earthquakes. Fuller was also suggesting that a centralized industry would reduce the power of special interests, such as lumber and cement, in the home-building field. Perhaps he was not conscious of it, but he was promoting his own special interest: the industrially reproduced house.

Fuller acknowledged that he was not the first to conceive of designing and marketing a manufactured house. Other companies marketed the basic shell and interior divisions but charged additional fees for accessories and labor. Fuller's concept differed because he would offer the house as a fully equipped unit instead of a divided container with optional accessories. As a newcomer to an established industry, Fuller wanted to give his product an edge by pointing out how much more progressive his idea was than the existing options.

Fuller was among the first to treat the house and its components as a unit. This was an idea he appropriated from the automobile industry. He understood that his innovative house with its unusual components would face strong opposition. He believed the most powerful opposition would come from established industries and trades threatened by the innovations incorporated into the house. He attempted to address anticipated criticism in chapter 5, *Analysis of the opposition*. He expected resistance from established companies since their products would no longer be necessary once the fully-equipped 4D House was on the market. As a case in point, he recounted problems encountered by a new building system (Stockade) at an "Own Your Home" exhibition, similar to those mentioned in "Lightful Houses." The story's purpose was to demonstrate

Fuller's familiarity with the obstacles, prejudices, and political backlash a new company faces when selfish interests are threatened by it.

The introduction of politics permitted Fuller to digress. He explained that rejection of the home-building field establishment was not communist since it could lead individuals to think for themselves rather than thoughtlessly follow the crowd. This led to criticism of current practices in collective bargaining as detrimental to "truth and TIME SAVING."[33] Fuller did not define truth although he posited that saving time was an economic law because it equaled saving capital. This was one reason historical styles were inappropriate for houses. Houses would be better designed through harmonizing mechanical functions and time saving. Fuller again referred to the automobile as a tool of persuasion. Advertising would remind his target audience it would not have cars if they were custom built and that industrial production would make it possible for individuals to have a new type of castle. Chapter 5 took many twists and turns to return the analysis of the opposition to the industrially reproduced house. Such wandering is characteristic of Fuller's writing in *4D Timelock* and makes it difficult to follow the text.

To Fuller, the deviations and digressions were connected to the theme of each chapter, as given in its title. For example, in chapter 6, *Analysis of the market — Its scope and demands*, Fuller began by drawing upon his experiences at Stockade that indirectly led him to solve the problem of the small house. He did not refer to Stockade by name; instead, he called it "the material" or "building system."[34] He used the company to show that the disorganized and old-fashioned home-building field did not want to improve through industrialization. Improvements, like those offered by Stockade and 4D, could lower the cost of a single-family house and invigorate the market. According to Fuller, there was "a falling off in the neighborhood of 50% in the erection of 5 room houses . . . during 1927" because "the small house has passed beyond the price limit of its market. . . . The latest model house of the NY-Herald-Tribune cost $45,000.00 of which but $800 was for mechanical time savers."[35] This was an outrage since industrial reproduction would both reduce the cost of a house and make life easier. The objective of *4D Timelock* was to convince people to invest in a company to manufacture low-cost, time-saving houses. No matter how far afield they might seem, the diverse arguments and comparisons were meant to persuade potential investors of the project's viability.

Fuller disclosed or created unusual relationships to support his claims. In one instance, he used population studies to justify promotion of the industrially reproduced house. He also compared the cost of the house to the cost of making a movie. Since the film industry kept its production costs low to generate more profit, it could serve as a model for the home-building industry. Some businesses, like car, rail, and airplane companies, served as models of what not to do. Fuller decided these were hastily set up without consideration for future development. The business that he was proposing would not suffer this fate because it would be centralized. In addition, his new, improved house would be harmonious and make life easier since he used advanced technology from existing industries connected to submarines, airplanes, hospitals, and theaters. In reconceptualizing the house, Fuller identified relationships that were normally overlooked.

He was able to discover these connections because he researched a number of different disciplines while trying to solve the small house problem. His research left no doubt that the type of house he proposed was inevitable: "By a reading of the articles referred to in the attached list of current references, written by acknowledged leaders in almost every great field of endeavor, the certain coming of an entirely modernized home, subject to the great benefits of mass production and transportation, will be evident."[36] The references, including contemporary architectural debates, were never included in *4D Timelock*. They are the subject of chapter 18 and are discussed here in that context. The only architectural text alluded to in chapter 6 is Le Corbusier's *Towards a New Architecture*; Fuller noted that others had realized that failure to improve the home-building field would lead to revolution. The indirect reference to Le Corbusier allowed Fuller to present his project as part of a larger, ongoing debate within contemporary architectural culture.

He also drew upon his familiarity with current architectural practices in chapter 7, *City vs Country design, criticism of both; indication of trends; and solution of technical design*. He began with the construction of tall buildings. Advanced technology was already being used in the construction of tall buildings and could be transferred to the home-building field. Yet he bemoaned the heavy masonry cladding placed on the exterior of skyscrapers that hide their structure the way a dowdy cotton stocking hides the leg under it. He proposed replacing masonry with a material that would reveal a skyscraper's form in the way a silk stocking compliments the leg on which it is worn. Some recent buildings, such as the Tribune Tower, however, used stone in a modern sense as exterior cladding to protect its internal frame or to provide a significant presence. He also applauded the Tribune Tower for its hexagonal plan that demonstrated rejection of the traditional orthogonal footprint, a design strategy he promoted.

In the Tribune Tower, Fuller saw hope that architects could cast off the yokes of masonry and designing from the outside in. Eliminating traditional construction and design methods would allow architects to comprehend the benefits of a circular plan and move away from boxy, preconceived designs. Here, Fuller displayed his affinity to and departure from Bach's article "Our Industrial Arts: Random Reflections on the State of Design." To Bach designing from the inside out meant letting the plan generate the form, whereas to Fuller it meant starting with a centered tower or support. Building with a central mast in combination with exploitation of metal's tensile strength would result in a new method of construction. Architects who failed to adapt to this new way of building would find their work obsolete.

The central mast would function like a tree trunk in a manner similar to the way the caisson mast of the "CHC/LTM" house would function like a backbone. It would support clusters of rooms as a tree trunk supports leaves and branches. If the weight were too great for one mast or stem, then a second mast could be added. In a rare acceptance of right angles, Fuller suggested that the clustered rooms on one stem could "be squared off to butt up" against those on another mast to create "a homogenous [*sic*] design of exterior covering, like a conventionalized clump or grove of trees."[37] The room clusters could obscure the masts just as leaves and branches veil their supporting tree trunks. Fuller was carefully informing his readers that this new type of construction was both efficient and aesthetic.

Fuller pointed out additional benefits offered by this new method of building. Taking another cue from Stockade, he explained it generated no waste materials. More important, eliminating wasted materials eliminated wasted time. Incorporating time would eliminate dishonest orthogonal forms whose origins lie in the fallacy that the world was flat. Honest design would be accomplished through the use of trigonometry or a mathematical system based on the circle instead of the right angle. Exactly how Fuller's new technical approach to construction, as manifested in the 4D House, related to the city or country design in the chapter heading, is not made clear. Perhaps Fuller was intimating that his new method of building would equalize the two.

If this were the case, Fuller may have considered the theme of chapter 8, *Analysis of standardization, truth, advertising and control*, as a means of achieving such equilibrium. He lauded the use of standardization and mass production within an individual structure to ensure consistent floor heights; standardization would stamp out arbitrary design decisions. Fuller never explained why individualism in design is undesirable while the type of individualism he was promoting, individual thought and action to oppose the status quo, was acceptable. He believed an individual thinker, a free thinker, understood the standardized, industrially reproduced house could reach a wider market than the one-off, custom-built, architect-designed house.

Fuller was also aware he would need to convince the general public of the benefits of standardized houses. He thought many people feared and mistrusted standardization because it implied an inferior product. If something was of quality and standardized, the general public would come to accept it. This was desirable since standardization signified both truth and progress. Acceptance of standardized houses meant rejecting the doctrines of traditional construction. Abstract thinking and a new beginning that erased old mistakes would help standardization and the industrially reproduced house gain approval. Advertising would assist in overcoming the distrust and fear of standardization.

Advertising appeals to the psychology of desire and replaces the psychology of fear as Fuller learned from Babson.[38] He would utilize all possible advertising venues to reveal the truth to the unenlightened masses. This truth would bring the new and efficient 4D House to scientific minds. Although more research and analysis were required before the final design could be determined, it was already patented. In truth, a patent application had been filed, but no patent had been awarded on this project. Fuller included this misinformation to warn potential competitors and copycats that his idea was protected. He believed when the design was determined and the advertising campaign set into motion, the demand for the 4D House would be so strong that other companies would begin to manufacture similar houses.

Even though the design was not yet finalized, Fuller insisted it would entail reduced building mass in chapter 9, *Weight in Building as the New Economical factor*. Making the house lighter would not compromise its quality because a lighter house would be a more perfect house. A lighter house would be more like other industrially produced objects, such as airplanes and automobiles, which also had to function efficiently.

The need for American architects to learn about the benefits of functional design and the use of industrial methods was the theme of chapter 10, *The Revolution in Design The Industrial ARTS vs Selfish Creation The New Scale and the Time dimension*. Fuller recommended Americans examine European design in order to apprehend its lessons. Stylism prevailed in America while Europe was experiencing a design revolution. Despite the advanced state of European design, Fuller warned, Americans should recognize that it was merely a trend.

A more important and permanent change was "PROGRESS BY CREA-TION as opposed to progress by destruction."[39] This meant using industrial methods to create houses instead of weapons. Abstraction and metal were critical to this transformation of the home-building field from a disorganized, client-oriented practice into a centralized industry. Fuller made another of his unusual connections by correlating the industrial production of the house to the shift of manufacturing from the house to the factory. Just as home manu-facturing was rendered obsolete by industrialism so would archaic construction methods be superseded by factory fabrication. Progress by creation meant bet-ter materials and better procedures would ensure better houses.

According to Fuller, the material best suited to machine production was metal, which he considered to be the fantastic new industrial tool. Metal would allow architects "to apply their [talents] to the new industrial canvas,"[40] as au-thors, composers, advertisers, and production glassmakers had done before them. Metal and industrial production in combination would produce a new type of house satisfying to both artists and industrialists.

This new type of architectural expression necessitated the use of modules, abstract thought, an understanding of the fourth dimension, and designing from the inside out. It did not mean abandoning the art of architecture. Rather, it brought the sculptor's art to the entire edifice, giving it an appropriate ap-pearance. Appropriate appearance meant the exterior reflected the interior to show that the house was designed from the inside out.

Building "From the Inside Out" as Opposed to building "From the Outside In" is the subject of chapter 11. According to Fuller, traditional architectural design meant starting with a plan's outer edges and then adjusting the design to fit the require-ments of the initial plan. Such an approach was old-fashioned, destructive, and wasteful. The natural way to build was from the inside out using a circular plan. He predicted the circle and trigonometry would end the tyranny of plane or cubical geometry and permit the incorporation of time or the fourth dimen-sion. Building from the inside out achieved progress through creation.

In chapter 11, Fuller repeated a few points, such as progress through creation, and used chapter 12, *Abstract Design, Harmony and Fourth Dimensional control*, to review information and address new topics. He again lamented that although European design was superior to American, it was still limited to surface decoration and stylism. This was because most contemporary design relied on Euclidian, or three-dimensional, geometry. The situation was not totally hopeless because some artists, whom Fuller considered the best of the day, were responding to the potential of mass production in their work. Mass production added time or the fourth dimension to design. With the introduction of the fourth dimension in chapter 12, Fuller switched from a summary of his previous points to an explanation of designing in the fourth dimension.

Designing in the fourth dimension meant designing according to time — the time it took to make an object as well as its longevity. Consideration of a material's life span was especially important in synthetics and combinations of materials. Only materials with equal longevity should be mixed. Adhering to this concept would produce more harmonious objects, reducing discord to a minimum. Fourth-dimensional design decreased weight, which in turn saved time, the new gold standard. A balance of "GOOD FAITH and TIME OR FAITH SAVING" produced "harmony of design as opposed to prosaicness (harmony is service, artistic appeal, etc.)."[41] This harmony was expressed in Fuller's industrially reproduced house whose radial design was based on the fourth dimension.

He believed designing in the fourth or time dimension, using radiating spheres and trigonometry, was truthful because matter is spherical. The length of a radius that extends from the center to the outer edge represented time. Fuller may have conceived this formula in February 1928 when he recorded that he formulated a theory about spheres in the diary; he made no comments in the entry about what the theory was. In *4D Timelock* he posited that if matter actually existed, it would have to be spherical. Fuller arrived at this conclusion through a reexamination of the principles of Euclidian geometry. According to Fuller, the failure to comprehend the spheroidal nature of matter was the reason the fourth dimension was denied. Unfortunately, the use of the phrase fourth dimension to denote time was also "incorrect and limiting" because it was based on the "fallacious three dimensions of cubism."[42] He would use the phrase because it was the contemporary representation of time. It was the closest approximation he had even though it was inadequate to express the relationships of geometry, industry, and time saving incorporated into the 4D House.

Fuller was eager to push the project to completion since he believed the house would help solve a multitude of social and personal problems. These benefits were advanced in chapter 13, *The Effect on Education and other problems of the new home — The New Home is applied Philosophy*. The new house would represent applied philosophy because it would contain mechanical appliances to ease menial labor and would be connected to an information network somewhat like the internet. Fuller anticipated some critics might find his goals for the house too far-reaching. Therefore, he argued that only when the patterns of life were understood would it be possible to solve the problem of the private house.

Fuller continued to explain how the 4D House would improve life in chapter 14, *Final Analysis and Guiding Considerations essential to a well rounded solution*. The new house would help eradicate low-paying jobs by helping people understand they could accomplish more through mental work than with manual labor. The inhabitants of this new house would be able to devote more time to mental activities because their physical labor would be lessened by mechanical shortcuts. Before the benefits of this new house could be enjoyed, however, it had to be designed and manufactured. All the details had to be worked out in advance because when capital, production, and distribution were in place all opportunities to invest would be lost.

Fuller wrote *4D Timelock* to help potential investors comprehend what he was trying to achieve and effectively communicate his goal. The essay treated an old topic in a new way. Those who understood the project's significance and its potential for generating income would help by investing in it. He again misleadingly stated that the idea was protected by patents. Fuller reassured his readers the project's details were the result of "protracted isolation for mental research, analysis, and design . . . aided by material self-negation."[43] He advised them that now was the time to take advantage of this opportunity.

Having made his argument about some of the intangible qualities of the house, Fuller next provided a description of it, its structure, and its accessories in chapter 15, *Some brief disclosures of the House itself as it will appear in the market. Separately marketable building products.* He again compared the house to automobiles. Like cars, the quintessence of industrial production to Fuller, the industrially reproduced house would have built-in mechanical equipment. This was as simple as built-in furniture and as complex as an air-cleaning, climate-control system to eliminate the need for bed linens and sweeping. The mechanically maintained environment would help keep the house so clean that the family would have more time for recreation. The purpose was to demonstrate the 4D House would care for the body as efficiently as it improved the quality of life.

The brief discussion of these features served as a prelude to the detailed description that was partially new and partially culled from earlier texts. Fuller started the description with what he considered the house's most attractive features: labor-saving devices and mechanical systems, assembled easily in one day, and designed according to 4D principles. The lead-in to the room-by-room description set the stage for the itemized list of appliances.

Fuller began with the kitchen, which would be equipped with an electric grill, electric range, electric refrigerator, dishwasher, sink, and cabinets with glass doors and shelves. From the kitchen, he turned to the laundry unit that would utilize domestically scaled industrial equipment. He reintroduced the automatic fine laundry cleaning feature. Then he moved to the garage with its machine shop, laboratory, and storage reached by chain hoist. He again envisioned the living room to be a combination entertainment/communications center and office. The two bathrooms in the 4D House would have facilities for personal hygiene and physical well-being. Fuller informed his readers all the parts of the house, from main rooms like the kitchen to auxiliary spaces like the garage, would be fully equipped.

Fuller not only outlined what would go into the house but also detailed its physical characteristics. All ceilings would be 9' high and the exterior walls would have 4D safety glass in varying degrees of transparency. Interior partitions would be pneumatic, unbreakable, and soundproofed. Flooring shared the latter two features and would be springy. The soft, bouncy flooring and built-in furniture would make the house safe for babies. Additional contributors to the ideal physical environment of the 4D House would be "overhead roller, inflation, or revolving type"[44] doors.

The revolving doors and windows would ensure environmental control. Such control would be necessary to allow the automatic ventilating system to keep the interior air dust-free, keep the humidity constant, and maintain an optimal temperature. When necessary, heat radiation drawn off the central lighting system would be blown into the rooms through ceiling openings and pulled down by floor vents. This system would not only circulate and remove heated air but also take away dirt, dust, and bothersome smells. The intrusion of offensive odors from the outside would be kept to a minimum by the revolving doors, windows, and air filters.

Fuller believed the complete, self-supporting 4D House required a central ventilation system with air filters in each room. It also needed septic and fuel tanks, energy sources, water supply, air and gas filters, clocks, and an alternative energy source. If any services were locally available, like sewage, water, or power, the price of the house would be prorated. If not, all facilities would be housed in the central caisson mast.

The house could be mounted on the central caisson mast at any point. Its position would be determined by climatic conditions, such as floods, or aesthetic considerations, like scenic views. If the house were above ground level, access would be via elevator. Although he did not indicate how, Fuller assured his readers that the 4D House was safe in the event of extreme weather, diseases, fire, and gas. An electronic security system would also be attached to the central caisson mast. Fuller was attempting to soothe any possible doubts about the safety and security of the house. The surveillance scheme would protect the house from human trespassers; the central caisson mast would protect it from natural as well as man-made disasters.

Not only would the house be safe and secure, it would be well made and require little maintenance. Nothing flammable would be used in it. Only rust-free or noncorrosive metals would be used. Surface finishes would never need retouching because the materials used would always retain their fresh-from-the-factory finish. The guarantees of safety and low-cost maintenance were echoes of the qualities assigned to Stockade houses.

If repairs, replacements, or improvements were required, these would be performed by the house's service station, a corporate maintenance and repair facility. The service station would deliver the house and assemble it in the following order: tank base planted; artesian well drilled; caisson mast raised; head trusses rigged out; and floors, partitions, and plumbing hung. The installation of factory made parts and segregation of functions would make it possible for the service station to quickly assemble the house.

Fuller again used the separation of functions to relate the house to the human body. For example, the caisson mast was like a skeleton and the "pumping or filtering units" like "the nervous system."[45] His argument was that as the separation of functions made the human body efficient, they would also make the house efficient. And, Fuller reasoned, the more efficient the house, the better life within the house. Because the mechanical systems incorporated into the house would perform the majority of the necessary, tedious tasks of daily life, the inhabitants would have more time to pursue their physical, intellectual, and aesthetic interests. The efficient segregation of functions would help business, selflessness, and creativity flourish in unprecedented ways.

Selflessness would increase as science continued to find the most efficient mechanical means to handle material affairs, allowing the 4D business to prosper. Like nature, science made segregated functions and the manufacture of standardized modular units possible. In terms of the 4D House, the modular units included arterial systems, support towers, pneumatic flooring, and isolation panels. Furthermore, these standardized units could be sold individually for incorporation into existing structures. Sales would only be through licensed vested interests. Business would be good, but only for those who were part of the 4D enterprise.

The structure of the proposed business is the subject of chapter 16, *Some remarks on the business organization*. After partnering with life insurance companies and securing legal and patent protection, 4D would use licensed contractors within the architectural and building trades. The contractors would market the house, foundation, and mechanical equipment at a fixed price plus any regional costs. The use of a standardized chassis would prevent architects from wasting time by repeatedly rendering the same details for different projects and would be complemented by standardized utility fixtures. Fuller argued that the novelty in this method of producing and assembling houses would attract more investors once they learned how profitable it could be.

Architects, to whom Fuller again credited only 5 percent of built houses, would serve as the engine through which this start-up company would become a successful corporation. They would facilitate the process by recommending either the entire house or different components to their clients. Architects would be required by agreement to share advertising revenues or participate in a shared advertising program.

In this way, the 4D corporation would be established. It was poised for take-off because most of the start-up capital was committed. A strategic move would be to shift much of the costs for research and development onto competitors who wanted to use 4D patents and products. Despite the personal and capital gains to be earned from the establishment of such an enterprise, Fuller feared greed would ultimately block its realization. Greed, which Fuller called the "truth of selfishness,"[46] could obstruct the growth of 4D since it controlled quite a bit of capital.

4D, like the Cosmopolitan Homes Corporation, consisted of twelve equal departments: Administration, Advertising, Architecture, Engineering, Fabrication, Financial, Information, Legal, Service, Personnel, Sales, and Transportation. These would be subdivided into the same four corporate activities — research, analysis, design, and practice — as CHC. The 4D Company would cycle through the activities to achieve its seven objectives:

1. long-term lease to establish exclusive rights to all patents relating to the 4D House terminated only by bankruptcy or disuse;

2. acquisition or licensing of any existing patents relating to any aspect of the 4D House and its components;

3. exclusive contracts for materials used in 4D products acquired by agreeing to share advertising costs;

4. exclusive contract with a national insurance company to both fund the marketing campaign and insure the 4D House;

5. exclusive contracts to fabricate, sell, and assemble patented 4D products;

6. exclusive contracts for worldwide distribution of 4D Houses and 4D products;

7. license contractors to market 4D merchandise.

These objectives outlined an important goal of the 4D company: dominate the market for industrially reproduced houses.

Fuller knew he would have to be completely focused and well organized to corner the market for industrially reproduced houses even if his particular version was not yet perfected. It was sound business to proceed, following the lead of the automobile industry. If automobile manufacturers had waited for the perfect design, no car would have been produced. Through repeated corporate research, analysis, design, and practice, the ideal house could be realized. The 4D

House could only be attained through industrial production and comprehensive, corporate organization.

The comprehensive corporation would facilitate control over all aspects of 4D. Fuller was determined to maintain control that was as strict as possible over the design and materials. According to the 4D objectives he would acquire all related companies. Another element of his comprehensive corporate control was to protect his idea by securing a patent on the 4D House.

The patent application was the subject of chapter 17, *The Patents*. This is an extremely short chapter because all the pertinent information was in the patent application, which was omitted.[47] Fuller claimed it was too costly to include the application instead of admitting his desire to protect his idea during the two years it took for issued patents to be published. Informing readers that he had filed the patent application, without revealing any of its details, helped him establish proprietorship of the 4D House and 4D products.

Fuller acknowledged the patent specifications and drawings were verbal and graphic representations of 4D philosophy, not artistic renderings, and he welcomed constructive criticism. He took the opportunity to announce that he would hold an international competition for the design of the 4D House after responses to the treatise were received and appraised. The essay was to serve as more than a business prospectus by sparking interest in the possibility of transforming the schematic patent drawings into an architectural classic.

Fuller was concerned about making an architectural statement with the 4D House. He planted the seed by announcing the forthcoming international design competition. In the first chapter he pieced together a quote from John Ruskin's *The Seven Lamps of Architecture*: "I would have our ordinary dwelling houses built to last and built to be lovely; as rich and full of pleasantness as any be within and without. When we build let us think that we build forever. Let it not be for the present life nor for the present use alone."[48] According to Fuller, Ruskin "did not confine himself to any stylistic description of the dwelling" but "called for character, harmony, and the best use of materials, methods, and thought."[49] Fuller used these criteria in the 4D House. He found them lacking in most contemporary structures that he dismissed as encumbered by stylism and surface design. He had addressed these issues in chapters 10 and 11 and echoed Le Corbusier's warning about architecture or revolution in chapter 6. For Fuller, it was necessary to start an architectural revolution by designing from the inside out and for industrial production.

Fuller believed that he was in position to initiate a revolution in the home-building field because he studied the problem of the house from a number of viewpoints. His research materials are the subject of chapter 18, *References and Dedications*. Fuller claimed that he had assembled "a 3,000 page scrap book of photographs and advertisements showing the fourth dimensional progress of various industries throughout the world, with architectural monstrosities and inefficiencies, as well as delights."[50] This scrapbook has not been located; in fact, given Fuller's propensity for overstatement, it may not exist. Or, he may be referring to the *Chronofile*. There is, however, an unpublished reference list attached to a copy of *4D Timelock* in volume 35 of the *Chronofile*, which reveals the diverse materials Fuller consulted as he explored the problem of the house.

Among the items on the reference list are a cartoon, numerous advertisements, articles, books, and, of course, architectural writings. Some are directly connected to Fuller's work on the 4D House whereas others have an obscure relationship to the project. Some were intended to situate the project within its historical context. Contextualization was important to Fuller because he believed that events do not occur in isolation. Although many of the seemingly odd sources on the reference list might appear unrelated to the text, to Fuller they were connected.

The items on the reference list regarding the current state of American industry, health, economics, design, and architecture are obviously related to the 4D House. Each subject influenced his decisions about the house and the company he was proposing to manufacture and market it. The numerous references related to architecture and design demonstrate a general awareness of coeval theories and debates. Fuller was informed enough to engage in the ongoing discussion about modern architecture in the late 1920s. Perhaps he felt that revealing his familiarity with Ruskin, Louis Sullivan, Frank Lloyd Wright, and Le Corbusier's call for architecture or revolution would signal a learned position. And, as chapter 18 confirms, the research also included topics such as sales techniques, economics, time, and individualism.[51]

Fuller used chapter 18, originally the last chapter, to reiterate some of his earlier points. The 4D House would specifically promote the creation of selflessness and individuality. It would also stimulate economic and industrial growth. The house would accomplish these things because it represented philosophy translated into contemporary form influenced by the fourth dimension and industrial processes.

Fourth-dimension thinking included fourth-dimension design that would stimulate creativity, not destroy it. Fuller did not explain how it would do this, although he was clear aesthetics and historicism were not to be the primary constituents of 4D design. Fuller was not completely eschewing aesthetics since the 4D House needed a pleasing appearance. Aesthetics occupied a secondary place in fourth-dimension design because Fuller believed the house's ability to improve the quality of life was more important than its appearance. The house improved life by fostering individualism and harnessing time. Harnessing time meant designing from the inside out, designing to facilitate life, and designing in metal. Stone and traditional design needed to be eliminated in order to improve the inhabitant's quality of life. Finding the best way to do this was Fuller's primary concern.

As he tried at the AIA convention, he requested input from his readers to help him arrive at the best solution. Fuller's activities at the AIA convention generated very little written response, although a number of questions were raised there. The additions of chapter 19, *Land to Sky The Outward Progression*, and its companion, *THE BEGINNING Rather than the end, for having started at dusk and traveled throughout the night do we not rest at Dawn? (A Footnote)*, were meant to address some of those questions.

Fuller attached the additions to the original text because it was wasteful to destroy the copies. He knew that comprehension of his message required deliberation, so he again advised his readers to carefully consider his message and not waste time by casually perusing it. Although the additions were mostly concerned with new information, some concepts, like selflessness and time, were thematically connected to the original essay.

When he repeated concepts, Fuller used the new treatment to expand upon his original discussion. For example, he strongly criticized consumption of alcohol as a waste of time and went so far as to suggest that the new house would end alcohol consumption; sober, healthy fun would become the norm. It would also bring out the presence of God in living persons, helping to diminish self-consciousness and expedite expansion toward God.

The 4D House would also be successful in obtaining its objectives and achieving capital growth even without salesmen. Perhaps his experiences at Stockade and Muller convinced Fuller to dismiss salesmen as a throwback to the days when a one-on-one approach was needed. In the media age, direct one-on-one sales were too personal, too limited. Therefore, impersonal but individual communication, such as broadcasting systems and written correspondence, would replace salesmen. Sales would not suffer because broadcasting the sales pitch would reach a greater audience than salesmen could.

The use of broadcasting reflected contemporary developments in technology and economics. Fuller prophesied that once broadcasting was perfected, real estate and railroad securities would be completely devalued. But, he cautioned, the owner of the new 4D home need not despair since the freedom it provided would eliminate both land mortgages and problems with moving. When the owners moved, the 4D House would be collected by the company's service station for storage or relocation. Such freedom of movement would eliminate the owner's servitude to a mortgage. Fuller also predicted the technology that made the 4D House possible would also create new economic and labor structures.

Some people in the 4D organization might work "one day per month at $1000. per day" and then spend the "rest of the time ... thinking, traveling, and gaining perspective [from] our old friends — Research, Analysis, Design, and Contact."[52] Those who persisted in being selfish or in being time wasters would remain "unenlightened" and "become sweepers in the ware houses of 4D. We may pay them $100. a day."[53] Fuller's proposed system, like his industrially reproduced house, dealt with work and play as well as physical and emotional well-being.

He knew that he was at the beginning of his crusade to realize this type of house and stated as much in the last addition to the text, the footnote to chapter 19. In a way, like the story about the jeweler exhibiting his goods he used in the preface, Fuller laid out his jewels in the preceding pages of his business prospectus. Although it was a difficult text, he felt anyone who read it in its entirety would become more of a free thinker, an individual. He also hoped those who reached the final paragraphs would be willing to invest.

They should invest in the company because "business of the new 4D House era is going to be damn good fun"[54] and make money. The individual could decide the appropriate amount of initial investment — in other words, the amount of involvement with the company. Having made and remade his case about the wisdom of investing in the 4D industry, Fuller informed his readers that he was going back to the laboratory, presumably to wait for responses.

He expected immediate, positive feedback since he was soliciting financial and ideological backing from his wide-ranging audience. The recipients included long-term associates, family members, new acquaintances, and powerful people. After the initial mailing, Fuller sent out more copies because he believed a copyright required verified receipt of two hundred copies. In 1928, however, a copyright could only be obtained by filing with the U.S. Copyright and Trademark Office.[55] Whether or not he knew this, Fuller desired formal copyright protection, like patent protection, to safeguard his own investments in the 4D project. Fuller also wanted the project to grow, so he encouraged his readers to help.

Fuller received a few replies, although no one signed on as an investor. Some reactions were positive whereas others were negative or politely dismissive. One supporter who served as a bearer of bad news was Fuller's friend and confidant, Larry Stoddard. Stoddard cheered: "You did a wonderful job, Bucky."[56] He also forwarded a copy of the text to his friend Bruce Barton requesting Barton consider it as thoroughly as possible. Barton may have devoted time to the book, but he was not impressed. He responded: "Possibly there is something in Mr. Fuller's idea, but if so it is so well concealed in his language that I have not discovered it."[57] In contrast to Barton's, there were a number of complimentary responses, most of them from people who were already admirers of the project. A few who were new to 4D reacted favorably. Gamaliel Bradford, a biographer of Fuller's great-aunt Margaret Fuller, was apparently one of these. He wrote, "[T]he subject is evidently of the first importance."[58] Fuller made no comment about the variety and low number of responses although they must have disappointed him. The text, like his efforts at the AIA convention, generated less interest than anticipated.

Given his frustration over the situation in St. Louis, Fuller may have decided a written prospectus would be more effective than an oral presentation. Fuller tried to put a positive spin on the events at the convention by including it in the experiment he described to John Boyd. According to Fuller, this trial convinced him to use the essay as an introduction to 4D: "For over six months prior to writing my manuscript, I carried out a very interesting experiment. . . . I formed a complete paper 4D company . . . which I proceeded to run . . . as if it were a real company. . . . While interviewing bus manufacturers, steel companies etc, the arguments would come up. I talked to . . . every type of person and I found that . . . the paper had to be written as the first contact."[59] The paper was not all that successful either. One reason is Fuller's verbose, convoluted, and seemingly aimless writing style. Barton complained about it, as did Fuller's brother, Wolcott. Anne also found it difficult, but she was more understanding than either Barton or Wolcott Fuller. She wrote to her brother-in-law: "I agree with you to a certain extent, that it is unnecessarily involved + too much philosophical digression + that it would be much more effective if it were shorter, snappier + more to the point, but Bucky certainly has had very enthusiastic comments on the book and it's brought surprisingly encouraging results. . . . Bucky feels it's all necessary and has all helped."[60] Even though Fuller believed everything in the text was necessary, its complexity and array of subjects made it difficult for some readers to grasp its purpose and meaning.

Fuller felt it was representative of his ideas and wanted the text to reach as wide an audience as possible. Therefore, he persuaded Francine Nelson, the French wife of the American architect Paul Nelson, to attempt a French translation. She began, but never finished.[61] Fuller also approached two or three publishers to make it available to the general public as a book.

He first negotiated with Charles Scribner's Sons, who insisted that he either rewrite the essay or use a ghost writer.[62] Scribner's must have convinced Fuller that reworking the text would improve its quality, because Fuller decided to seek input by making the book cooperative. He planned to lecture at the Architectural League in July 1929 and solicit commentary from the audience for possible incorporation into the text.[63] If the afternoon proceeded as planned, Fuller elected not to incorporate the suggestions. He did, however, write a table of contents for a general interest book. Despite Fuller's efforts, Scribner's ultimately rejected the manuscript.

Characteristically, one rejection did not dissuade Fuller. He simply fine-tuned the outline and then offered it to Harcourt Brace & Company. Harcourt Brace also declined because the company thought everyone who wanted to know about it already did. Therefore, "it would be almost impossible to attract a sufficiently large number of buyers."[64] Harcourt Brace's viewpoint is quite understandable. By the time he approached the company, Fuller had regularly lectured on the house and written numerous articles about it. If Fuller's intention was to publish the original essay as a book, its contents would have seemed outdated even though Fuller had refined and polished them. *4D Timelock* was in limited circulation until 1970 when Fuller chose to republish the essay and its additions.

Its limited circulation might have been another reason why Fuller decided to make the text into a diary, a history of the project's development. Unfortunately, the project did not proceed as expected. Successful realization of the 4D project would require different tactics, such as promotional lectures. These were very rewarding and drew upon Fuller's sales experience at Stockade and Muller. Reluctance to go back into the field may have prompted his initial use of the 4D essay. The essay was impersonal and could not make the persuasive argument Fuller could in person. To bolster his written argument, Fuller joined the lecture circuit to promote his concept of the industrially reproduced house and its benefits.

6

PROTOTYPE

Fuller may have preferred a written marketing campaign, but he was prepared to serve as the project's and the company's spokesman. He did not abandon writing. He was simply much better at communicating the urgency of his message through the spoken word instead of the written one. Whether employing oral or verbal strategies, Fuller was certain his 4D project would be successful. He briefly outlined his plans and expectations for his childhood friend, Lincoln Pierce: "I expect to write articles and get the business started as well. . . . The sincere interest of extraordinarily important people already heard from, seems to vindicate my conclusion that this is soon to be the greatest industry in the world."[1] He also confidently informed his mother that his houses would probably be ready in under three years.[2] This was before he knew the AIA would not help him develop the project. Fuller's certainty that 4D Houses would go into production was not diminished with the organization's rejection. He modified his plan and more actively began to look for other sources of support.

Exactly how much support Fuller secured in the early stages of the project is uncertain. Without specifying from whom or how much each contributed, Anne explained to her brother-in-law, Wolcott: "The organization . . . is just a preliminary agreement between Bucky and a few friends who are to put up enough money for current expenses in connection with 4D and to partly cover our living expenses (so that R. B. F. can devote his time to it) in exchange for a percentage of his personal interest in its sales."[3] These friends included Russell Walcott and John Douglas who signed on before the AIA convention. Paul Nelson, a Beaux Arts–trained American architect, also agreed to help. Nelson was in Chicago with the hope of repeating the success he had achieved abroad. They met as Nelson was preparing to return to Europe. Fuller felt that destiny had brought them together because 4D demonstrated a way for Nelson to reconcile modern design with economic considerations. Fuller enlisted him to serve as the 4D foreign representative and design supervisor. Nelson's primary role was to develop the European market. His contributions to the house's formal properties are not clear. Since he was acquainted with the work of Auguste Perret and

Le Corbusier, Nelson may have suggested that Fuller study it. He might have argued that elements of European modernism would improve the clumsy design in the patent application. It is unknown if Nelson contributed financially to the project.

Until Fuller began to lecture extensively on the project in the winter of 1929–1930, his income and funding were sporadic at best. The 4D company could never pay him a salary and he was not otherwise gainfully employed. His earnings were limited to the seed money he could secure and lecture fees he received. Fuller may also have tapped into the family's savings and investments to help make ends meet. Some fortuitous funds arrived from the sale of family properties in Cambridge, Massachusetts.[4] Anne and Fuller supposedly received small inheritances and a few old debts were paid.[5] In addition, Anne received her money, perhaps a trust payment or inheritance. During Fuller's troubles at Stockade, she had written to him that they could live on this if necessary.[6] But when she received it, she shielded it from her husband and entrusted its care to her brothers, an act Fuller considered to be selfish betrayal.[7] He was desperate for funding. Fuller knew that the costs of establishing the company were high; he needed lots of money. He also knew that strong consumer support would help convince investors of the soundness of the project. One method of attracting both was to lecture about the house as often as possible to as diverse an audience as possible.

It took time to organize lectures and exhibitions on the project. According to the "Dymaxion House Chronology," Fuller scheduled only one venue in 1928. This was on May 21 at the AIA convention where he appeared at the invitation of the Chicago Chapter.[8] Obviously, the chronology contains some errors: Fuller was not invited to the convention by anyone, and he could not have lectured on the 21st because it ended on the 18th. The next presentations are listed as "Jean Toomer Group" and "Chicago Artists Weisenborn Studio" in early 1929.[9] These would have been private events arranged by friends for select audiences. They would have helped Fuller prepare for the project's public debut at the Marshall Field Department Store in the Chicago Loop.

Fuller claimed the store invited him to present the 4D House to help promote a selection of modern furniture purchased at the 1925 Art Deco Fair in Paris. The store's intention was to create a "dramatic setting" in which the "advanced design of the furniture" would "appear conservative — new, but not too new."[10] The store's furniture ads in the *Chicago Tribune* during the two weeks in April 1929 when the model was exhibited feature traditional designs with cabriole legs, wingbacks, and overstuffed, upholstered cushions. Modern-style furniture is mentioned in small, unillustrated blurbs. Neither the 4D model nor Fuller's talks are promoted in any of these *Tribune* ads, not even in the store's full-page home furnishing advertisements on Tuesdays. The model was shown in the Interior Decorating Galleries on the ninth floor,[11] although how it was exhibited or among what items, if any, are not known. Nothing in Fuller's papers or in the Marshall Field archives provides information about the exhibition.[12] Whatever the department store's motivation for hosting Fuller and the model, it gave the aspiring industrialist a venue in which to personally present his project to the general public for the first time.

Fuller intended to make the most of this opportunity. Between April 6 and April 20, he gave a brief lecture about the house on the hour from noon to five o'clock each day (figure 6.1). He even agreed to change the name of the project, from 4D to Dymaxion, to make it more appealing. The change was suggested by "promotional minds" at the store, the advertising department, to prevent the house from being associated with "a grade in public school, or . . . living quarters on the fourth floor of an ordinary apartment" instead of the "fourth dimension."[13] Waldo Warren, an employee in the store's advertising department, created the new name, Dymaxion. According to Fuller, Warren took notes as he spoke about the house and its underlying philosophy. He then chose words from Fuller's vocabulary and broke them into their component syllables. He used these syllables to create words that reflected the meanings of the originals.

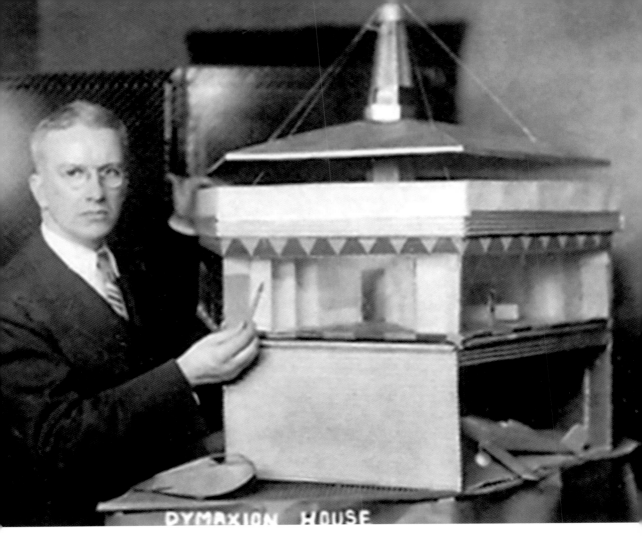

DYMAXION HOUSE

6.1

Buckminster Fuller pointing out
features of the Dymaxion House,
ca.1929. This was a staged photograph
used in various promotional materials.
It was not taken during one of the
lectures at Marshall Field.

Warren next asked Fuller to consider these and reject the inappropriate ones. In the end, "'Dymaxion,' a fusion of syllables related to 'dynamism,' 'maximum,' and 'ions,'"[14] remained. Again, no documents have been located to corroborate this story. In 1933 Fuller received a letter from Mary Reynolds, who worked with Warren, confirming Warren's involvement, although it does not shed light on his participation.[15] Fuller's willingness to attribute the creation of "dymaxion," a word that became synonymous with him and his work, to Warren lends credibility to the story. It also serves to demonstrate how easily someone outside the building and architectural trades could comprehend Fuller's message. A clearly articulated message and a snappy title were two important components of the aspiring industrialist's formula for success.

A third was a detailed model to translate Fuller's design and philosophy into three dimensions. Fuller could have, but probably did not, make a model for the patent application and AIA convention. It is, therefore, safe to conclude the first model is the one Fuller exhibited at Marshall Field (figure 6.2). Fuller acknowledged he had assistance without disclosing how or if his helpers contributed to the design: "I have a voluntary designing class that meets two nights a week and works even more frequently composed of young architects. . . . Their enthusiasm at having a problem so real and so full of creative possibility . . . is truly astounding."[16] Fuller's former coworker, Martin Chamberlain, became caught up in the excitement: "Hoping your plans are working out . . . and hoping that you will show me some of the designs that the boys have worked out for your new 4D houses."[17] The excitement was justified if the description Fuller sent to Nelson of the "exceptionally able men comprising the first 4D class" was accurate:

> The leader . . . is Leland Atwood, 27 years old, artist and draftsman. He has studied at the University of Michigan. . . . Others . . . are Robert Paul Schweikler, 25 . . . who won the scholarship of the Chicago Architectural Sketch Club, which sent him to the Yale University Architectural School

. . . Another is Clair Hinkley, 30 . . . who attained the highest marks at the

Armour Institute Architectural School. . . . A young member is . . . Tad E.

Samuelson, honor student of the Armour Institute.[18]

Of the class, Atwood remained close to Fuller and orchestrated the exhibition of the Dymaxion Car at the 1933 Chicago Century of Progress Fair.[19] The talented class, like Paul Nelson, may have been fundamental to the transformation of the ungainly patent drawing (figure 3.12) into the chunky, but more modern, first model (figure 6.1).

Another influence on the design was Mr. Hansel, head of the Chicago branch of the N. W. Ayer and Co. advertising agency. Fuller met with him at the urging of an unidentified but interested manufacturer. Hansel asked Fuller to draft the simplest plans possible and then construct a model based on them. He basically requested that Fuller design the model from the inside out, reflecting Fuller's own approach to architectural design. Fuller described the model to his mother as "a one deck solution, that is one living deck, for there is also a sky promenade deck, and an open plaza below which is used as garage and airplane hangar."[20] He also explained that there were two models, one for exhibitions and one for demonstration purposes.

Fuller left out most of the unusual characteristics in the description he gave to his mother. He did not state the living area was raised one full floor above ground level, though he hinted at it by mentioning the open plaza parking area. This allowed Fuller to avoid clarifying that the single-family house, or one-deck living area, was supported by a central mast and stabilized by cables (figure 6.3). Since he was not offering details about the model's structure, he did not tell her that its minimal frame consisted of hollow metal tubes at the floor and roof levels. Although he pointed out the roof deck, he omitted important details about the model's formal qualities, such as its hexagonal plan, triangular rooms, window walls, and built-in furniture. He did not refer to the materials from which the model was constructed: aluminum, wood, and transparent casein (figure 6.4).

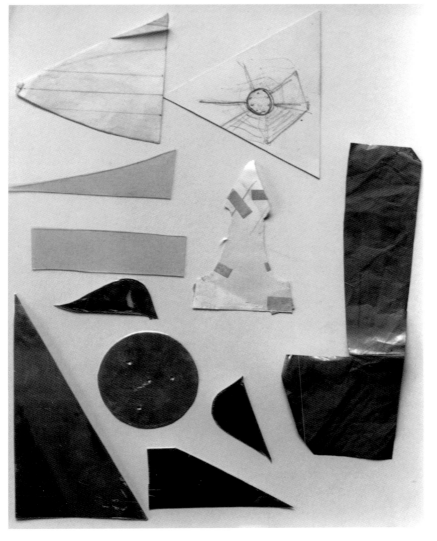

Sample materials used
in first Dymaxion House
model, 1928.

6.5

Jeannette Shirk, "A House Party
Bungalow" from *Pencil Points*,
January 1929.

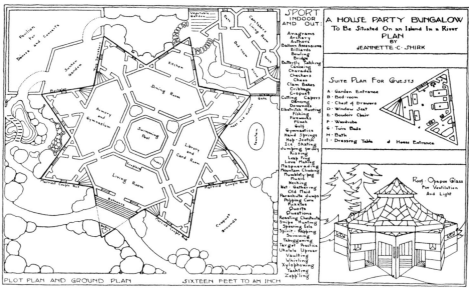

DESIGN FOR "A HOUSE PARTY BUNGALOW"
BY JEANNETTE C. SHIRK
Awarded honorable mention in our recent competition.

Fuller may have kept these features a secret in order to surprise his mother with its uniqueness. He also may not have wanted to worry her by making the model, and the house it represented, seem too far-fetched to realize.

Even though Fuller knew the design was unconventional, he was convinced it represented the most recent developments in appliances, utilities, mechanical systems, and architecture. This assessment is at variance with the generally accepted notion that the project represented a house of the future, a view fostered by Fuller when he knew it would not go into production. Fuller was not originally interested in a house for tomorrow; he wanted to establish a company to industrially reproduce a house for today. When he began to discuss the project, he explained that the house would be realized in the future since it was not yet in production. He initially referred to the immediate future, not the distant future or the twenty-five-year time frame he later gave for its development.[21] In his article "The House of the Future," Theodore Morrison noted that "Mr. Fuller . . . may well hold the key to an actual and imminent future with his revolutionary Dymaxion house."[22] Morrison claimed it was "a startling new conception of housing. Every element of tradition, every empirical assumption and casual accident or habit which has influenced the development of our modern houses, is thrown overboard."[23] Taken by the idea, it is not surprising that Morrison found no similarities between the Dymaxion House and other houses.

But there are. Fuller kept examples of contemporary designs that share some of its unusual qualities. Two are award-winning designs by Jeannette C. Shirk. Her octagonal design for "A House Party Bungalow" earned honorable mention from the magazine *Pencil Points* (figure 6.5).[24] A few months earlier, the same periodical bestowed the second-place prize in its competition for a "Suburban Love Nest or Snuggery" to Shirk for her circular, multilevel structure with its round staircase encased in a tower (figure 6.6).[25] There are references to a spherical building at the 1928 Centennial Exhibition of the Saxony Technical Schools in Dresden. One is a newspaper clipping sent to Fuller by Arthur Holden who emphatically pointed out the circular structure was "built on the post, not hung

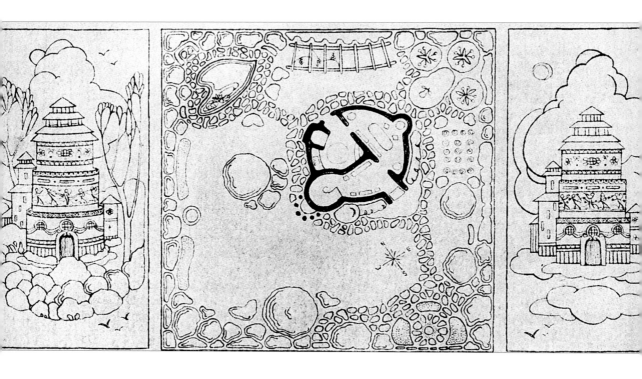

6.6

Jeannette Shirk, "Suburban Love
Nest or Snuggery" from *Pencil
Points*, September 1928.

from it."[26] When the same building appeared in the *New York Herald Tribune* with the caption "What the Offing Holds," Fuller clipped it for the *Chronofile* (figure 6.7).[27] The building met specific requirements in innovative ways. Fuller wanted the Dymaxion House to be special, ingenious, and appealing, which is why he referenced traditional domestic elements in its design.

Among these are the central mast with its ventilator hood rising above the roof line that reads as an abstracted chimney. A sheltering roof, albeit made of metal, shields the sky promenade deck, just as a porch roof does. The attention given to the ventilator hood and roof belies an affinity, however subtle, with the Prairie Houses of Frank Lloyd Wright in which a strong chimney anchors the structure and overhanging eaves shelter the interior.

More obvious is Fuller's reworking of Le Corbusier's five points of architecture: pilotis, free façade, free plan, roof garden, and ribbon windows. Fuller transformed Le Corbusier's pilotis into the central mast; his roof garden became Fuller's sky deck; the narrow ribbon windows were stretched into windows walls indicating a free façade or nonsupporting exterior walls. Both Le Corbusier and Fuller used interior partitions instead of dividing walls to reflect the open plan concept.[28] Fuller acknowledged parallels with Le Corbusier's work in his article "A Tree-like Style of Dwelling Is Planned." It included a drawing of a 4D tower labeled "Toward a New Architecture"[29] (figure 6.8). Fuller believed Le Corbusier privileged aesthetics over industrial production because the Swiss architect failed to grasp the latter's full potential: "Corbusier has picture of a roof tile at the beginning [of *Towards a New Architecture*] which is typical of his lack of hitting the bulls [*sic*] eye."[30] In other words, Le Corbusier was content to mass-produce architectural elements that would be assembled into a coherent whole whereas Fuller advocated mass-producing the house as a fully equipped unit.

Fuller co-opted Le Corbusier's design principles and book title to show that he was familiar with contemporary developments in architecture. He was also correlating his work to that of an important European modernist. He carefully

6.7
....

What the Offing Holds
from the *New York
Herald Tribune*, 1928.

What the Offing Holds

The world's first spherical building. It is at Dresden, Germany, the
feature of the Centennial Exhibition of the Saxony Technical Schools.
The structure is six stories, thirty meters high and twenty-four meters
in diameter. It is equipped with an elevator. On the fifth and sixth
floors is a restaurant. There are ten stores on the ground floor. The
building covers an area of 100 square meters.

6.8

Buckminster Fuller,
annotated drawing for
the article "Toward a
New Architecture,"
1928.

pointed out to his sister Rosamund that his work was developed independently; it was not derivative of Le Corbusier's:

> *Le Corbusier the great revolutionist in architectural design whose book should be read in conjunction with my own 4D. My own reading of Corbusier's "Towards a New Architecture" . . . when I was writing my own, nearly stunned me by the almost identical phraseology of his telegraphic style of notation with notations of my own set down completely from my own intuitive searching and reasoning and unaware even of the existence of such a man as Corbusier.*[31]

Fuller's appropriation of Le Corbusier's title and five points was a clever strategy to hint that his own design was more in tune with modern methods of production than that of the European architect's.

Fuller also needed to communicate his own design principles and philosophy through the formal properties of the Dymaxion House. Foremost among these were industrial production and time saving. The former was expressed primarily through the use of metal and clean lines. He articulated the latter in the hexagonal shape of the living deck that more closely approximated his intentions than the orthogonal footprint of the patent application house. He preferred a circular plan since he thought it was the most efficient in terms of time saving: all points within a circle are equidistant from the center. But the way the hexagonal shape flared from its narrowest at the mast to its widest at the outer edge was more dynamic. Fuller may have discovered this when looking at the exhibition building from Dresden (figure 6.7). Even if persuaded to remove the reference to time from the project's title, Fuller still wanted to convey its presence in the design. According to Morrison: "[T]he inventor . . . refers to [the houses] as examples of '4D' design; 4D is . . . an expression symbolic of 'fourth dimension.' The fourth dimension . . . is allied to time, and much attention has been paid to the time dimension in this new conception of the house."[32] To the uninitiated eye the model's hexagonal shape probably did not denote saving time, which could be more easily comprehended by the inclusion of appliances and environmental systems.

The use of mechanical devices and services brought technology inside the house to emphasize the time saved and the comfortable, clean interior gained from machines. Mechanical services in the mast would filter and condition incoming air to maintain an optimal temperature and keep the house dust-free. Eliminating the onerous task of dusting was one time-saving technique. The cooking grill, dishwasher, washer/dryer, and central vacuum were time-saving apparatuses clustered around the central mast.

The combination of the house's unusual shape and the inclusion of appliances illustrate how Fuller rethought the organization of domestic space, how he understood that technological advancements in the domestic sphere required an innovative approach to home design. Reyner Banham acknowledged that the Dymaxion House was not simply about creating a new image for the private house; it was also about creating a new approach to living with technology:

> Fuller . . . advanced, in his Dymaxion House project, a concept of domestic design that . . . had it been built, would have rendered [Le Corbusier's] Les Heures Claires, for instance, technically obsolete before design had even begun. The Dymaxion House concept was entirely radical . . . hung by wires from the apex of a central . . . mast which also housed all the mechanical services. . . . Even those like Le Corbusier who had given specific attention to this mechanical revolution in domestic service had been content for the most part to distribute it through the house according to the distribution of its pre-mechanical equivalent. Thus cooking facilities went into the room that would have been called "kitchen" even without a gas oven, washing

machines into a room still conceived as a "laundry" in the old sense . . . vac-
uum cleaner to the "broom cupboard", and so forth. In the Fuller version
this equipment is seen as more alike, in being mechanical, than different be-
cause of time-honoured functional differentiations, and is therefore packed
together in the central core of the house.[33]

Banham did not note that Le Corbusier and Fuller differed about who would
reap the benefits from the use of mechanical equipment. Le Corbusier included
appliances to lessen the workload of servants whereas Fuller incorporated them
to make the workload lighter for the housewife.[34]

Although Fuller's concern with making housecleaning easier was unusual,
the inclusion of technology and mechanical equipment in residential design
was not. One historical precedent, featuring an unusual floor plan, which Fuller
may have known, was the Octagon House promoted by Orson Fowler in the
mid-nineteenth century.[35] The Octagon House, like the Dymaxion House, was
designed to create a healthy environment through the use of modern conveniences. By the 1920s these included indoor plumbing, mass-produced kitchen
appliances like stoves and iceboxes, furnaces, gas, and electricity. Fuller's inclusion of household appliances went beyond the standard equipment and the
residential designer's standard interest in it. One reason is provided by Alden
Hatch, who explained that after Fuller's father died, his mother needed to reduce her household expenses so she let the handyman go. Fuller took over many
of his chores and claimed it was "a very, very rich part of my life experience to
learn so much about how houses run. I imagine this must have affected a lot
of my feelings about what needs to be done to make things work."[36] A second
influence was watching his wife repeatedly perform the same mundane tasks,
particularly washing diapers.[37] A third was the image of the modern home, full
of time-saving equipment and electric helpers, as promoted by contemporary
trade journals, women's magazines, and Ideal Home Exhibitions.

Fuller studied the necessity of mechanical instruments in a modern house by consulting a number of sources. Architectural and building magazines offered advice about necessary advancements in household technologies in articles such as "How Many Outlets?" and "Consider the Refrigerator When Planning Homes."[38] Articles highlighting the advantages of mechanized appliances, sometimes called slaves or servants, were regularly featured in periodicals.[39] The annual Ideal Home Exhibitions sponsored by the *Daily Mail* in England also stressed the use of new construction methods and labor-saving devices. Fuller listed a review of the 1928 exhibition with its modernist *House of the Future* in the *4D Timelock* reference list.[40] Machines performed all household tasks in the *House of the Future*, which included a futuristic combination car/boat/airplane vehicle.[41] These features were similar to components of the Dymaxion House and helped validate its status as an ideal house. They also reinforced the different magazines' messages that a modern house was more than a modern design: it was full of modern appliances essential to modern housekeeping.

Fuller drew upon the concept of modern housekeeping as it was defined and specifically marketed to women in the late 1920s. Electric companies and appliance manufacturers were reaching out to women to increase electricity consumption. Electricity was promoted as healthier and cleaner than the use of coal or wood.[42] Although electric appliances were primarily directed at the most difficult and time-consuming household tasks, such as cooking, laundry, ironing, and vacuuming, there were also a number of gadgets to assist with minor chores, like making toast.[43] Anne was supportive and understood the value of the different devices. While setting up house after returning to Long Island in mid-1929, she wrote to Fuller: "I'm working out plans to make it easy without a maid . . . + I think if we work out different labor saving things a la 4D it will be quite simple."[44] Fuller hoped other women would respond to "different labor saving things a la 4D" as positively as his wife did.

Unlike periodicals and Ideal Home Exhibitions that featured detailed interiors, Fuller provided few hints about how the mechanical devices would fit into the Dymaxion House (figure 6.9). The kitchen and its appliances, for instance, can be visualized from its description in *4D Timelock*. A black-and-white photograph of the model shows a sparsely furnished living room with a built-in couch and a large, backless cushion in the center (figure 6.10) with no apparent mechanical gadgets. A slightly confusing chart lists the colors of some rooms (figure 6.11). A small watercolor by Lee Atwood coordinates with Fuller's color scheme for the study (figure 6.12). On the chart Fuller noted cerise as the living room color, and Anne used red for the living room in a watercolor of the model from the 1930s (figure 6.13). She must have taken artistic license since the interior in her painting is more developed, but offers no more information about the incorporation of appliances, than those shown in the photographs (figures 6.14, 6.15, and 6.21).

Like the awkward early version exhibited at Marshall Field, the final model is a three-dimensional representation of Fuller's ideology and design principles as they applied to the house (figure 6.15). Fuller wrote to Henry Saylor at Scribner's in 1929 that he was working on a new, larger model, whose parts were better integrated; it was easier to move than the first.[45] This was a sleeker, more streamlined version that represents the mature design of the house. Outtakes from a 1929 Movietone newsreel feature the boxy first model of the house (figures 6.16–6.20). By February 1930, a model "much larger and improved in detail over the original" was exhibited at the Architectural League in Manhattan.[46] The first version is very obscure and rarely reproduced, like the patent drawing; the 1930 model is the one now associated with the Dymaxion House. Its suspended living deck, strong central mast, exposed cables, and shiny metal exterior make it look futuristic (figure 6.21).

Even though it looked futuristic, Fuller was still trying to get the Dymaxion House into production when the mature model was created. It is uncertain at what point he conceded that it would never be mass-produced. The futuristic design and the futuristic treatment of the interior as a type of mechanical paradise made it easy for the project to be transformed from a potential new

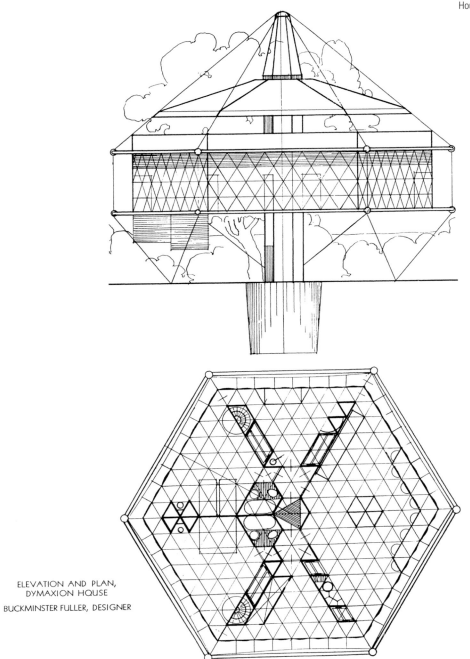

6.9

Elevation and plan of final
version of the Dymaxion
House, ca. 1930.

ELEVATION AND PLAN,
DYMAXION HOUSE

BUCKMINSTER FULLER, DESIGNER

6.10
....

Undated photograph of
first Dymaxion House
model interior, ca. 1928.

6.11
....

Buckminster Fuller,
sample Dymaxion House
color chart, ca. 1928.

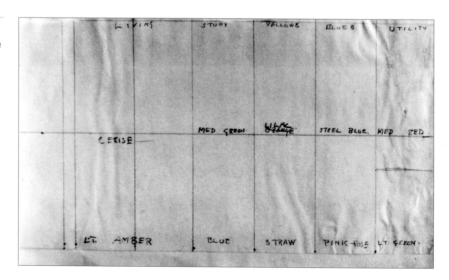

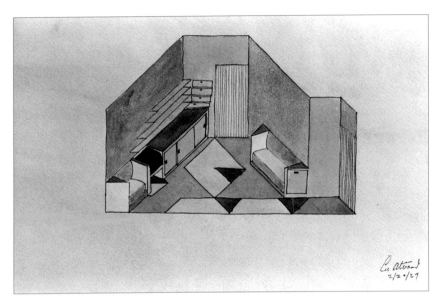

Undated photograph of
third Dymaxion House
model showing interior
and screen around
ground level, ca. 1930.

6.15
....
Undated photograph of
third Dymaxion House
model from above,
ca. 1930.

6.16

Buckminster Fuller with
hollow structural tubes
of first model of the
Dymaxion House in Fox
Movietone outtakes,
1929.

6.17

Buckminster Fuller
discussing hollow
structural tubes of first
model of the Dymaxion
House in Fox Movietone
outtakes, 1929.

Buckminster Fuller with
assembled first model of
the Dymaxion House in
Fox Movietone outtakes,
1929.

Undated photograph of
third Dymaxion House
model showing chassis,
ca. 1930.

type of contemporary dwelling into a house of the distant future. Fuller encouraged this perception as a way to keep the Dymaxion House in the public arena. At some point in the 1930s he began to claim a twenty-five-year lag period for its realization, disguising his disappointment that it was not already in production. He also began to treat some of the appliances as beyond the capabilities of contemporary technology. For example, the washer and hot air dryer of *4D Timelock* became an automated washer-dryer-ironing unit.[47] The former existed in the late 1920s, but the latter was not yet available in 2007. Fuller included appliances and mechanical services because articles and advertisements told him these were necessary components of a modern house. In the Dymaxion House, Fuller responded to various ideas of what a modern house should be. He was working within the limits of contemporary technology in terms of designing, manufacturing, and equipping the house. He was familiar with debates about the design of modern houses and the role of machine production in the realization of those designs. He was also informed about the different machines required by the contemporary housekeeper. His version of the ideal house represented an affordable solution to both.

Low cost, or affordability, was another key element in Fuller's argument in favor of the industrially reproduced house over the custom-designed one. To him an ideal house would not only facilitate the lives of its inhabitants but also avoid burdening its owners with a long-term, interest-laden mortgage. Industrial reproduction of the house and its components meant low overhead for the manufacturer who could pass on the savings to the consumer. Start-up costs would be high, but once production was under way the cost-per-house would be low. Fuller argued as much when he presented his case for manufacturing houses in a manner similar to the way cars are made. He was not the only one to have this idea. In 1929 Edward A. Filene also predicted that houses would be built like Fords in the near future.[48] Producing houses like cars would not eliminate payments for those who could not pay the balance upon purchase. What it would do was reduce the cost of the house and lower the overall number of payments.

Industrial reproduction would lower the cost of the Dymaxion House without compromising its structural integrity. Fuller explained his theory in "A Tree-like Style of Dwelling Is Planned": "[A] house . . . fabricated industrially, centrally wrought, and assembled in the course of a day . . . will cost approximately $500 per ton. . . . [They] are structured after the natural systems of humans and trees with a central stem or backbone, from which all else is independently hung. . . . This results in a construction similar to an airplane, light, taught [*sic*] and profoundly strong."[49] Although he gave the cost as "$500 per ton," Fuller did not specify how much the house would weigh. The projected weight must have been six tons since Morrison reported it would "cost about $3,000."[50] In addition, Morrison noted "all the essential services can be operated for perhaps as little as $5.00 a month."[51] These were two more benefits offered by the Dymaxion House: freedom from the economic tyranny of equity-building debt and monthly bills.

Fuller's understanding of monetary troubles and his desire to ease them is expressed by a cartoon entitled *The World's Strong Man* by Albert T. Reid, which is in his papers (figure 6.22). This man, an allegorical figure representing the American public, struggles to support a mound of "goods bought on installment plan."[52] His burdensome load includes a car, piano, furniture, clothes, and household appliances. Through the industrially reproduced house Fuller was offering the American public a way to acquire some of these items without straining their budgets or their backs. Even though individuals would need to purchase vehicles, clothing, and pianos, the purchase price of the Dymaxion House included household appliances and some furniture. Dymaxion House mortgage owners would pay one low monthly installment for many factory-installed accoutrements of modern living rather than separate payments for the same things independently purchased for other houses.

Fuller wanted to reassure consumers that the low cost of the industrially reproduced house and its components did not mean poor quality. He addressed the issue in *Analysis of standardization, truth, advertising and control*, chapter 8 of *4D*

Timelock. He needed to assure interested consumers that he offered a product of good quality. His goal was to use industrial reproduction to supply a safe, sturdy house at a reasonable price. This was another reason he used the analogy of automobile production: he wanted to associate the quality of mass-produced cars with the quality of the mass-produced Dymaxion House.

The focus on quality allowed Fuller to sidestep the issue of individuality. The automobile industry again provided a model since mass-produced cars were personalized by their owners. The message that industrially reproduced houses could also be personalized was implicit, not explicit, in the car analogy. In early 1930, he thoughtfully responded to a reporter's question "Won't the standardization remove all individual possibilities?":

> *No, it multiplies them. First because such order is a kind of beauty. . . . In such a house there is an infinitude of possibilities for color harmonies in the lighting system alone. The walls are not arbitrary partitions controlling the sizes and shapes of rooms as in the ordinary house. They can be adjusted to please the individual dweller. The sizes and shapes and arrangement of Dymaxion houses would not necessarily have any more similarity to each other than do the oblong houses of brick and stone. . . . The infinitude of beautiful color in modern materials that come to hand for the fabrication of Dymaxion houses would individualize them to some extent, even if the same general model were used in many thousands of cases.*[53]

His answer was a new response to reservations about standardized design, not a reworking of his previously expressed notions of standardization. In "Lightful Houses" and *4D Timelock*, he argued that a number of standardized, mass-produced objects were already used frequently in modern life — for example, paper, the alphabet, fabrics, and automobiles. As emphasized at the AIA convention, architecture was a fine art and standardization of design was antithetical to the art of architecture. Fuller was not as concerned with designing a good-looking house as he was with establishing a company to manufacture and market an affordable, industrially reproduced house of good quality that could be personalized by its inhabitants.

Fuller needed to address the issue of aesthetics when he translated his ideas into a model. His emphasis may have been on mass production, but an unattractive model would have been a drawback, not a selling point. In *4D Timelock* he admitted that he had not yet finalized the design and would allow more qualified persons to assume that responsibility. The process through which Fuller arrived at the definitive, sleek, clean-edged model is unclear. The use of industrial processes did not imply a mediocre commercial product to Fuller. In fact, prompted by Russell Walcott, Fuller came to believe that Leonardo da Vinci[54] would have designed for industrial reproduction had he lived in the twentieth century: "Making no self swelling comparison, we . . . perceive that were Leonardo da Vinci a contemporary, he would have been lending his intuitive genius not to stylistic copying of medieval arts and crafts, nor to art institute and church craft, but to the vastly greater and more abstract revelation and contact, of industrial reproduction and composition of business."[55] Although it was conjecture, Fuller's reference to Leonardo was intended to add a bit of credibility to his own use of industrial reproduction. One might also surmise that if Leonardo were to design a house for industrial reproduction, aesthetics would play as much of a role, if not more, as quality, affordability, and comfort.

Fuller's version of the ideal house was not a tabula rasa — he did not create the concept of the industrially reproduced house. He drew upon existing technologies to create a new paradigm of the industrially reproduced house as a factory-made, fully equipped unit. Amenities, such as electrical wiring and interior plumbing, were figured into the cost of the house, not options tacked onto the initial price as they were in the houses sold by companies like Sears and Gordon-Van Tine. In addition, Fuller rejected his competitors' conservative approach to design. He interpreted some elements of traditional and modern architecture and incorporated these into the Dymaxion House. It was not a collage of mass-produced and custom elements arranged by an architect as were Le Corbusier's houses. In designing his ideal industrially reproduced house, Fuller tapped into existing ideas about quality houses, notions of comfort, the image of modernity, and industrial reproduction.

In contrast to his insistence on industrial reproduction, Fuller intended to use manual labor at the site to assemble the Dymaxion House from its components. This is paradoxical since Fuller wanted to use industrial reproduction to keep the cost of the house low and the use of manual labor in the final stage seems like an unnecessary, hidden expense. Fuller believed it was too difficult to ship the assembled house directly from the factory to its location. It would therefore be necessary to ship the components individually until it could be delivered as a complete unit by airplane. Even though the Dymaxion House would be put together at the site by hand, it is still important to remember that this was manual labor, not manual fabrication. It was a complete ready-to-assemble manufactured house.

It was also rather well received by the general public and architects. He picked up a few loyal supporters at the AIA convention; Arthur Holden and John Boyd Jr. were two of the most important. Ralph T. Walker became mildly interested, but as Fuller happily replied to Eugenia Walcott's inquiry as to whether he needed the rest of her subscription, "Mr. Corbett and Raymond Hood have taken up the cudgets for me. Both are extremely helpful."[56] Hood primarily assisted through monetary donations. Corbett actively endorsed the project by networking, contributing money, soliciting money, and arranging promotional venues. Corbett was so effective that Fuller asked him to raise money for the preparations of the 1933 Chicago Fair.[57] Corbett secured $100 from Hood and a pledge from Eli Jacques Kahn who eventually contributed $50.[58] While Fuller must have felt a bit vindicated by the backing of professional colleagues, he also knew the project's successful realization would require widespread support.

Fuller courted the general public through articles and the Marshall Field exhibition, which generated enthusiastic inquiries from individuals and organizations. Bernard Newman of the Philadelphia Housing Association and Sidney Wilcox from the Illinois Industrial Commission requested detailed information about the house. Carleton Washburne, a public school superintendent, invited Fuller to lecture. The Chicago Home Owners Institute and *Nation's Business* asked for articles. R. C. Sacketter of Advertisers Incorporated asked if the house could be included in a publicity campaign for all-steel mono-bodies. Fuller declined since the house was not made of one piece of metal.[59] If possible Fuller accommodated the inquiries, even though he could not fulfill the requests of persons desiring to live in a Dymaxion House.

Many individuals were anxious to acquire a Dymaxion House. Mrs. Helen Hodgdon of Medford, Massachusetts, offered her family's services as live-in company agents:

> *I think your radical idea of house building sounds wonderfully practical. . . . My husband, who is a doctor, thinks your idea is the solution of hygienic housing, and worked out to a nicety. I wish you would let us be pioneers in your scheme. Build us a house . . . for demonstration purposes, and give us an agency. We'll boost it with pep and enthusiasm. . . . Please, please, give us a chance and we will put the best there is in us, into it.*[60]

If Fuller replied to Mrs. Hodgdon, his answer is lost as was the one to George Olmstead who simply inquired: "[W]ill you kindly let me know if you are proceeding with the manufacture of your "DYMAXION HOUSE" as I am much interested in your splendid invention."[61] Fuller did reply to Mrs. Rothwell Hyde. She wrote to him because she was planning to build a new house upon her move to California and figured she would best be served by a Dymaxion House. When her first inquiry went unanswered, she sent a second more impatient letter. Fuller finally answered her with the sad news that production of Dymaxion

Houses would be delayed until 1933.[62] Yet, by 1934, the house was still not in production as Fuller had to inform Richard Reed.[63] He hinted to Mrs. Hyde that he hoped to use the 1933 Chicago Fair as a catalyst to propel the Dymaxion House into production.

The factors preventing the inclusion of the Dymaxion House in A Century of Progress are not clear. In his recollection of the events, Fuller claimed that money was the reason the house was not exhibited and consequently never went into production. He recounted a clever story about being approached by one of its promoters a short while before the fair opened. Fuller explained he was only willing to exhibit the house as a full-scale, production-ready model. When asked what the cost of creating this model would be, Fuller estimated a hundred million dollars. He was basically asking the fair's organizers to finance the set-up costs of industrially reproducing the Dymaxion House—a request they declined. Fuller used this tale to lament another opportunity lost because of the selfishness of others as he admitted he wanted the fair to bear the financial burden of creating a new industry.[64] Nothing in Fuller's papers corroborates this account. It is also doubtful that Fuller would have been approached shortly before the fair's opening had there been serious interest in including the house. A somewhat grounded version of the Dymaxion House appeared at the fair in the form of George Keck's *House of Tomorrow* (figure 6.23). When motivated, the fair's organizers could obviously secure funding to create a model house. The documents in Fuller's papers do not tell the entire story, but they hint that once again Fuller was approaching a third party, in this case the fair's organizers, as he did the AIA with the hope it would assume financial responsibility for bringing his project to fruition.

At first Fuller was quite confident that the Dymaxion House would be exhibited at A Century of Progress. He wrote as much to Glendenning Keeble: "The proposed series of lectures and shows of the dymaxion architecture seems to point significantly towards . . . their application to the World's Fair of [19]33 in Chicago, in which it is tentatively planned to at least exhibit one complete

6.23

Hedrich-Blessing, *House of Tomorrow* by Keck & Keck, A Century of Progress, Chicago, 1933.

model. . . . Of this I have been advised by Mr. Harvey Wiley Corbett and Mr. Raymond Hood of the World's Fair Architectural Committee."[65] He subsequently wrote to Saylor about negotiations and backroom deals that thwarted his ambition.[66] He kept entreating Corbett to raise money since it was "only three years to World's fair and a promethean task to develop Dymaxion design and public appreciation thereof. Yet if successful, it will make it the greatest designing triumph of all Fairs and a successful Worlds Fair."[67] The money never materialized, and there is nothing more in Fuller's papers about exhibiting the house at the fair until 1932 when he was informed it would not be.

J. C. Folsom, the exhibition director, explained that lack of funding on the part of Fuller and the fair's organizers meant the house would not be included: "Last spring . . . I saw Mr. Fuller for a few moments at the office of Fortune Magazine and . . . brought up the matter of the possibility of such an exhibit but Mr. Fuller did not seem to feel that it would be possible to finance the project. Unfortunately, the Exposition has no funds to set up such exhibits no matter how desirable they may be."[68] This notice confused and angered Fuller who wrote on it that he had never spoken to Folsom. Under Fuller's direction, L. Levinson in Fuller's office at *Shelter* magazine urged Folsom to reconsider since a house was being assembled and would be ready for the opening:

> *A copy of your letter of 12/14/32 was forwarded to Mr. Buckminster Fuller [who] noted that in regard to your reference to a meeting at the office of Fortune Magazine, the meeting was proposed but never occurred. He also noted that he did not say that it would not be possible to finance the exhibition of the Dymaxion House. . . . If the Dymaxion House now under construction is completed in time for the Exposition . . . it would be a simple matter to arrange for its display — if not at the Fair, in the major cities.[69]*

Perhaps to ensure delay, Folsom did not respond until more than a year later when he conclusively informed Fuller: "I very much regret to advise you that we have already made complete arrangements for exhibit houses at the 1934 Exposition and that I know of no possible way in which we could find space for another house."[70] The length of time between the original and second notices confused Fuller who did not remember Levinson had hinted in his reply that the house might still be included. He curtly answered:

> *I am still curious to know why you wrote me on March 10 regretting that it would be impossible to exhibit one of my houses. I do not recall having made any application for such an exposition. A year ago I received a similar letter from you without solicitation on my part. Is someone trying to play a joke on me? My only recollection of . . . you was when you called at the offices of Fortune in July 1932 and asked for an appointment with me which you failed to keep.*[71]

Fuller's irritation at Folsom is justified, but also a bit unnecessary. By 1934 Fuller was no longer sincerely interested in exhibiting the Dymaxion House at A Century of Progress since Lee Atwood, the leader of Fuller's 4D design class, had made arrangements to add the Dymaxion Car to the Crystal House exhibit.

Fuller did not abandon the Dymaxion House project in the 1930s. It would have been foolish to do so since manufactured houses were gaining more acceptance, especially within architectural culture. In 1930 Lewis Mumford published an important article, "Mass-Production and the Modern Home," exploring the virtues of the manufactured house. Mumford was cautious and echoed AIA concerns about the possible detrimental effects of industrial production upon architectural design. Mumford actually lauded Fuller's work because the inspiring industrialist "kept, with charming unconsciousness, the most traditional and sentimental tag of all, namely, the free-standing individual house."[72] Yet, as he became more and more convinced that the Dymaxion House would not be manufactured, Fuller began to focus on more viable projects.

The first was related to the Dymaxion House. He was contracted in April 1931 to develop a mass-produced bathroom by the John B. Pierce Foundation. He tendered his resignation three months later citing ideological differences with Robert Davison, the director of research.[73] His next major undertaking was to acquire *Shelter* magazine in early 1932 as a vehicle for the promotion and realization of the industrially reproduced house. This was another short-lived venture; *Shelter* under Fuller's directorship published its last issue in November of that same year.[74] He then began work on the Dymaxion Transportation Unit, a promising three-wheeled car of which only three prototypes were produced. He abandoned this project in the mid-1930s and accepted a position at the Phelps Dodge Corporation for whom he was to design a one-piece bathroom for mass production. The prototype was of copperplated antimony, and only twelve were made.[75] After Phelps Dodge, Fuller became a technical consultant for *Fortune* magazine through the influence of Claire Booth Luce, whom he met while working for the Pierce Foundation. His responsibilities included editing, fact checking, and researching new technical developments. Beginning in 1940 Fuller worked for the Foreign Economic Administration as a special assistant to the deputy director. It was during this tenure that Fuller was given his first opportunity to realize an industrially reproduced house, the Dymaxion Dwelling Unit (DDU). The DDU was not as complex as the Dymaxion House although it was Fuller's first patented design for an industrially reproduced house.[76]

Despite the diversity of these projects, many shared the idea of industrial reproduction with the Dymaxion House. In a sense the Dymaxion House was Fuller's bread-and-butter project, the one guaranteed to capture the public's attention. He continued to exhibit the house throughout the 1930s, even when the model began to show wear and tear. One model was damaged while on loan to Donald Deskey who informed Fuller:

Unfortunately one of the truck men in moving furniture to one of the back

rooms seems to have heaved no less than a steel couch thru your nice model. I

don't think any of the parts are damaged but it certainly looks like a wreck.

I am awfully sorry because I have been showing it whenever I have the

chance to people that I think are interested. . . . Perhaps the only thing we

can do is to wait until you get back to NY so you can reassemble it from the

wreckage.[77]

The fate of this particular model is unknown, but Fuller continued to exhibit the Dymaxion House throughout the decade. He declined to exhibit it at the 1934 Own Your Home Show in Yonkers, New York, because he needed to make a new model.[78] In 1939, Fuller agreed to lend a model to exhibitions by the United States Department of the Interior in Washington, D.C., and the Museum of Modern Art (MoMA) in New York.[79] Fuller was at first reluctant to lend MoMA the model because it was ten years old, in bad shape, and meant to illustrate lectures, not serve as an exhibition model.[80] It is uncertain whether there were different models exhibited at these two exhibitions, or one rickety Dymaxion House model that went from one to the other.

What is certain is that a model of the Dymaxion House was destroyed while on loan to the Architectural Forum Offices in 1939 and another was not made. According to Pamela Wilson, manager of the archives, the model was dismantled and packed into boxes that were accidently discarded as garbage.[81] After this, the Dymaxion House was not exhibited again.

At the end of twelve years of work, Fuller had not realized the Dymaxion House project. He downplayed his disappointment later by insisting that he had known from the beginning it would take at least twenty-five years for such a project to go into production. Even though the legacy of the Dymaxion House claims it was designed as a house of future, Fuller's original intention was to found a company that would use available technology to industrially reproduce it.

As he struggled to secure funding for the start-up costs, the house went through different phases, from Fuller Houses to Lightful House to 4D House to Dymaxion House. The changes were steps Fuller took to bring the house closer to production, the company nearer to incorporation. He was able to attract some capital and some support, enough to be assured that the project was feasible. Despite his skills as a salesman, he was never able to close this deal. Fuller worked hard, but his efforts to manufacture the Dymaxion House, his ideal, industrially reproduced house, were unsuccessful.

7

END PRODUCT

The inability to put the Dymaxion House into production did not stall Fuller's career. He used its unusual characteristics to keep it and himself in the public arena. The basis of his business proposal was cleverly translated into the house of the future. In the process Fuller was transformed from a potential corporate executive into a prognosticator of what a house could be. He did not mind being considered a visionary but claimed he found it distasteful to be treated like a prophet.[1] He, of course, learned to use such treatment to his advantage. The image of the visionary Buckminster Fuller became a tool to help the man Buckminster Fuller promote his ideal, industrially reproduced house.

An early step was to strongly identify Fuller with the project. He may have changed the name from Fuller Houses to get away from the personal, as Anne wrote to her brother-in-law, but he never distanced himself from the project. Throughout its development, it was his project—he conceived it, he wrote about it, he promoted it. The Dymaxion House was neither generic nor anonymous. It was the brainchild of its creator who was ready to answer questions and dispel doubts. As the house was more and more understood as belonging to the distant future, Fuller more and more became the ideologue who struggled to make it a reality.

To accomplish his goal, Fuller would have to overcome many obstacles, especially the bias toward mass-produced, standardized houses. Not only was the use of industrial processes unusual, the materials specified for the house, metal and plastic, were atypical (figure 6.4). The mature model of the Dymaxion House echoed some elements of traditional housing, yet its central mast, suspended hexagonal living area, and shiny exterior made it look like something from a science fiction novel. Fuller's emphasis on labor-saving devices made it seem like a mechanical paradise, an ideal house of which the housekeeper could only dream. While these characteristics put the house on the cutting edge of the home-building field, they also made it seem beyond the reach of contemporary technology.

Fuller, however, knew how to reconstruct a problem into a promotional strategy. Just as he reworked the AIA's stance against standardization of design into a battle between tradition and progression, he commuted his first unsuccessful attempt at establishing a company to manufacture houses into a lifelong mission. Fuller knew the perception of what happened, the spin put on it, was more important than the event itself. He utilized this knowledge well when he turned his failure and the house's uniqueness into powerful talking points as it became clear the Dymaxion House would not be realized.

As the one with the vision who conceived the project and with the drive to realize it, no matter how long it took, Fuller was its perfect spokesperson. He was willing to buck the status quo of the largely craft-based home-building field to bring the project to fruition. His Stockade experience taught him how to overcome difficulties blocking new developments. It also demonstrated that he had the strength and courage to carry the task through to completion. In addition, he came from a long line of radicals who went against the odds when convinced they were in the right. The implication was Fuller could be counted on to accomplish his goal because he was following a family tradition.

When Fuller believed the house would go into production, he stood alone as an entrepreneur, like Henry Ford, who would create a beneficial industry. The earliest articles focused on the house and its accessories; there was no interest in Fuller's background.[2] Fuller's role was as the originator of the project, not as an object of interest.[3]

By 1930 Fuller was also a topic of interest, almost as intriguing as his unconventional Dymaxion House. His background and family history began to be used as important components of the story. Their use was immediately codified. For example, Inez Cunningham wrote in "Fuller's Dymaxion House on Display":

> *Here is this young man with his Dymaxion house. He comes of five generations of New England Americans. The men of his family were preachers and*

lawyers. He is the grand nephew of Margaret Fuller, and all these people,
who attacked the moral and social problems of a new world, are alive in
him . . . a young person capable of such intense suffering that he must in self-
defense refer to the race of man as the human family and attack its problems
to forget his own.[4]

Mme. X, author of "Buckminster Fuller Explains His New Housing Industry,"
followed suit, but added a few facts about Fuller's personal history and his
mother's family:

This is a youngish man, Buckminster Fuller, who on his father's side is re-
lated to some of the most famous New England families and on his mother's
side to one of the best known Chicago families. . . . He is descended from
a long line of ancestors, among whom there were in five generations five
Harvard graduates. He himself was also a student at this first of Ameri-
can universities, though without any embarrassment, he says he was twice
dropped. . . . He has all the air of alert independence of thought which have
animated so many celebrated Americans. . . . He is now profoundly inter-
ested in putting before the world a scheme of house building which differs
entirely from any hitherto presented to this country.[5]

Mme X's article is one of the few places where any mention is made of his ma-
ternal relatives. His mother's relatives were accomplished, although Fuller did
not find the inspiration in their achievements that he did in those of his father's family: his paternal ancestors were lauded for their fortitude in the face
of opposition and their independent thinking. Both authors credited Fuller's
initiative and determination to his New England heritage, a legacy he would
continue to draw upon throughout his career. As a man with rebellion, struggle,

and triumph in his blood, Fuller was an object as curious and fascinating as the Dymaxion House.

He was not merely using his lineage as a public relations ploy; he was very proud of his background, especially proud of his distinguished ancestors. He was particularly fond of Margaret Fuller Ossoli, whom he learned about during the project's early phase. The discovery excited him. In his great-aunt he saw a kindred spirit, someone with whom he could identify in his efforts to overcome unjust opposition.

Unlike the accomplishments of Margaret, which were unknown to him until he was in his thirties, Fuller had heard stories about the exploits of the male members of his family throughout his childhood. Lieutenant Thomas Fuller, his great-great-great-great-grandfather, emigrated to the New World from England in the seventeenth century and founded the American branch of the family. Thomas's grandson, Reverend Timothy Fuller, a Massachusetts delegate to the Federal Constitution Assembly, had refused to sign the Constitution because it did not abolish slavery. Timothy, his son, had helped found the Hasty Pudding Club at Harvard where he was forced to graduate in second place as punishment for participating in a student revolt. Arthur Buckminster Fuller, Bucky's grandfather and a minister, had been an abolitionist who died leading a charge in Fredericksburg, Virginia. His son and Fuller's father, Richard, was a merchant-importer and the first Fuller male in many generations to reject law and the ministry as his profession.[6] Such family legends may have fueled a desire in Fuller to attain an appropriate personal history.

Until he became an advocate of industrially reproduced houses, Fuller's life was fairly average with typical low and high points. Among the distressing moments were the death of his father and first child, being forced out of Stockade, and his thwarted attempt to set up a company to mass-produce the Dymaxion House. Successes included his climb through the ranks at Armour, becoming an officer in the navy, his marriage, the birth of the Fullers' second child, and the rapid growth of Stockade. No matter how personally devastating or satisfying these events, they constitute a rather ordinary set of ups-and-downs. Yet, with the right twist, they could be made into appropriate material for a tragic biography. Bucky's life story could also become a Fuller legend with careful handling.

Creative manipulation of the facts of his life began after the publication of the articles by Cunningham and Mme X. One of the earliest examples is a press release for a 1932 lecture in Philadelphia. His life was presented in a positive light: he was from Boston, the great-nephew of Margaret Fuller, and Fuller men went to Harvard. He, too, had gone to Harvard but was twice expelled. No explanation was offered. He recovered nicely and eventually earned a commission in the United States Navy. He then successfully manufactured construction materials, one of the rare instances in which his Stockade experience was treated favorably. Hewlett, his father-in-law, gave him entrée into the world of architecture.[7] These facts were basically accurate. What were altered were the origins of the Dymaxion House, the project under discussion: "How the Dymaxion House Came Into Being — The Dymaxion house has been a conception in the mind of Buckminster Fuller since 1922, when he was thinking loosely upon the subject. In 1927 he went into the slums of northwest Chicago and spent eighteen months in systematic thought upon the subject."[8] Nothing in Fuller's papers suggests that he did any thinking, loose or concentrated, about industrially reproduced houses in 1922. He lived in the fashionable Lakeview area of northwest Chicago in 1927. While there he did more than think about the project; he doggedly pursued its realization. Such creative twists characterized Fuller as patient, thorough, and determined.

In the late 1930s, Fuller began to alter other facts of his life. He consciously did so in a six-part, fifty-seven-page, autobiographical essay for Joe Bryant, a coworker, at Time, Inc.[9] The purpose was to provide Bryant with material for an article, perhaps in response to the success of Fuller's book *Nine Chains to the Moon*. Although Bryant's article never appeared, Fuller's text was not written in vain. While composing it, Fuller figured out which parts of his life he would tamper with and which phases he would not alter.

Fuller's lengthy essay to Joe Bryant was a comprehensive, if manipulated, narrative of his life. Fuller used it as an adjustable template of his pre-1939 life and work; it was repeatedly recycled. An excerpt from this imaginative recollection, in which he calls himself "B," follows:

> *B resigned from the service in Sept. 1919 . . . daughter ill. . . . Got his job back at Armour . . . $55 a week as asst manager of the NY division of the export dept. Raised to $80 a week when he quit in Feb 1922 to go with Eddie McDonnel . . . to be his national account sales manager for Kelly-Springfield Truck . . . but Co was soon liquidated. . . . Another friend . . . had him recalled to active navy service. . . . B decided to quit the Navy . . . his father-in-law had invented a system of wall building with reinforced concrete — pressed bricks of grass, excelsior, and any vegetable fibrous material. . . .*
>
> *They started serious work on the building blocks — "Stockade." B had to invent the machinery for building the blocks. That fall, 1922, he went to H[arvard] P[rinceton] game at Cambridge, his wife and daughter Alexandra . . . coming to see him off. Just before her fourth birthday. "Daddy, will you bring me a cane?" Returning, he phoned . . . she had pneumonia again and was unconscious. Woke to ask "Daddy, did you bring me a cane?" No; had forgotten. She never spoke again. . . .*
>
> *Threw himself into the job. For five years worked intensely. Built, invented, and installed machinery in 5 factories around the country to fabricate units of a new building system. Built 240 houses out of shredded wheat bricks . . . put on an exhibit in the Own Your Own Home show at the new Madison Square Garden and got 21,000 queries, with 50% return*

contacts. . . . But no house was built of it, because no responsible firm, nor integrated industry was handling the whole thing. . . . B's nebulous deduction; people wanted good homes; they didn't care about style, as long as they contained certain conveniences. . . .

On August 18, 1927, he was forced out of the company and out of the shares. . . . Ten days later, when he was broke and out of a job, his daughter Allegra was born. He didn't tell his wife . . . until two weeks after the baby's birth. They were living in the Virginia, a little old hotel north of the river in Chicago. He had only $50 to his name. . . . Had only this $50 because . . . sales manager had borrowed $700 from him and had skipped to the West Coast.

Now came the great crisis in his life. No job, no money, infant daughter, betrayed by people he had trusted. He walked over to the lake and thought about suicide. Should he call his life a bad job and throw it away? Or should he try to figure out some way to make it (all the experiences of it bitter or happy) useful? He took stock of himself, and realized that he had had a full life. . . . Here, on the lake shore, was his first real thinking about life objectively; its bigger meanings — hitherto he had been part of it without perspective. . . .

Within a few hours of this realization, an old friend from NY invited him to dinner at the Blackstone Hotel. Later, walking up Wabash Ave., he reached Monroe St. when a colored taxi-driver asked him the time. As B reached for his watch, another man slugged him with brass knuckles, breaking his cheek bone. Unconscious, he was robbed of his watch and his few remaining dollars. . . .

Instead of crushing him, the blow was what he needed to send him into action. He resolved to stay in Chicago and work out his fate. . . . Money? No matter; don't worry; it will be provided. Self must be dismissed. The business must be straightened out, no matter how long it took.

The first thing to do was to install his family in a small, clean, safe place. He found a one-room flat in a new fire-proof apartment building at Clark and Belmont, at $22 a month. . . .

B said to himself, "If you're going to learn to think clearly, you must get into training." For six years he neither drank nor smoked; he took vigorous exercise and became a vegetarian. . . . Decided never to speak unless every word was a necessity, coming from inside out. . . .

The day before Thanksgiving 1927, a friend in Joliet got him a job as Chi. sales representative of a Waukegan firm manufacturing floor tiles. Salary: $50 a week. . . . He worked for this firm for 3 months, but found that the time he should have been putting into the tile business he was using for thinking. His thoughts were coming too fast. As a matter of integrity, he resigned. . . .

In Feb. (28) he was walking down town to see Ford's industrial show . . . when he encountered the man who had fired him. B's first impulse was to kill him, but with his new found strength, he resolved instead never to mention the circumstances of his firing again, and told the man so. A few minutes later . . . he heard a voice say: "You think truthfully. From now on, you need never await temporal attestation to your thoughts." On the way home came another thought: "From now on, write down everything you think."

For 3 months he was like a man with ague . . . thoughts came so fast and covered so much that all his subsequent developments derived from them — Dymaxion car and so on. At the end of three months, the compulsion [ended] as suddenly as it had begun. By this time it had totaled some 5,000 double-spaced typewritten pages.

Rereading his writings, he would clip each item as he came to it and say, "This idea might appeal to so-and-so" . . . he would distribute them in 40 different envelopes. When the distribution was finished he found that the different sheaves of items had definite continuity, so he clipped the names off them, put them together and made them separate chapters of his book "Time Lock."

He had no money to publish this book, and knew that it was too wild for any publisher . . . a mimeograph firm lent him a machine to be used at night, and gave him ink and paper. He even mimeographed his illustrations. He boiled his book down took out all the "ands", and bound up 200 copies. While he was putting the book together, another thought came to him: "You must crystalize this philosophy in design. Say nothing until then." . . .

"Dwelling is the largest objective use to which I could apply my philosophy." Used to think sitting beside the water at Lincoln Park. Trees there impressed him particularly, by their ability to support at a height volumes and weights equivalent to those of shelters, also snow loads and wind pressures, and all on slender single supports. "There is a structural secret here." . . .

Meanwhile, the Dymaxion house was taking form in his mind. He showed his drawings to the Chicago architects he knew. One, Pierre Blouke, sicced a reporter on him. In April [19]28, the first news of the Dymaxion house was published. He was invited to speak at the Architects Club and did so; they invited him to go, expenses paid, to the Am. Architects convention at St. Louis in May; exactly one year after Lindbergh's Spirit of St. Louis flight to Paris. Half the city had just been blown down in a storm, which gave him his thesis. (His father-in-law was there; had just been elected 1ˢᵗ VP of the Inst.) B made no speech; he talked to architects individually and gave them his books. Back in Chi., he mailed out the rest of his books to a selected list. . . . He spent the whole summer and winter answering letters and making models. . . .

That June, he patented the designs of the house and offered them to the Inst. as permanent custodians, so that they could never be privately exploited. Ironically, his father-in-law received them and turned them down as of no use to the Inst., missing the point of the gift. B found that the world adopted the house enthusiastically, but that engineers turned it down. . . .

In March 1929, Marshall Field asked B to show his house in place of an exhibit of futuristic European architecture. . . . They said, "This house is so extreme that it will make our modernistic furniture seem mild and old-fashioned, and therefore saleable." He accepted, giving half-hour talks with ten-minute intermissions all day for three weeks . . . people began coming to see his plans and models . . . His ideas were taking hold. . . .

In July 1929 . . . his family took a house at Woodmere, LI. . . . He gave 20 lectures that winter. Had gained fame in a little over a year. . . . He figured that if he could convince the "intelligentsia" of NY of his Dymaxion theories, he would be alright. . . .

> *That winter (29–30) he made a new and larger model of the Dymaxion*
> *House. . . . The whole year of 1930 was spent in lectures, and that winter*
> *(30–31) as well. . . .*
>
> *The designing for the Chi World Fair was allocated in 30–31. . . . Har-*
> *vey Wiley Corbett . . . was chairman of the architectural board. . . . He*
> *became disciple (theoretically only) . . . B spent hours with him trying to*
> *"make him conscious of his social responsibility in incorporating the Dy-*
> *maxion attitude of design." No luck . . .*[10]

Fuller referred to himself as "B" because he was drafting an article someone else would rewrite. He wanted to set the tone, the direction of the narrative. It is indicative of his tendency to dissociate himself from his public persona. In the Bryant essay, he created a dramatic narrative of misfortune, enlightenment, and rebound out of the basic facts of his life.

As previously discussed, some of this story was true, and some was not. A few of the fabrications were only used in this context. For example, a Stockade sales manager did not borrow $700 from him and skip to the West Coast, leaving him with only $50. Nor was his cheekbone broken when he was robbed of his last dollars and watch while walking home one evening in Chicago. Fuller dropped these fictional encounters since they did not fit comfortably into his saga. Writing these subplots was not fruitless. They helped him figure out what type of character he would be in his life's story: he would be strong and resourceful in the face of adversity and hardship. Fuller realized that he did not need to fabricate such calamities since he could depict himself as routinely persecuted then redeemed by misrepresenting the events of his life.

The biography Fuller constructed was cyclical: he would do well, run into problems, bounce back, only to find himself in another bad situation, and so forth. Sometimes his misfortunes were commonplace, such as a death in the family or the loss of a job. Sometimes the problems were his fault, like his troubles at Harvard.[11] Fuller preferred to present his difficulties as if they were caused by others, usually people who took advantage of his naïveté or misunderstood him. He also liked to add theatrical touches to make ordinary occurrences seem particularly noteworthy (his reason for resigning from Muller) and his life more meaningful (his unsuccessful struggle to get the Dymaxion House into production). Analysis of this excerpt from the Bryant essay reveals how astutely Fuller engineered a personal narrative of struggle, accomplishment, disappointment, and rebound.

As Fuller wrote to Bryant, he resigned from the navy in 1919 because he wanted to remain close to his family. Armour rehired him at $50 a week, not at $55, and his salary was not raised to $80 as an incentive to remain with the company instead of accepting the Kelly-Springfield job. Arthur Meeker, a family friend who arranged Fuller's first job at Armour, encouraged him to accept the Kelly-Springfield offer because it was a good opportunity. Fuller, however, worked at Kelly-Springfield for only a few months. His employment did not end because the company closed; his position was officially terminated because business was slow.[12] After this, he reenlisted in the navy reserves as a lieutenant, the same rank at which he had resigned.

It is also true that he again chose family over the navy in 1922 when he left the latter to go into business with his father-in-law. They founded the Stockade Building System based on the rough-surfaced blocks Hewlett invented; Fuller's first task was to figure out the best way to manufacture the blocks. Fuller did invent some of the machinery required to produce the blocks and patented the mold and the process. He also attended the Harvard–Princeton football game and may have promised to bring his daughter a cane, which he forgot. There is no way to confirm or contradict his story. Although she was healthy at birth, Alexandra contracted a number of diseases. Among these were spinal meningitis, pneumonia, pyrosis and pysoloszis.[13] She died on November 14, 1922, a Tuesday,[14] three days after Harvard shut out Princeton.[15] The two dates are very close, and guilt about attending the game when his daughter was ill may have made it seem as if they happened on the same day. The combination of beginning a promising, new business with his father-in-law and his daughter's death made 1922 a bittersweet year for Fuller.

Whether motivated by guilt over his daughter's death and his forgetfulness or by a desire to succeed or by an amalgam of the two, Fuller worked hard to make Stockade a success. His diligence was rewarded; the company grew and expanded rapidly. Many types of structures, not just houses, were built using the Stockade system. He was explicit that Stockade's problem was that it only built the shell and interior partitions, not an integrated house — a subtle plug for the Dymaxion House.

Fuller's efforts on Stockade's behalf did not provide him with a secure future. He resigned as president of the parent company in February 1927, and Farley Hopkins's restructuring of the company forced Fuller out. When his second daughter, Allegra, was born on August 28, 1927, he was still employed by Stockade, if beleaguered by its management. Anne and Fuller were living in the Virginia Hotel when Allegra was born and stayed there until their December relocation to the Lake View. The Virginia's manager allowed them to leave without settling their account,[16] but they were never completely broke or down to their last $50 as the diary and brokerage account confirm. Anne knew about her husband's problems. She was sympathetic and supportive. Portraying himself as downtrodden, dejected, and desperate after being ousted from Stockade was a prelude to the next stage in his dramatic reworking of this period.

The loss of his Stockade position and its income was a problem, not a great crisis, as the diary entries convey. Even though Fuller was upset and angry, he was already working on his next project and had a new job within a month of being forced out of Stockade Midwest. The diary depicts a time of great activity and networking. There is nothing in his papers to corroborate his assertion in the Bryant essay that he contemplated suicide. He went to Lincoln Park many times, walking the baby or jogging, and could easily have found himself staring at the water in deep thought. In *4D Appendix No. 3* Fuller described his state of mind as "mental anguish such that must end either in jumping into the lake, or getting up and bowling over selfish materialism."[17] Ironically, this passage does not make Fuller seem depressed; rather, he seems so excited that he could jump in the lake or start a revolution. In American English, the phrase "go jump in a lake" is used to tell someone to calm down, or go away, which is consistent with Fuller's usage; it is not used to direct the person toward suicide. As with so many other components of his life, Fuller reworked this simple statement into a declaration of despair.

Characterizing himself as so distraught and demoralized that he was one jump away from suicide meant he needed to explain why he elected to live. The story presents him as broke, without options, unable to care for his family, and betrayed. Fortunately, he realized while standing by Lake Michigan that he had gained perspective on life and its meaning.

Now he simply needed to figure out how to put his knowledge and experience to use. To begin required pulling himself together and dealing with his responsibilities. He moved his family into a small, affordable apartment in a safe building, established a personal regime to clear his head, and accepted a job in late November. In subsequent versions, the apartment in a safe building became a tenement in a slum, the head-clearing regimen was transformed into a year of silence, and the job was omitted.[18] It is easy to understand why Fuller later made his circumstances during this time seem so bad: his recovery was more impressive. The silent period is more difficult to appreciate. He planted its seed in *4D Timelock* when he wrote that he spent time in "protracted isolation" and suffered "material self-negation"[19] while working on the project. According to Sidney Rosen, as he was standing at the edge of Lake Michigan Fuller realized:

> *A man could only know if his genius was real and worthwhile by doing nothing except thinking for a long time. This was how a great philosopher named Descartes, over three hundred years before, had given birth to his genius; he had locked himself away in a little hut for the winter with*

nothing but a little food, a stove, and his thoughts. This was how Henry Thoreau . . . found his genius—alone in the country near Walden Pond in Massachusetts.[20]

For Rosen, his subject's refusal to speak established a connection between Fuller and important men. It is also used to signify a time of self-control and unwavering concentration. This part of the story was not formulated in the Bryant essay where he needed to present himself as focused on his potential and how to act upon it.

This required intense concentration. He was too distracted to continue working; therefore, to be fair to his unnamed employer, he left the company after three months. This would make February the month of his departure from Muller although diary entries indicate he was still there in March.[21] Fuller may have been truthful about why his position at Muller ended or he may have adjusted the facts. It does seem likely that concentrating on his own project interfered with his ability to fulfill his duties for Muller. In any case, by February 1928, he was no longer thinking about Fuller Houses—he was taking action to make his idea a reality.

His strategy included visiting trade shows to see if there was anything he could use. At the beginning of February, Fuller recorded his visit to the Ford Industrial Exhibition, but he made no note of seeing Hopkins or of a vision or of any insight.[22] Fuller might not have mentioned his desire to attack Hopkins to avoid worrying his wife. He was being honest in one aspect: he never again discussed the exact circumstances surrounding the loss of his Stockade job. In recounting the story, he imparted only those details befitting his side of the story. And, given the amount of trivia in the diary, it hardly seems likely that he would have failed to record such a momentous occurrence as receiving affirmation from a voice, presumably a spiritual voice. The voice he heard that day telling him his thinking was truthful may have been his own internal voice. It was "another thought," not another voice, he informed Bryant, that instructed him to "write down everything you think." The inconsistency is not obvious and may have resulted from Fuller's struggle to create an auspicious beginning for the project. This voice informed him he no longer needed earthly confirmation of his ideas since he was receiving spiritual approval. He did not immediately recognize the significance of the voice's message. On his way home, he realized he might not need temporal attestation, but he did need temporal expression: he should write down his thoughts. In reality, Fuller was hard at work on the project and had written one or two outlines.

Fuller was disguising the origins of *4D Timelock* and the Dymaxion House. The book was a business prospectus and an architectural manifesto; the house was a product the 4D company would manufacture and sell. Fuller never pretended he did not want to put the house into production, although he later claimed he had arrived at the idea by chance: "I did not set out to design a house that hung from a pole . . . or to manufacture a new type of automobile. . . . I started with the Universe. . . . I could have ended up with a pair of flying slippers."[23] The only chance was whether or not the house would become a reality. He knew he wanted to start a business to manufacture houses.

His first step may have been to jot down his thoughts, but writing down his ideas was not his main focus in the project's early stages. Since he was working as many angles of the project as he could (networking, research, patent application, design development, corporate structure, and business proposal), he may have been "like a man with ague," or in a feverish, agitated state. Nothing indicates that any of the months, especially not any specific three-month period during the development of the project and the writing of *4D Timelock*, were more hectic than any other. His anxiety probably increased as he prepared the patent application and for the AIA convention in St. Louis. The compulsion to record his ideas may have stopped once he felt he had adequately expressed them on paper. It could have taken three months and fueled his drive to realize the project.

Exactly how many drafts and pages were required to record his thoughts is unknown. If the existing drafts, fragments of essays, and completed texts are totaled, there are fewer than five hundred pages. This is a much smaller than the "5,000 double-spaced typewritten pages" Fuller cited to Bryant. Exaggerating the number of pages, like an external voice telling him his thoughts were true, helped make the project seem bigger than one person could manage and too important to selfishly keep quiet. Five thousand pages would probably contain redundancies. This may be what he meant by boiling down the book. In addition to taking out all the "ands," removing repetitious points would help resolve how the original five thousand pages were reduced to ninety.[24] He might have discovered the redundancies as he reread the pages and divided them into envelopes for different people. Through his classification system Fuller discovered cohesion among the ideas and decided to merge them into one big composition, *4D Timelock*, instead of separate letters. Fuller did not elaborate on the problems he encountered while reorganizing the envelopes' contents into the book's chapters. He made it appear to be an easy, seamless evolution. Fuller camouflaged the fact that *4D Timelock* was a carefully composed essay intended to attract investors by describing its creation as an almost accidental, three-step process.

On the other hand, printing multiple copies of the book could not be treated as unintentional. It could be construed as an act of generosity. According to the Bryant narrative, the book was mimeographed in May (he was hired by the Waukegan firm in late November; he left after three months' employment, which would be in February; and it took him another three months, or until May, to write out his ideas). Even though he realized the book was a little unorthodox, he wanted to put it into print. He decided to publish it himself but did not have the money because he had been unemployed for three months. The situation was not hopeless; a mimeograph firm granted him use of its equipment and supplies to produce two hundred copies of the book, complete with illustrations. Fuller never provided a motive for the firm's generosity, although many possibilities exist. He could have known the owner, been a long-term customer, or negotiated a trade of some kind. Instead, the mimeograph firm suddenly appears, like the voice, to provide reassurance in the form of materials and machines. In reality the production of the book was not an act of charity. Fuller explained to Hewlett that preparations for the AIA convention left him broke. The mimeograph firm may have been generous enough to let Fuller use its supplies and equipment, but it charged for its services and materials.

Since he mimeographed two hundred copies of *4D Timelock* and its illustrations as a way to publicize his ideas about industrially reproduced houses and to generate interest in his business venture, Fuller's statement that he realized as he assembled the book he needed to "crystalize this philosophy in design" is dubious at best. There are descriptions of the house and its components, especially in chapters 15 and 16. Furthermore, the illustrations are primarily of multilevel dwellings. Fuller obviously had a design concept by the time he mimeographed the book even if it did not adequately represent his philosophy.

By this point in the Bryant essay Fuller had not explained his philosophy, only that he should remain quiet until he figured out a design to depict it. Unfortunately, he could not determine a design until he had an application. After much consideration in Lincoln Park, he settled on the house. Since his philosophy was not defined, his desire to express his general idea could have led him first to houses, then to transportation, and so on. There is also no justification for why dwelling was "the largest objective to which could apply philosophy." The undefined philosophy could have led him anywhere, even to flying slippers. Fuller did not end at houses, he began with them, and his desire to manufacture houses motivated the production of the book.

His design concept for manufactured houses may have been generated by a "structural secret" he learned by observing the way tree trunks support limbs and leaves. Trees were not, however, the only influence on the design. By the time he circulated *4D Timelock*, the project had taken form in his mind. He did discuss it with many Chicago architects, including Pierre Blouke. Blouke was supportive and suggested that he send a copy of *4D Timelock* to a Mr. Sternfeld, whom Fuller identified as the winner of the 1925 Beaux Arts Institute of Design Paris prize.[25] Blouke may have introduced Fuller to reporters. But the "first news of the Dymaxion house was" not published in April 1928, nor was Fuller "invited to speak at the Architects Club," which did not sponsor his trip to the AIA convention in St. Louis. On the other hand, Fuller's historical context was basically correct: Lindbergh had made his solo transatlantic flight in the previous May, St. Louis had recently suffered a devastating storm, and his father-in-law had recently been elected vice-president of the AIA. Fuller explained to Bryant that he only spoke to architects on an individual basis and gave them a copy of the mimeographed book at the convention; he "made no speech." Fuller also made no comment to Bryant about the AIA's stance on standardization of design; perhaps he had not figured out how to make it seem as if the institute had responded to his project. After the conference he began a letter writing campaign that had run its course by September. Finally, Fuller and his associates made a model, or three-dimensional representation of his design concept, during the summer following the AIA convention.

Although there is no record of it, a model may have been produced in conjunction with the patent application. If this was the case, then the model produced after the convention would have been a refinement of Fuller's ideas in the abandoned patent application. He offered permanent custodianship of the patent to the AIA, more likely to procure funding than to prevent private exploitation of the house. Fuller approached Hewlett to act as his mediator with the organization. Hewlett may have missed the point of the gift, but he understood how undeveloped the project was and recognized the conservative nature of the AIA. Even though the AIA was not interested in Fuller's project, there were architects, engineers, and investors who were. As with most new products, some people accepted it while others rejected it. There was no one group, such as engineers, who categorically dismissed the project whether they had been introduced to it through *4D Timelock*, newspaper articles, lectures, or exhibitions.

In less than a year after the AIA convention, Fuller generated enough interest in the project to justify an exhibition of the model at a major Chicago department store for three weeks in April, not March, 1929. Whether the store, Marshall Field & Company, asked Fuller to exhibit the house in order to make modern furniture look "saleable" [*sic*] or to make unfamiliar furniture designs seem exciting is not known. The opportunity's importance, however, cannot be underestimated. The project was renamed the Dymaxion House, a more appealing although no more descriptive title than 4D. It was also the project's debut to the general public, some of whom enthusiastically accepted it. Fuller could use the positive reactions in his negotiations with potential investors to show the project might be unusual but acceptable. Fuller's ideas "were taking hold" by the middle of 1929.

Fuller and his family did move to Woodmere, Long Island, in July of that year even though he initially planned to stay in Chicago. Their return to New York was more likely motivated by marital problems than by Fuller's desire to "convince the 'intelligentsia' of NY" of the value of the Dymaxion House. After being forced out of Stockade, Fuller wrote to his uncle Alfred and aunt Pauline that he planned to stay in Chicago since it was "a 'hard boiled' business section of the country but it is at the same time pretty much the center of the building and building material world. I am therefore planning to stay here for some time as I have plans for a new undertaking which looks even more promising than Stockade did."[26] In the year and a half between this letter and his return to New York, Fuller's project progressed nicely. There was a good chance that he and his project would be fine in the Midwest. His marriage might not have been as Fuller reminded Anne a few years later:

> *All our troubles started back in Chicago — both our faults; mine for a stupid*
> *notion of a martyristic [sic] monk's . . . which had a horrible reaction . . .*
> *on both of us and nearly wrecked everything. Your fault was over money.*
> *When you deceived me first and then excluded me from your financial*

affairs, because you had lost confidence in my acumen; and . . . your brothers
. . . seemed to offer so much more security and gain to you than I could, that
you deserted me in many ways.[27]

At the time of this letter, Fuller and Anne were living apart in a "partial estrange-
ment."[28] He was in Buffalo working on a prefabricated bathroom, and she was
on Long Island. The letter helps explain the distance that had developed between them. When they first returned to the New York metropolitan area,
Anne preferred to be on Long Island near her family and Fuller spent most of
his time in Manhattan working on the Dymaxion House (figure 7.1). He and
Anne were not as close as they had been in Chicago, but Fuller worked hard to
support his family.

In New York Fuller's goal was to put the Dymaxion House into production.
He worked to expand his supporters by lecturing and networking. Lectures were
his main source of income, although some supporters gave him money. It is unlikely he "gave 20 lectures" during the 1929–1930 winter as he wrote to Bryant.
His claim that he "gained fame in a little over a year" is true. In May 1928, Fuller
went to St. Louis to interest architects in his idea; in April 1929, he introduced
the Dymaxion House to the general public at Marshall Field; and, by January
1930, he was lecturing in different cities about the project.

It is not clear when Fuller realized the house would never go into production.
He may have known this when he made the new, futuristic model during the
winter of 1929–1930. At some point he must have comprehended that his own
future was secure even if the house did not go into production. As time progressed the issue changed from the specific house to the possibilities the house
represented. Fuller became known as a man who wanted to help make those
possibilities a reality. It is also why he later used the fact that the house was not
part of A Century of Progress in Chicago as the point at which he understood
the Dymaxion House would never be manufactured.

7.1

Buckminster Fuller in
Manhattan, ca. 1931.

Despite his relationships with Harvey Wiley Corbett and Lee Atwood, Fuller did not seriously push to have a model of the house built for the Chicago Fair. By 1933 his focus was on the Dymaxion Car, of which there were working prototypes. He put the house on the back burner as he concentrated on the project, the car, that seemed more likely to go into production. The automobile industry already existed, and it would have been easier to adapt an existing industry to produce a new type of car than to create an entirely new industry to produce a new type of house. A Century of Progress provided Fuller with an opportunity to exhibit a functioning prototype of the Dymaxion Car instead of a model of the Dymaxion House that was still in development. As with so many other facts of his life, Fuller later transformed his decision into another stumbling block. According to Fuller, he was asked to exhibit the house at the Chicago Fair a short while before its scheduled opening. He would, but only if a full-scale prototype of the house ready for production were created. When asked about the cost to develop the prototype, which to Fuller meant developing the entire industry, he estimated it to be in the hundred-million-dollar range. The cost was too high for the fair's organizers, the prototype was not realized, and, consequently, the house never went into production.[29] Even though his request meant the fair's budget would finance the development of a new industry, the implication is that the organizers failed to act because they failed to understand the significance of his proposal. Fuller deftly transferred the responsibility for his failure to get the Dymaxion House into production onto the organizers of the 1933 fair.

Once again, Fuller presented himself as a misunderstood idealist whose efforts were undermined by powerful opposition. For Bryant, he treated his life experiences like a continuous cycle of achievement, stumbling block (such as misunderstood intentions or persecution by foes), and failure followed by a new effort. The Bryant essay became the template on which Fuller modeled his life story, with its cycles of trials, tribulations, and triumphs.

The Bryant essay is, therefore, the first installment of the personal myth Fuller created to explain his life, achievements, and failures. In *The Stories We*

Live By: Personal Myths and the Making of the Self, Dan McAdams defined "personal myth" as follows:

> *a special kind of story that each of us naturally constructs to bring together the different parts of ourselves and our lives into a purposeful and convincing whole. Like all stories, the personal myth has a beginning, middle, and end, defined according to the development of plot and character. We attempt . . . to make a compelling aesthetic statement. A personal myth is an act of imagination that is a patterned integration of our remembered past, perceived present, and anticipated future. As both author and reader, we come to appreciate our own myth for its beauty and its psycho-social truth . . . in moments of great insight, parts of the story may become suddenly conscious, or motifs we had believed to be trivial may suddenly appear to be self-defining phenomena.*[30]

McAdams also explained that individuals discover value and direction through development of a personal myth: "We each seek . . . a sense of coherence by arranging the episodes of our lives into stories. This is not the stuff of delusion or self-perception. We are not telling ourselves lies. Rather, through our personal myths, each discovers what is true and what is meaningful in life. In order to live well, with unity and purpose, we compose a heroic narrative of the self that illustrates essential truths about ourselves."[31] Fuller's personal myth helped identify and clarify his purpose in life. It also served as the basis of his public persona. According to McAdams, "In moments of great intimacy, [individuals] may share important episodes with another person."[32] To Fuller, almost every episode of his public life, not his personal life,[33] was important. Fuller effectively conflated his personal myth and public persona to create a seemingly interpersonal intimacy with his supporters.

The use of Fuller's personal myth as a public relations tool is one reason for the cultlike devotion of some of his supporters. The documents contradicting Fuller's personal myth are both a revelation and an unmasking. As McAdams explained, the sharing of one's self "with another is the hallmark of interpersonal intimacy. To be intimate with another means to share one's innermost self."[34] Such intimacy implies honesty. The knowledge that Fuller's life story is a construction could be understood as betrayal by those who accept it as an honest struggle of good (Fuller) against evil (his opponents). Fuller may not have consciously been telling himself or his supporters lies; he may have understood his past as such a struggle. Over time the lines between his personal myth and the actual past may have become too blurred for Fuller to distinguish. Personal myth may have become personal history for him.

A significant influence on the development of Fuller's personal myth was Bertrand Russell. Fuller was familiar with Russell's writings and discussed them with Bob Hussey in early 1928.[35] Two books and an article by Russell are in the *4D Timelock* reference list: *Education and the Good Life*, *Selected Papers of Bertrand Russell*, and "The Training of Young Children."[36] Fuller owned *Selected Papers* because Hussey purchased it for him and Anne.[37] "A Free Man's Worship," from *Selected Papers*, reads like an inspirational model for the Bryant essay.

In it Russell argues that the renunciation of self and selfish desires in combination with submission to Power (presumably God) allow a person to become a free thinker and escape the confines of fate:

> *From the submission of our desires springs the virtue of resignation, from the freedom of our thoughts springs the whole world of art and philosophy, and the vision of beauty . . . the vision of beauty is possible only to unfettered contemplation, to thoughts not weighted by the load of eager wishes; and thus Freedom comes only to those who no longer ask of life that it shall yield them any of those personal goods that are subject to the mutations of*

Time . . . by death, by illness, by poverty, or by the voice of duty, we must

learn. . . . It is the part of courage, when misfortune comes, to bear without

repining the ruin of our hopes, to turn away our thoughts from vain regrets.

This degree of submission to Power is . . . the very gate of wisdom . . . there

is a cavern of darkness to be traversed before that temple (for the worship

of our own ideals) can be entered. The gate of the cavern is despair, and its

floor is paved with the gravestones of abandoned hopes. There Self must die;

there the eagerness, the greed of untamed desire must be slain, for only so can

the soul be freed from the empire of Fate.[38]

In his personal myth, Fuller crossed the "cavern of darkness" to stand at the "gate of wisdom" and entered the "temple (for the worship of [his] own ideals)" where his "Self" died and his "untamed desire [was] slain" between the summer of 1927 and the spring of 1928. Correlating, albeit misdated, events in the Bryant essay are his being forced out of Stockade in August 1927 and the patent application for the 4D House in April 1928. It was also when he learned the folly of selfishness and gained the courage to pursue his own path.

These lessons were not easily comprehended. Their meanings were learned through despair, which Russell called the "gate" to "the cavern of darkness." Despair, Russell posited, could be induced "by death, by illness, by poverty, or by the voice of duty."

In the Bryant essay, Fuller basically used each of Russell's conditions as a metaphor for his own experiences as he struggled to find meaning in his life and to believe in himself. The first crisis was the death of his daughter in 1922, after which he was so despondent he threw himself into his work. Five years later, despite his hard work, he was forced out of Stockade. The combination of the loss of his Stockade position and the money he lent to a Stockade sales manager left him broke, poverty-stricken. No money, no job, and no prospect for a new position meant that he would have difficulty providing for his family, the second crisis. Such a wretched situation could easily have forced Fuller to evaluate all options, including suicide. As previously argued, Fuller did not consider physical suicide, although he may have experienced an epiphany or a moral suicide of his former self, or both. As a result, he found the inspiration to reject his past as well as the perspective to redirect his life along a new path because he understood that there was light at the end of the tunnel. Unfortunately, this insight did not end his trials, because shortly after his realization he was mugged, robbed, and, one must imagine, left bleeding on the sidewalk with a broken jaw. The physical assault, however, strengthened his resolve to learn to think clearly and made him more determined to follow the new, as yet unidentified, direction he had so recently found.

Fuller wrote the Bryant essay before any of his inventions went into production and just as his ideas were beginning to be widely circulated through the successful publication of *Nine Chains to the Moon*. Over time he reworked the text and discarded certain episodes, like the mugging, to make the story less dramatic, more cohesive, and more believable. He also switched "the voice of duty" from the need to care for his family to the need to follow his new direction, to use his knowledge and experiences for the selfless benefit of others. Even though he changed some of the details he described to Bryant, Fuller retained both the structure from the Bryant essay and the concept of a life-changing revelation from the Russell essay in the later versions of his personal myth.[39]

It is more likely that Fuller was calculatedly creative instead of purposefully deceptive in the construction of his personal myth. He may also have believed the misrepresentations were accurate if he viewed his life as a series of successes and failures. As McAdams explains: "Though we may act out parts of our personal myth in daily life, the story is inside of us. It is made and remade in the secrecy of our own minds, both conscious and unconscious, and for our own psychological discovery and enjoyment."[40] Fuller did not keep the "discovery and enjoyment" he derived from his personal myth to himself; he used it as the basis of his public persona. Through careful design the story of his 1920s activities became one of his most successful public relations tools. This may have been the most important contribution the early period made to his career. Ultimately, Fuller's work on the Dymaxion House project did not launch a new industry to manufacture houses. It did, on the other hand, provide a foundation for the building of Fuller's career.

NOTES

PREFACE

1.   J. Baldwin, *Bucky Works: Buckminster Fuller's Ideas for Today* (New York: John Wiley & Sons, Inc., 1996), 62–65. An anticipatory comprehensive designer is a generalist who tries to use current technology to anticipate future needs.

2.   Ibid., 197.

3.   Ibid., 74–75. Two scientists, Harry Kroto and Richard Smalley, confirmed tetrahedra in nature in the 1980s when they discovered C_{60}, a carbon molecule named buckminsterfullerene and called buckyball.

4.   For typical treatments of Fuller's work, see Kenneth Frampton, *Modern Architecture: A Critical History*, 3rd ed. (New York: Thames and Hudson, 1992), which discusses Fuller's work as an alternative to modernist architecture, and Reyner Banham, *Theory and Design in the First Machine Age*, 2nd ed. (Cambridge, MA: MIT Press, 1980), which praises Fuller's use of technology. Fuller's designs, especially the Dymaxion House and the Wichita House, 1944–1946, are often treated as prototypes for futuristic housing as in H. Jandl Ward, with John A. Burns and Michael J. Auer, *Yesterday's Houses of Tomorrow: Innovative American Homes 1850 to 1950* (Washington, DC: Preservation Press, 1991).

5.   Richard Hamilton, "Work of R. B. Fuller: Design Initiatives and Prototype Engineering," *Hamilton Extracts*, R. Buckminster Fuller Papers, Department of Special Collections, Stanford University Libraries, Stanford University, Stanford, CA.

6.   Y. C. Wong, "Geodesic Works of Richard Buckminster Fuller, 1948–68 (The Universe as a Home of Man)" (Ph.D. diss., Massachusetts Institute of Technology, 1999).

7.   Karl M. Conrad, "Buckminster Fuller and the Technocratic Persuasion" (Ph.D. diss., University of Texas at Austin, 1974).

8. R. Buckminster Fuller, New York, NY, "Letter and Autobiographical Essay to Joe Bryant," New York, NY, July 1, 1939 (typed October 2, 1939), *Chronofile*, vol. 46 (1939), R. Buckminster Fuller Papers, Department of Special Collections, Stanford University Libraries, Stanford University, Stanford, CA. The first example of Fuller's manipulation of the development of the Dymaxion House is found in the draft for a press release Fuller noted was written by Miss Dorothy Baker. See "Draft of Philadelphia Art Alliance Press Release," *Chronofile*, vol. 42 (1932). The press release may have served as the starting point for Fuller's further elaboration in the Bryant essay.

1 BUILDING STOCKADE

1. Anne Hewlett Fuller (henceforth AHF), *Diary*, August 7, 1927, *Chronofile*, vol. 30 (1927). Anne had sole responsibility for the diary until December 14, 1927, when she stopped making entries. Buckminster Fuller (henceforth RBF) began the diary again on January 1, 1928. After this, Anne and Fuller both wrote entries. For a complete transcription of the diary, see L. Lorance, "Building Values: Buckminster Fuller's Dymaxion House in Context" (Ph.D. diss., CUNY Graduate Center, 2004), Appendix 1.

2. Hewlett was granted patent number 1,450,794 on April 3, 1923, for the Stockade Building System. In 1926 and 1927, Hewlett and Fuller were awarded additional patents for improvements to the Stockade system. See chap. 1, n. 30

3. *Stockade Patented: The Invention of James Monroe Hewlett, F.A.I.A.* (New York: Stockade Building System, n.d.), [2]. This brochure probably dates from 1925. It is identical to the Stockade brochure published in *The American Architect*, January 5, 1926.

4. Ibid., [1–2]. Emphasis in original.

5. James Monroe Hewlett (1868–1941) graduated from Columbia University in 1890 and briefly worked for McKim, Mead, and White before studying in Paris. He

became a partner in the New York–based architectural firm of Lord & Hewlett upon his return in 1894. The firm designed a number of public and residential buildings in the New York metropolitan area and throughout the United States. He also served as the president of the Architectural League and was a director and fellow of the American Institute of Architects. Although a respected architect, Hewlett is now more known for his mural paintings than for his architecture.

6. C. W. Young, New York, NY, to J. McCarthy, Quebec, Canada, June 6, 1922, *Chronofile*, vol. 23 (1922). The $69 weekly salary was determined by dividing $3,600 by 52, the number of weeks in a year. In 2007 dollars, Fuller was earning an equivalent of $863.23 per week and $45,037.93 annually (www.bls.gov).

7. R. Buckminster Fuller, "Résumé" (hand-dated 5/18/44), *Chronofile*, vol. 93 (1944), 5. In the semi-autobiographical *The Dymaxion World*, Fuller also claims that Kelly-Springfield went out of business (Buckminster Fuller and Robert Marks, *The Dymaxion World of Buckminster Fuller* [Garden City, NY: Anchor Books, 1973], 13). His job at the company may have ended in May 1922 as listed in his 1944 résumé, but nothing in the *Chronofile* supports or negates this claim.

8. The 2007 monetary equivalents for $50 and $100 in 1922 are $625.53 and $1,251.05 respectively (www.bls.gov).

9. *Chronofile*, vol. 17 (1920). Fuller attended a naval training camp in Plattsburg, NY, during July 1916 where he made corporal and won the marksmanship award (*Chronofile*, vol. 3 [1916]). Fuller next volunteered his mother's boat, the *Wego*, to patrol the Maine coast. He was enlisted as chief botswain in the Fourth U.S. Naval Reserve Force on April 18, 1917, and was given active duty for the duration of the war. He served in this capacity until September 25, 1917 (*Chronofile*, vol. 10 [1917]). Then, with the support of his superiors, he eventually became a junior grade lieutenant in 1918. He resigned from the navy on September 2, 1919 (*Chronofile*, vol. 17 [1920])

10. Robert Snyder, *R. Buckminster Fuller: An Autobiographical Monologue/Scenario* (New York: St. Martin's Press, 1980), 25. It is difficult to verify many of the specifics of Fuller's life and experiences during this period. In *Chronofile*, vol. 1 (1895–1917), are letters postmarked 1914 from his mother, Caroline Wolcott Fuller, to him in

Sherbrooke in response to correspondence he sent her about his activities in Canada. His letters, however, are not in the *Chronofile* in its present state. They may be in some of the damaged volumes.

11.   *Chronofile*, vols. 6–11 (1917).

12.   RBF, Hampton Roads, VA, to C. W. Fuller, New York, NY, December 2, 1927, *Chronofile*, vol. 9 (1917).

13.   Rebecca Livingston, National Archives and Record Administration, Washington, DC, to the author, June 11, 2002.

14.   Alden Hatch, *Buckminster Fuller: At Home in the Universe* (New York: Crown Publishers, 1974), 59. According to Teri Hedgpeth, National Archives and Records Administration, Washington, DC, nothing in Bellinger's files supports this claim (letter to the author who was not granted access to the files, January 24, 2002). Fuller wrote to his mother on February 4, 1918, that Bellinger wanted him to stay in Virginia (*Chronofile*, vol. 12 [1918]).

15.   Beverly Lyall, United States Naval Academy, Annapolis, MD, to the author, January 25, 2002. According to Lyall, this "was a 90 day program established at the Naval Academy during World War I and II to provide the Navy with sufficient officers."

16.   RBF, Hampton Roads, VA, to C. W. Fuller, New York, NY, February 4, 1918, *Chronofile*, vol. 12 (1918).

17.   RBF, Hampton Roads, VA, to C. W. Fuller, New York, NY, May 2, 1918, *Chronofile*, vol. 12 (1918).

18.   Beverly Lyall, United States Naval Academy, Annapolis, MD, to the author, July 18, 2002.

19.   *Chronofile*, vols. 13–17 (1918–1920).

20.   Hatch, *Buckminster Fuller*, 23.

21.   Barry Farrell, "The View from the Year 2000," *Life* 70, no. 7 (February 26, 1971): 46–48, 50–51, 53, 55–58.

22. RBF, "Summary of Developments October 1st, 1922, to October 1st, 1923," *Chrono-file*, vol. 24 (1923–1924), 1.

23. Ibid.

24. Hatch, *Buckminster Fuller*, 80.

25. RBF, "Summary of Developments," 1.

26. Ibid., 1–2.

27. Ibid., 2. $900 in 1923 is equivalent to $11,061.95 in 2007 (www.bls.gov).

28. *Stockade Building System, Inc., A New and Better Method of Home Construction with Proven Units* (New York: Stockade Building System, Inc., 1927), 17.

29. *Chronofile*, vols. 24–34 (1923–1928). There are many letters debating or declining various opportunities for expansion. Stockade Corporation of Florida letterhead exists, but no franchise was set up in that state. In an August 9, 1926, letter to Fuller, Sam Hoffman, SBS general manager, informed Fuller of a cable from Havana inquiring about licensing the patents to manufacture blocks in Cuba (*Chronofile*, vol. 26 [1926]). Fuller responded on January 15, 1927, to an inquiry from Kiam Hoa Seng & Company, Bangkok, Siam, about the costs of setting up a plant and the different types of materials appropriate for the blocks (*Chronofile*, vol. 31 [1927]). To protect his interests, Hewlett took foreign and American patents on Stockade. To officially present their product as Stockade, foreign companies were required to pay a licensing fee to use the name and the method of construction.

30. *Hamilton Extracts*, volume 14, box 3. The patent numbers and dates are as follows: number 1,631,373 on June 7, 1927, to Hewlett for a Stockade partition wall; number 1,633,702 on June 18, 1927, to Hewlett and Fuller for a supporting wall made of Stockade blocks; and number 1,634,900 on July 5, 1927, to Fuller for the mold and the process to make Stockade blocks.

31. "Order Blank and Guaranty," Gordon-Van Tine Company, *117 House Designs of the Twenties: Reprint Edition of the Gordon-Van Tine Co.'s 1923 Catalog* (New York: Dover Reprints, 1992), 135, and "Easy Payment Plan," Sears, Roebuck and Company, *Honor Bilt Modern Homes* (Chicago: The Company, ca. 1927), 144.

32. RBF, "Summary of Developments," 2. The equivalent production cost of 8¢ in 2007 would be 98¢ per block (www.bls.gov).

33. Scott Derks, ed., *The Value of a Dollar: Prices and Incomes in the United States 1860–1999* (Lakeville, CT: Grey House Publishing, 1999), 486. The 2007 equivalent of $19.81 in 1923 is $243.49, which means the blocks would cost about 25¢ each. In 1924, the price per 1,000 bricks was $17.04 ($209.44 in 2007) ; $14.70 in 1925 ($176.55 in 2007); $16.46 in 1926 ($195.45 in 2007); $13.88 in 1927 ($167.66 in 2007); and $13.00 in 1928 ($159.78 in 2007) (www.bls.gov).

34. RBF, "Summary of Developments," 2. In 2007, the cost of the 15¢ block would be around $1.84 (www.bls.gov).

35. *Stockade Building System, Inc.*, 4–7. In 2007, Gill's 20¢ block would be about $2.40 and the 4,000 blocks purchased by Skinner would cost about $10,088.50 and be around $2.88 each (www.bls.gov). The two letters were dated 1925; therefore, the equivalents are adjusted for 1925, not 1926.

36. "Copy of Report by the Mechanical Engineering Laboratory," Massachusetts Institute of Technology, Cambridge, MA, April 1924, *Chronofile*, vol. 32 (1927).

37. "Copy of Test Results Performed by the Department of Acoustics," Riverbanks Laboratories, Geneva, IL, July 23, 1927, *Chronofile*, vol. 32 (1927). According to Riverbanks, the acoustic absorption of other materials was: 1 inch hair felt: 50 percent; heavy rugs: 25 percent; and hard plaster on tile: 2.5 percent. Perhaps because their textures were similar, hair felt blocks (cattle hair free from excessive dirt and felted together to a uniform thickness) were often compared to Stockade blocks in these types of tests.

38. "Copy of Test Results by Robert W. Hunt Company, Engineers," Chicago, IL, May 3, 1927, *Chronofile*, vol. 32 (1927).

39. "Report of Architecture and Allied Arts Exposition," New York, NY, April 1925, *Chronofile*, vol. 32 (1927).

40. RBF, Chicago, IL, to Robert McAllister Lloyd, New York, NY, July 12, 1927, *Chronofile*, vol. 29 (1927).

41. Hatch, *Buckminster Fuller*, 85.

42. RBF, Chicago, IL, to E. B. Millar, New York, NY, January 14, 1927, *Chronofile*, vol. 31 (1927).

43. B. T. Betts, New York, NY, to RBF, New York, NY, June 1, 1925, *Chronofile*, vol. 25 (1925–1926).

44. *The American Architect: Golden Anniversary Issue*, vol. 129, no. 2488 (January 5, 1926): 81.

45. See "Sources," in Robert L. Sweeney, *Wright in Hollywood: Visions of a New Architecture* (New York: Architectural History Foundation, 1994), chap. 8.

46. RBF, "Later Developments of My Work," in *Ideas and Integrities: A Spontaneous Autobiographical Disclosure* (Englewood Cliffs, NJ: Prentice-Hall, 1963), 44.

47. RBF, Chicago, IL, to Alfred and Pauline Fuller, Daytona Beach, FL, January 9, 1928, *Chronofile*, vol. 34 (1928).

48. Carl Condit, *American Building: Materials and Techniques from the First Colonial Settlements to the Present*, 2nd ed. (Chicago: University of Chicago Press, 1982), 43.

49. Ibid., caption to illustration 42, n.p.

50. "Blocks of Straw Yet Houses of Reinforced Concrete," *Scientific American*, vol. 134, no. 5 (May 1926): 331.

51. "Lower-Cost Houses Coming," *Babson's Reports* (June 1, 1926): 1. This weekly newsletter kept tabs on financial developments in the United States.

52. The balance sheet of December 31, 1925, shows Stockade even with assets of $122,282.03 and liabilities of $122,282.03 (which is approximately $1,468.621.16 in 2007 [www.bls.gov]). It was prepared by W. S. Whittlesey, CPA, 101 Park Ave, New York, NY. *Chronofile*, vol. 25 (1925–1926).

53. Sam Hoffman, New York, NY, to RBF, Chicago, IL, *Chronofile*, vol. 26 (1926).

54. Wolcott Fuller, Boston, MA, to RBF, Chicago, IL, August 17, 1926, *Chronofile*, vol. 26 (1926).

55.   "Report of Stockade Building System, Inc. Board Meeting," *Chronofile*, vol. 26 (1926).

56.   "Report of Stockade Midwest Corporation Board Meeting," *Chronofile*, vol. 26 (1926).

57.   Mr. and Mrs. A. C. Strong, Lisle, IL, "To Whom It May Concern," Stockade Midwest Corporation, Chicago, IL, undated, *Chronofile*, vol. 27 (1926).

58.   William Otterley, Lisle, IL, to The Stockade Building Company, Chicago, IL, November 16, 1926, *Chronofile*, vol. 27 (1926).

59.   RBF, Chicago, IL, to Mac (Robert McAllister Lloyd), New York, NY, January 10, 1928, *Chronofile*, vol. 33 (1928). Mac is not identified beyond the nickname but the sequence of their correspondence and its content indicates Mac is Robert McAllister Lloyd.

60.   Ibid.

61.   Ibid.

62.   Ibid. $1,000 in 1927 is about $12,079.14 in 2007 (www.bls.gov).

63.   "Balance Sheet," *Chronofile*, vol. 26 (1926). $57,177.58 in 1927 is equivalent to $690,655.88 in 2007 (www.bls.gov).

2 CORPORATE RESTRUCTURING

1.   Correspondence between Sam Hoffman, New York, NY, and RBF, Chicago, IL, *Chronofile*, vols. 25–32 (1926–1927).

2.   DeCoursey Fales, New York, NY, to RBF, Chicago, IL, October 19, 1926, *Chronofile*, vol. 27 (1926).

3. RBF, Chicago, IL, to Sam Hoffman, New York, NY, November 15, 1926. *Chronofile*, vol. 27 (1926).

4. Minutes, November 18, 1926, SBS Board Meeting, *Chronofile*, vol. 27 (1926).

5. Farley Hopkins's papers have not been located. His involvement with Stockade is only known through the company papers in the Fuller archives.

6. J. M. Hewlett, New York, NY, to RBF, Chicago, IL, September 27, 1926, *Chronofile*, vol. 25 (1925–1926). In 2007 Hewlett would need around $59,372.03 (www.bls.gov).

7. Telegram, J. M. Hewlett, New York, NY, to RBF, Chicago, IL, September 27, 1926, *Chronofile*, vol. 25 (1925–1926). Unfortunately, the whereabouts of Hewlett's papers are not known, and the story can only be pieced together from documents in Fuller's papers. Hewlett's financial problems also prompted him to sell part interest in the Stockade foreign patents. Hopkins purchased a one-third interest in these. Foreign patent ownership did not affect Fuller's relationship with Stockade and will not be discussed in more detail.

8. Snyder, *Autobiographical Monologue/Scenario,* 34, and Fuller and Marks, *The Dymaxion World*, 13. Stockade was a privately owned and traded company, there is no public record of its financial transactions.

9. Sam Hoffman, New York, NY, to RBF, Chicago, IL, January 4, 1927, *Chronofile*, vol. 31 (1927).

10. RBF, Chicago, IL, to SBS Board of Directors, New York, NY, February 10, 1927, *Chronofile*, vol. 32 (1927).

11. RBF, Chicago, IL, to W. J. McCarty, Detroit, MI, February 16, 1927, *Chronofile*, vol. 28 (1926–1927).

12. *Chronofile*, vol. 28 (1926–1927). Fuller gave his talk "New and Better Methods of Home Construction" at 1:00 p.m. on the Chicago radio station WMAQ. Fuller's notes for the talk are primarily drawn from a Stockade brochure.

13. Telegram, Andrews King, unknown city, to RBF, Chicago, IL, February 17, 1927, *Chronofile*, vol. 28 (1926–1927).

14. Sam Hoffman, New York, NY, to RBF, Chicago, IL, February 28, 1927, *Chronofile*, vol. 28 (1926–1927).

15. J. M. Hewlett, New York, NY, to RBF, Chicago, IL, undated letter, *Chronofile*, vol. 28 (1926–1927).

16. Frances Freeman, New York, NY, to RBF, Chicago, IL, March 14, 1927, *Chronofile*, vol. 28 (1926–1927). In 1931, when Fuller was trying to establish a Manhattan office, he contacted her about working for him. She was willing, but there was not much work for her. Eventually, she took another job and offered to moonlight for him. No work materialized for her (*Chronofile*, vol. 38 [1931]).

17. RBF, Chicago, IL, to DeCoursey Fales, New York, NY, March 8, 1927, *Chronofile*, vol. 32 (1927).

18. RBF, Chicago, IL, to Mr. O. A. Rasin, New York, NY, July 1927, *Chronofile*, vol. 29 (1927).

19. Minutes, Special Meeting of Board of Directors [Stockade Midwest], *Chronofile*, vol. 32 (1927). Hopkins would be proposing close to $2,415,827.59 in 2007 dollars (www.bls.gov).

20. RBF to Mac, *Chronofile*, vol. 33.

21. Ibid. Emphasis in original.

22. AHF, *Diary*, November 21, 1927.

23. AHF, *Diary*, November 23, 1927.

24. AHF, *Diary*, November 22, 1927.

25. W. R. Smythe, F. R. Muller Co., Inc., Waukegan, IL, to RBF, Chicago, IL, November 22, 1927, *Chronofile*, vol. 37 (1927). $50 per week in 1927 is equivalent to $603.96 in 2007; 1¢ in 1927 is about 12¢ in 2007 (www.bls.gov).

26. RBF to Mac, *Chronofile*, vol. 33.

27. See AHF diary entries for November 21 and 23, 1927.

28.   RBF to Mac, *Chronofile*, vol. 33.

29.   Ibid.

30.   AHF, Chicago, IL, to J. M. Hewlett, New York, NY, September 14, 1927, *Chronofile*, vol. 29 (1927).

31.   Fuller traced the American branch of his family to Thomas Fuller, a lieutenant in the British navy who arrived in the colonies in 1630. Many of Thomas Fuller's male descendants, primarily Harvard-educated lawyers and ministers, were community leaders and political activists. Margaret Fuller, the nineteenth-century feminist, author, and editor, was Buckminster Fuller's great aunt. His father, Richard Buckminster Fuller Sr. attended Harvard but did not graduate although his bachelor of arts, out of course, was given to him in 1908 ("Notice from Harvard University," *Chronofile*, vol. 1 [1895–1917]). Fuller Sr. was a "merchant-importer" and "the only Fuller in eight generations who had not been either a minister or lawyer" (Fuller and Marks, *The Dymaxion World*, 11). Other sources give the number of generations as five. Whether it was five or eight generations, his son, Buckminster, was the first (male) Fuller not to earn a degree from Harvard.

   The Hewlett family began to climb the social ladder in 1824 when Anne's great-grandfather, Thomas, purchased Rock Hall, a house with 124 acres of farmland, in Lawrence, Long Island. Thomas was from a family of small farmers of "respected and industrious Long Island Stock" (Shirley Hibbard, *Rock Hall: A Narrative History* [Lawrence, NY: Friends of Rock Hall, 1997], 31). Thomas's second son, James Augustus, became a prominent Manhattan businessman, securing the family's place in New York society.

   See *Chronofile*, vols. 17–22 (1920–1922), for information about Anne's and Fuller's listings in the New York Social Register.

32.   AHF, Lawrence, NY, to RBF, Chicago, IL, July 21, 1927, *Chronofile*, vol. 29 (1927). These letters demonstrate Anne knew about Fuller's problems with Hopkins as well as Stockade Midwest's reluctance to reimburse his expenses. She wrote to him on July 13: "What does old skunk Farley say about your expense acct. I was wild when I heard the 1000 was from your stock & not the account money at all. You are going to get that paid aren't you darling?" A few days later she wrote, "I guess with

Geo. Cross around you can fix things so that Farley can't do any nasty tricks while you're away" (*Chronofile*, vol. 29 [1927]).

33. Hatch, *Buckminster Fuller*, 39–40.

34. RBF, Chicago, IL, to Uncle Waldo, unknown city, January 10, 1928, *Chronofile*, vol. 34 (1928).

35. The rate for number 922 was $12.50 per week (about $150.99 in 2007) and for number 823 was $15.55 per week (about $187.83 in 2007) (*Chronofile*, vol. 29 [1927] and www.bls.gov).

36. AHF, *Diary*, December 5, 1927.

37. *Sandborn Fire Insurance Maps: Chicago 1905–1951*, vol. 9, reel 24.

38. Unidentified clipping from the *Northside Sunday Citizen* (December 30, 1927) from *History of the Lakeview Community* in *Chicago Historical Society: Documents: History of Chicago*, 6 vols. (Chicago: Chicago Historical Society, 1925–30): document 16.

39. RBF, "Letter and Essay to Joe Bryant," and Richard Hamilton, "Notes on [RBF's] Career," 11.

40. This story is drawn primarily from Fuller and Marks, *The Dymaxion World*, 13–14, and Snyder, *Autobiographical Monologue/Scenario,* 34–40. It is the accepted account of his life immediately after Stockade. Variations of it are found in every synopsis of his late 1920s activities that are too numerous to list.

41. RBF, "Letter and Essay to Joe Bryant." In 2007 dollars, the $22 apartment would be about $265.74 (www.bls.gov).

42. Richard Hamilton, "Buckminster Fuller: Comprehensive Designer," unpublished manuscript, n.d., 11, in *Hamilton Extracts*, vol. 2, box 2.

43. Hatch, *Buckminster Fuller*, 91. Hatch is discussing room 411, which was $17.50 per week (about $211.38 in 2007), *Chronofile*, vol. 29 (1927). This was probably not their first Lake View quarters since it was more expensive than number 823 in the Virginia (www.bls.gov).

44.   RBF, *Diary*, February 1, 1928.

45.   Martin Chamberlain, Joliet, IL, to RBF, Chicago, IL, November 6, 1927, *Chronofile*, vol. 32 (1927).

46.   AHF, *Diary*, November 23, 1927.

47.   RBF, *Diary*, January 28, 1928.

48.   RBF, *Diary*, February 25, 1928.

49.   Cover letter and patent application, Martin Chamberlain, Joliet, IL, to RBF, Chicago, IL, November 6, 1927, *Chronofile*, vol. 32 (1927).

50.   Ibid.

51.   Ibid.

52.   Ibid.

53.   Martin Chamberlain, Joliet, IL, to RBF, Chicago, IL, October 24, 1928, *Chronofile*, vol. 34 (1928).

54.   RBF, *Diary*, February 20, 1928.

55.   AHF, *Diary*, March 8, 1928.

56.   RBF, *Diary*, March 17, 1928.

57.   Ibid.

58.   RBF, Chicago, IL, to J. M. Hewlett, New York, NY, handwritten copy of telegram sent March 28, 1928, *Chronofile*, vol. 33 (1928).

59.   J. M. Hewlett, New York, NY, to RBF, Chicago, IL, March 19, 1928, *Chronofile*, vol. 34 (1928).

60.   Handwritten draft or copy of undated letter from RBF to J. M. Hewlett in response to his letter of March 19, 1928, *Chronofile*, vol. 34 (1928). Fuller was not honest in claiming complete dissociation from Chamberlain. They kept in touch and

Chamberlain invited the Fullers to his wedding; they did not attend. Fuller and Chamberlain never again collaborated.

61. J. M. Hewlett, New York, NY, to RBF, Chicago, IL, March 26, 1928, *Chronofile*, vol. 34 (1928).

62. Handwritten draft or copy of undated letter from RBF to J. M. Hewlett.

63. Sam Hoffman, New York, NY, to RBF, Chicago, IL, March 28, 1928, *Chronofile*, vol. 34 (1928). Hoffman was employed by Stockade for about a year longer. He wrote to Fuller in May 1929: "You have no doubt heard that I am through with Stockade, our Chicago friends having used me to clean up a lot of dirty work and suddenly informing me that they had decided to close the New York office, and left me practically stranded without paying me the last two week's salary while I was still in their employ. I suppose this is typical of their business ethics and altogether in line with their methods" (*Chronofile*, vol. 34 [1928]).

64. Legal agreement signed by RBF and Farley Hopkins, March 29, 1928, *Chronofile*, vol. 33 (1928).

65. RBF, *Diary*, March 21, 1928. Hopkins may have been willing to accept Fuller's stock as a way to keep the company's problems under wraps, avoid negative publicity, and prevent a drop in the share price.

66. Andrews King, Chicago, IL, to RBF, Chicago, IL, January 21, 1929, *Chronofile*, vol. 36 (1929).

67. RBF, Chicago, IL, to The Stockade Corporation, Chicago, IL, February 18, 1929, *Chronofile*, vol. 36 (1929).

68. RBF, Chicago, IL, to George Buffington, Chicago, IL, August 31, 1928, *Chronofile*, vol. 35 (1928).

69. RBF to Mac, *Chronofile*, vol. 33. $200,000 in 1928 is equivalent to $2,458,210.53 in 2007 (www.bls.gov).

70. The pain of his father's death must have been amplified by its date. Fuller was open about the anguish caused by his father's death, but he did not publicly acknowledge that his father died on his fifteenth birthday. Fuller noted the fact on an envelope

in *Chronofile*, vol. 17. He hand-dated the envelope "March 23, 1917" and wrote on it: "My Father Richard Buckminster Fuller died on my birthday July 12th, 1910." In the unpublished essay to Joe Bryant, he wrote: "He was married on July 12, 1917, with three days' leave from the Navy. This was his birthday, his grandfather Fuller's birthday, the anniversary of his father's death, his wife's brother's birthday" (RBF, "Letter and Essay to Joe Bryant").

71.   Conrad, "Buckminster Fuller and the Technocratic Persuasion,"74.

72.   Snyder, *Autobiographical Monologue/Scenario,* 34, and Fuller and Marks, *The Dymaxion World*, 13.

73.   Sydney Rosen, *Wizard of the Dome: R. Buckminster Fuller, Designer for the Future* (Boston: Little, Brown and Company, 1969), 41.

74.   Hatch, *Buckminster Fuller*, 86.

75.   Ibid.

76.   Fuller and Marks, *The Dymaxion World*, 13.

77.   RBF, "Résumé," *Chronofile*, vol. 93.

78.   Fuller and Marks, *The Dymaxion World*, 13.

79.   Snyder, *Autobiographical Monologue/Scenario,* 40.

3 PROJECT DEVELOPMENT

1.   AHF, *Diary*, November 26, 1927.

2.   AHF, *Diary*, November 29, 1927.

3.   RBF, *Diary*, January 27, 1928, and AHF, *Diary*, March 1, 1928. Fuller regularly manipulated his financial portfolio with stock holdings of Bancitaly, Curtiss Aero, Radio

A, Auburn Com., TransContinental Air Way, Wright Aero, and Casein Co. (See *Chronofile*, vol. 34 [1928]. Investing $128 in 1928 is like investing $1,573.25 in 2007 [www.bls.gov].)

4.   AHF, *Diary*, March 1, 1928.

5.   Hatch, *Buckminster Fuller*, 91.

6.   AHF, "Budget," *Chronofile*, vol. 34 (1927). Missing from Fuller's papers during this time are bank statements and tax forms that would shed much light on his financial situation. Some tax returns for earlier years are in the *Chronofile*, but not for the late 1920s. The 2007 equivalents of $1,153.41 and $842.25 are $13,932.20 and $10,173.65 respectively (www.bls.gov).

7.   AHF, Lawrence, NY, to RBF, Chicago, IL, July 17, 1929, *Chronofile*, vol. 29 (1927).

8.   RBF, Chicago, IL, to The Goodrich Transportation Co., Municipal Pier, Chicago, IL, January 17, 1928, *Chronofile*, vol. 34 (1928). In 2007, Fuller would be paying $921.83 in monthly rent (www.bls.gov).

9.   This is typical for Fuller. He had a tendency to enter into a contract and then ignore the commitment. For example, even though he did not graduate, Fuller pledged $100, payable in $25 installments, in 1920 to the Harvard Alumni Fund. By 1927, he had only paid $10 toward the pledge despite Harvard's threats to send his account to a collection agency. In her summary of their financial situation at the end of 1927, Anne included the remaining $90 in the accounts payable column (*Chronofile*, vol. 34 [1927]). It is not known if the pledge was fulfilled, but, on March 27, 1939, Harvard again requested Fuller fulfill it (*Chronofile*, vol. 64 [1939]). In 2007, Fuller's 1920 $100 pledge is the same as a $1,050.88 pledge; he paid the 2007 equivalent of $105.09, which left a balance equivalent to $845.79 (www.bls.gov).

10.   RBF, "Letter and Essay to Joe Bryant."

11.   AHF, *Diary*, December 3, 1927.

12.   RBF, *Diary*, March 16, 1928.

13.   RBF, *Diary*, March 27, 1928.

14. RBF, *Diary*, January 28, 1928.

15. RBF, *Diary*, January 26, 1928.

16. RBF, *Diary*, February 3, 1928.

17. RBF, "Reference List for *4D Timelock*," *Chronofile*, vol. 35 (1928). The entire reference list can be consulted in Lorance, "Building Values," Appendix 5.

18. RBF, *Diary*, February 4, 1928.

19. RBF, *Diary*, February 5, 1928.

20. RBF, *Diary*, February 23, 1928.

21. RBF, *Diary*, January 30, 1928.

22. RBF, *Diary*, February 21, 1928.

23. RBF, *Manuscript 28.01.01, Folder 9*, R. Buckminster Fuller Papers, Department of Special Collections, Stanford University Libraries, Stanford University, Stanford, CA.

24. French was a required subject at Milton Academy, which "takes its French seriously." According to Mr. Feather, the Milton Academy archivist, Fuller's Milton transcript has disappeared so it is difficult to gauge his proficiency in the language (telephone conversation with the author, March 13, 2002). On his unsuccessful application for a Simon Guggenheim Memorial Foundation Fellowship for Advanced Study in 1934, Fuller wrote that he adequately read and wrote both French and German, but needed practice in order to speak them (*Chronofile*, vol. 41 [1932]).

25. All texts mentioned in the diary and in the reference list are in English. As the notes about *Urbanisme* and *L'Art Decoratif d'Aujourd'hui* show, Fuller knew of developments in architecture outside the United States, or at least in France. There are also reprints of buildings at the Weissenhofseidlung, Stuttgart, Germany, 1927, from the French magazine *L'Architecture d'Aujourd'hui* slipped into *Chronofile*, vol. 33 (1928). Fuller never referred to these. When he acquired them and when they were slipped into the volume are not known. They are loosely placed inside the back cover, not incorporated into the volume.

26. RBF, *Diary*, February 21, 1928. He does not state whether this is the diary of Reverend Timothy Fuller, his great-great-grandfather, or that of the Honorable Timothy Fuller, his great-grandfather. On May 3, 1928, he wrote to his mother: "I am . . . astounded further that I should have gown to this age + never have read anything of [the writings of Margaret Fuller Osoli] or Grandfather Fuller's. His artistry is excellent." He does not clarify which Grandfather Fuller (*Chronofile*, vol. 34 [1928]).

27. AHF, *Diary*, March 28, 1928.

28. AHF, *Diary*, December 12, 1927.

29. AHF, *Diary*, January 7, 1928.

30. RBF, *Diary*, January 24, 1928.

31. AHF, *Diary*, January 23, 1928.

32. AHF, *Diary*, February 6, 1928.

33. RBF, *Diary*, February 5, 1928.

34. Ibid.

35. AHF, *Diary*, March 4, 1928.

36. RBF, "Sketches for 4D Furniture," R. Buckminster Fuller Papers, Department of Special Collections, Stanford University Libraries, Stanford University, Stanford, CA.

37. AHF, *Diary*, March 4, 1928.

38. RBF, *Diary*, March 5, 1928.

39. AHF, *Diary*, January 10, 1928.

40. RBF, *Diary*, March 5, 1928.

41. AHF, *Diary*, January 23, 1928.

42. RBF, *Diary*, January 24, 1928.

43. Ibid.

44. AHF, *Diary*, March 8, 1928. To which drawing Anne is referring is not known.

45. RBF, *Diary*, February 4, 1928.

46. Ibid.

47. RBF, *Diary*, January 26, 1928.

48. RBF, *Diary*, February 3, 1928. How this outline relates to the one given to Bob Hussey on March 8 and the one given to Mr. Morgan on November 29 is not clear. None of these outlines have been identified, although they may relate to the early Cosmopolitan Homes Corporation texts or "Lightful Houses"; see chapter 5. It is also not known if they were incorporated into *4D Timelock*.

49. RBF, *Diary*, February 20, 1928.

50. Ibid.

51. RBF, *Diary*, February 1, 1928.

52. RBF, *Diary*, February 23, 1928.

53. AHF, *Diary*, March 2, 1928.

54. RBF, *Diary*, March 6, 1928.

55. RBF, "Fuller Houses," *Manuscript 28.01.01, Folder 6*, 10.

56. Ibid., 2–3.

57. Ibid., 8.

58. Ibid., 5.

59. Ibid.

60. Ibid.

61. AHF, Chicago, IL, to Wolcott Fuller, Boston, MA, August 10, 1928, *Chronofile*, vol. 35 (1928). Fuller had an affinity for the name Fuller Houses; he revived it for the

name of the corporation he set-up in the mid-1940s to manufacture the Dymaxion
Dwelling Machine, popularly known as the Wichita House.

62. RBF, *4D Timelock* (Albuquerque, NM: Lama Foundation, 1972), 10.

63. Rosen, *Wizard of the Dome*, 59–60. Emphasis in original.

64. RBF, "Lightful Houses," *Manuscript 28.01.01, Folder 3*, 16. Emphasis in original.

65. RBF, *Manuscript 28.01.01, Folder 9*, 7.

66. RBF, "Lightful Houses," 16. Emphasis in original.

67. Linda Dalrymple Henderson, *Fourth Dimension and Non-Euclidian Geometry in Mod-
     ern Art* (Princeton, NJ: Princeton University Press, 1983), 235. Emphasis in original.

68. RBF, New York, NY, to Paul Nelson, Paris, France, August 10, 1928, *4D Timelock*
     (1972), 85.

69. Ibid. Emphasis in original.

70. American Institute of Architects, *A Filing System for Architects' Offices: What It Is and
     How to Use It (A.I.A. Document, No. 172)* (Washington, DC: AIA, 1928), 5.

71. R. Buckminster Fuller, *Inventions: The Patented Works of R. Buckminster Fuller* (New
     York: St. Martin's Press, 1983), 11.

72. D. H. Sweet, of Emery, Booth, Janey and Varney, Chicago, IL, to RBF, Chicago, IL,
     November 1, 1928, *Chronofile*, vol. 34 (1928).

73. D. H. Sweet, of Emery, Booth, Janey and Varney, Chicago, IL, to RBF, Chicago,
     IL, January 22, 1929, *Chronofile*, vol. 36 (1929).

74. D. H. Sweet, of Emery, Booth, Janey and Varney, Chicago, IL, to RBF, Chicago, IL,
     January 24, 1929. In this letter, Sweet informed RBF of costs and "requirements
     for filing and prosecuting patent applications in various countries based on your
     U.S. patent application (our file 1793)" (*Chronofile*, vol. 36 [1929]).

75. Roland C. Rehm, of Emery, Janey and Varney, Chicago, IL, to RBF, Chicago, IL,
     May 29, 1929, *Chronofile*, vol. 36 (1929).

76. L. A. Janey, Emery, Booth, Janey and Varney, Chicago, IL, to RBF, Chicago, IL, June 29, 1929, *Chronofile*, vol. 36 (1929).

77. Invoice, Emery, Booth, Janey and Varney, Chicago, IL, to RBF, Chicago, IL, July 1, 1929, *Chronofile*, vol. 36 (1929). In 2007, $75 is equivalent to $921.83 and $342.20 is like $4,206.00 (www.bls.gov).

78. Roland C. Rehm, of Wilson, Dowell, McCanna & Rehm, Chicago, IL, to RBF, New York, NY, October 27, 1930, *Chronofile*, vol. 37 (1930). Rehm must have been referring to Fuller's desire to take out American and foreign patents.

79. Ibid.

80. RBF, Chicago, IL, to J. M. Hewlett, New York, NY, June 8, 1928, *Chronofile*, vol. 34 (1928). Emphasis in original.

81. Sweet to RBF, November 1, 1928. On the back of this letter, RBF made a list of the claims included in these nine patents; all forty-three claims in the 4D House application are on his list.

82. United States Patent Office, Letters Patent No. 236,141, dated January 4, 1881, to William F. Beecher, Cleveland, OH, for "Heating and Ventilating."

83. United States Patent Office, Letters Patent No. 1,026,406, dated May 14, 1912, to Charles W. Nichols, Rahway, NJ, for "Arrangement for Inclosing Vacuum Conduit Systems."

84. United States Patent Office, Letters Patent No. 504,544, dated September 5, 1893, to William van der Heyden, Yokohama, Japan, for "Sanitary House."

85. United States Patent Office, Letters Patent No. 1,667,484, dated April 24, 1928, to Paul Liege, Berlin-Tempelhof, Germany, for "Translucent Wall, Ceiling and Floor Structure."

86. United States Patent Office, Letters Patent No. 439,376, dated October 28, 1890, to Dudley Blanchard, Brooklyn, NY, for "Tornado-Proof Building," 1.

87. United States Patent Office, Letters Patent No. 1,470,935, dated October 16, 1923, to Allan C. Rush, Los Angeles, CA, for "Observation, Amusement, and Utility Tower," 1.

88. United States Patent Office, Letters Patent No. 1,529,516, dated March 10, 1925, to Alexander Thomson Thorne, Tulsa, OK, for "Cantilever Building Construction."

89. United States Patent Office, Letters Patent No. 1,543,134, dated June 23, 1925, to Libanus M. Todd, Rochester, NY, for "Shelter."

90. United States Patent Office, Letters Patent No. 1,683,600, dated September 11, 1928, to Archibald Black, Garden City, NY, for "Building Construction."

91. Ibid., 1. Fuller and Black both proposed manufacturing and assembling entire sections of the house at the factory and then shipping those to the site, like modular housing. This is in contrast to the type of prefabricated houses manufactured by companies such as Sears, which sold the house as a kit of individual pieces that were assembled one-by-one much like custom housing.

92. RBF, *Inventions*, 11. Fuller acknowledged problems with the claims resulted in the abandonment of the application without revealing all the claims were problematic. According to Marjorie Ciarlante, archivist, National Archives and Records Administration, a patent application is abandoned when "the applicant fails to pay fees or submit documentation requested by the examiner within the allowed time; when claims made for the invention are not patentable or were previously patented; or when another applicant has filed an application for the same invention and can demonstrate an earlier date for the conception of the invention" (Marjorie H. Ciarlante, National Archives and Records Administration, College Park, MD, to the author, April 11, 2002).

93. RBF, *Inventions*, 12.

94. For examples of the treatment of the 4D House patent application, see Fuller and Marks, *The Dymaxion World*, 87; RBF, *4D Timelock* (1972), 55–69; and RBF, *Inventions*, 10–29 (figure 7 is correctly numbered in this reproduction).

95.   RBF, "What I Claim Is," *Chronofile*, vol. 35 (1928). For a complete transcription of the forty-three claims from the patent application, see Lorance, "Building Values," Appendix 2.

96.   Ibid., 12, and RBF, *4D Timelock* (1972), 55.

97.   RBF, *Inventions*, 11.

98.   RBF to J. M. Hewlett, June 8, 1928. Emphasis in original.

99.   RBF to J. M. Hewlett, June 8, 1928.

100. RBF, *Diary*, February 23, 1928.

101. RBF, *Diary*, February 22, 1928.

102. ABF, *Diary*, January 21, 1928.

103. RBF, *Diary*, February 3 and 4, 1928.

4 TRIAL OFFER

1.   Inventors customarily include a model with their patent application. Yet, no model of the 4D House is mentioned in reprints of the patent application and Fuller's description of the patent process includes only drawings and verbal instructions. It is now impossible to consult the original 4D patent application because patents dated before June 8, 1995, are destroyed twenty years after closure unless they are referred to in an issued patent (M. H. Ciarlante to the author, April 11, 2002).

2.   Earl Reed, Chicago, IL, to RBF, New York, NY, February 13, 1940, *Chronofile*, vol. 75 (1940). In St. Louis Fuller discussed the 4D House with Reed and gave him an essay. On May 21, 1928, Fuller sent him additional material (*4D Timelock* [1972], 45.). Reed probably confused the 1928 convention in St. Louis with the 1930 convention in Washington, DC. At the Washington convention, Reed and Fuller shared a

room and Fuller made an unofficial presentation about the project (*Chronofile*, vol. 37 ([1930]).

3.   See various letters from RBF to persons he hoped to interest in the 4D House in *Chronofile*, vol. 34 (1928), and *4D Timelock* (1972).

4.   American Institute of Architects, *Program of the Sixty-First Annual Convention* (Washington, DC: AIA, 1928), and Board of Directors, AIA, *Proceedings of the Sixty-first Annual Convention of the American Institute of Architects* (Washington, DC: AIA, 1928).

5.   RBF, "Essay about the May 1928 AIA Convention," *Chronofile*, vol. 33 (1928). For a transcription of the essay, see Lorance, "Building Values," Appendix 3.

6.   RBF, *4D Timelock* (1972), 31.

7.   RBF, Chicago, IL, to H. W. Tomlinson, Joliet, IL, undated draft of letter, *Chronofile*, vol. 34 (1928). He made the same claim in other letters he wrote immediately after the convention.

8.   Author's correspondence with Sarah Turner, AIA Library and Archives, Washington, DC; Mary Sullivan, St. Louis AIA Chapter; and Joan Pomaranc, Chicago AIA Chapter.

9.   RBF to J. M. Hewlett, June 8, 1928.

10.   RBF, *4D Timelock* (1972), 38.

11.   RBF, "Draft of Speech for May 1928 AIA Convention," *Chronofile*, vol. 33 (1928). Emphasis in original.

12.   RBF, "Essay about the May 1928 AIA Convention." Emphasis in original. The essay is in Fuller's characteristically difficult, convoluted prose and typically highlighted by a few words of his own invention.

13.   RBF to Tomlinson, undated draft of letter.

14.   Fuller made no notes on the program or on any other documents from the St. Louis convention confirming that he had made a presentation. This is in contrast to his handwritten entry on the program of the AIA convention in Washington, DC. At

the bottom of the schedule for May 22, 1930, he wrote: "10:30 [p.m.] talk by Buck-minster Fuller at request Chicago Chapter." The Chicago Chapter did support Fuller this time, and Earl Reed tried unsuccessfully to get Fuller slated into the convention schedule. Reed contacted Charles Butler, the convention organizer, on May 10, 1930, to request that Fuller be added to the program. Butler responded: "Regret no time for Fuller." Fuller and his supporters must have chosen that evening as the most opportune time to insert his presentation into the convention (*Chronofile*, vol. 37 [1930]).

15. RBF, Chicago, IL, to A. P. Herman, Seattle, WA, May 21, 1928, *4D Timelock* (1972), 45.

16. RBF, Chicago, IL, to T. R. Kimball, Omaha, NE, May 21, 1928, *4D Timelock* (1972), 45.

17. J. M. Hewlett, New York, NY, to RBF, Chicago, IL, June 4, 1928, *4D Timelock* (1972), 50.

18. A. E. Erickson, Chicago, IL, to RBF, Chicago, IL, June 12, 1928, *4D Timelock* (1972), 50.

19. Boyd and Holden were much taken by the 4D House project and they corresponded with RBF about it. Their unedited letters are in *Chronofile*, vol. 34 (1928). Some of their correspondence was reprinted in *4D Timelock*, although a few important details were edited out. For example, beginning on page 49 is a May 31, 1928, letter "To R.B.F. from a New York Architect and Architectural Author," which refers to "Mr. X." The "New York Architect and Architectural Author" was John Boyd Jr. and "Mr. X" was Arthur Holden. Their identities are confirmed through consultation of the original letter. Fuller may have wanted to keep Holden's and Boyd's identities secret because their office related high housing costs to land and financing. Holden had already published some of his findings and these may have influenced Fuller's thinking. It is not known if he read Holden's work, but the references to them in Boyd's letter to Fuller were edited out (see page 50).

Fuller offered to make Holden his representative in New York. Although Holden declined, he was willing to help: "I feel that it would be a grave injustice to you to accept this because I am not able at the present time to put the time that should be given to work in your behalf. . . . I am anxious to support and help you. I don't think you ought to count on me to be an official representative, as you put it, but I will do what I can for you, especially if you give me concise and brief information as to what you want" (A. Holden, New York, NY, to RBF, Chicago, IL, August 13, 1928, *Chronofile*, vol. 34 [1928]).

20. Fuller and Marks, *The Dymaxion World*, 20, and Snyder, *Autobiographical Monologue/ Scenario*, 57.

21. "Cities Becoming 'Peas of a Pod,' Architects Warn: Report of Board to American Institute Here Deplores Standardization," *St. Louis Star* (May 17, 1928), 11. Excerpts are in *Chronofile*, vol. 35 (1928).

22. Ibid.

23. Ibid.

24. Kenneth Frampton, *Towards a Critical Regionalism: Six Points for an Architecture of Resistance*, in Hal Foster, ed., *The Anti-Aesthetic: Essays on Postmodern Culture* (Port Townsend, WA: Bay Press, 1983), 16–30. According to Frampton: "The fundamental strategy of Critical Regionalism is to mediate the impact of universal civilization with elements derived *indirectly* from the peculiarities of a particular place" (21; emphasis in original). The AIA's concerns about the disappearance of local architectural character in 1928, generally accepted as conservative in the wake of increasing modernism, makes an interesting companion to Frampton's criticism of the lack of local architectural character, generally understood as progressive given the challenges to modernism's hegemony in 1983. In one sense, Frampton's essay serves as a confirmation of the AIA's assessment that restricting architectural design to a few proscribed characteristics would have negative effects.

25. "Cities Becoming 'Peas of a Pod,'" 11.

26. Board of Directors, AIA, *Report to the Sixty-First Annual Convention of the American Institute of Architects* (Washington, DC: AIA, 1928): 33.

27. Ibid.

28. Ibid.

29. Ibid.

30. "Cities Becoming 'Peas of a Pod,'" 11.

31. Fuller, *4D Timelock* (1972), 3.

32. Fuller Houses, Inc., *The Fuller House* (Wichita, KS: Fuller Houses, Inc., 1945): 29.

33. The final version of the 4D/Dymaxion House was realized by the time it was exhib-
     ited at the Architectural League in Manhattan in February 1930 (*Chronofile*, vol. 37,
     1929). There are at least three variations of this project. Fuller did not discuss the
     formal changes and chose to represent the last version as if it were the only one.
     Fuller included the patent application as part of the house's history, but he did not
     point out that it was much different in appearance than the well-known model.

34. RBF, "Essay about the May 1928 AIA Convention."

35. Ibid. Ataxia is loss of muscle coordination, especially in one's limbs.

36. RBF, "Form Letter for First Announcement Letter, May 21, 1928," *4D Timelock*
     (1972), xiv. This letter was adjusted to appeal to the specific recipient. For example,
     the letter he sent to the author Gamaliel Bradford praised Bradford's book *Life and
     I* and his brief biography of Fuller's great-aunt, Margaret Fuller.

37. Ibid.

38. Ibid.

39. AIA, *Program of the Sixty-first Annual Convention*, [2].

40. RBF, handwritten note on Milton B. Medary, "Opening Address," *Report of the Board
     of Directors to the Sixty-first Convention of the American Institute of Architects* (Washing-
     ton, DC: AIA, 1928), 7–8, *Chronofile*, vol. 35 (1928).

41. E. V. Meeks, "Collaboration in Art Education," *Journal of the American Institute of
     Architects*, vol. 16, no. 2 (February 1928): 45–53, and R. F. Bach, "Our Industrial Arts:
     Reflections on the State of Design," *Journal of the American Institute of Architects*, vol.
     16, no. 2 (February 1928): 53–59.

42. RBF, Chicago, IL, to E. V. Meeks, New Haven, CT, May 21, 1928, *4D Timelock*
     (1972), 47.

43. Meeks, "Collaboration in Art Education," 51.

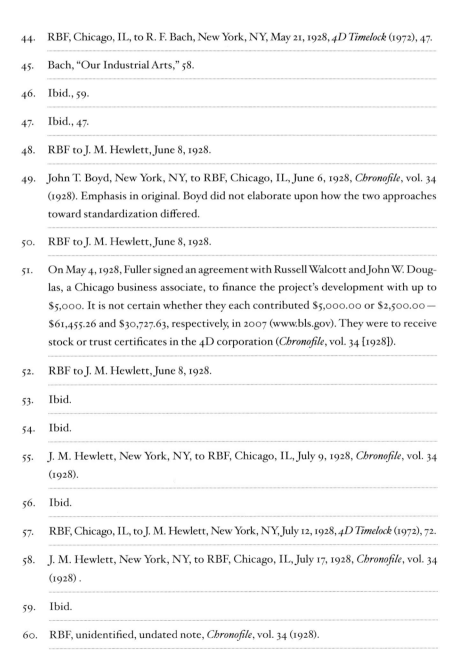

44. RBF, Chicago, IL, to R. F. Bach, New York, NY, May 21, 1928, *4D Timelock* (1972), 47.

45. Bach, "Our Industrial Arts," 58.

46. Ibid., 59.

47. Ibid., 47.

48. RBF to J. M. Hewlett, June 8, 1928.

49. John T. Boyd, New York, NY, to RBF, Chicago, IL, June 6, 1928, *Chronofile*, vol. 34 (1928). Emphasis in original. Boyd did not elaborate upon how the two approaches toward standardization differed.

50. RBF to J. M. Hewlett, June 8, 1928.

51. On May 4, 1928, Fuller signed an agreement with Russell Walcott and John W. Douglas, a Chicago business associate, to finance the project's development with up to $5,000. It is not certain whether they each contributed $5,000.00 or $2,500.00 — $61,455.26 and $30,727.63, respectively, in 2007 (www.bls.gov). They were to receive stock or trust certificates in the 4D corporation (*Chronofile*, vol. 34 [1928]).

52. RBF to J. M. Hewlett, June 8, 1928.

53. Ibid.

54. Ibid.

55. J. M. Hewlett, New York, NY, to RBF, Chicago, IL, July 9, 1928, *Chronofile*, vol. 34 (1928).

56. Ibid.

57. RBF, Chicago, IL, to J. M. Hewlett, New York, NY, July 12, 1928, *4D Timelock* (1972), 72.

58. J. M. Hewlett, New York, NY, to RBF, Chicago, IL, July 17, 1928, *Chronofile*, vol. 34 (1928) .

59. Ibid.

60. RBF, unidentified, undated note, *Chronofile*, vol. 34 (1928).

61. RBF, Chicago, IL, to Mr. Sternfeld, unknown city, July 30, 1928, *Chronofile*, vol. 34 (1928) and RBF, Chicago, IL, to Raymond Hood, New York, NY, July 30, 1928, *4D Timelock* (1972), 76.

62. RBF, Chicago, IL, to George Buffington, Chicago, IL, August 31, 1928, *Chronofile*, vol. 35 (1928).

5 SUPPORTING DOCUMENTS

1. RBF/CHC, "Lightful Products," *Manuscript 28.01.01, Folder 3*, [1]. For a transcription of the Cosmopolitan Homes Corporation documents, see Lorance, "Building Values," Appendix 4.

2. Conrad, "Buckminster Fuller and the Technocratic Persuasion," 220.

3. RBF/CHC, "Lightful Products," [2]. Emphasis in original.

4. RBF/CHC, "Lightful Products Trademark," *Manuscript 28.01.01, Folder 3*, [3].

5. RBF, Chicago, IL, to J. M. Hewlett, New York, NY, June 6, 1928, *Chronofile*, vol. 34 (1928). This article is in the *4D Timelock* reference list.

6. Fuller revisited the concept of the drudgery-proof home in the 1940s as he developed the Dymaxion Dwelling Machine (Wichita House). In the mid-1920s, the discussion of reduced drudgery was equivalent to the discussion of industrial production. In the mid-1940s, industrial production was forefronted.

7. RBF/CHC, "Lightful Products," [1]. Emphasis in original.

8. RBF, Chicago, IL, to C. W. Fuller, Deer Isle, ME, July 16, 1928, *Chronofile*, vol. 34 (1928).

9. RBF/CHC, "Lightful Products Trademark," [1].

10. Ibid., [2].

11. Ibid.

12. Ibid., [3].

13. Ibid.

14. Ibid.

15. Ibid.

16. Ibid., [4].

17. Ibid.

18. RBF, "Lightful Houses," 68. Fuller meant Holy Week. Since Easter was on April 8 in 1928, Holy Week was from April 1 to April 7 (www.timeanddate.com/calendar). For a transcription of "Lightful Houses," see Lorance, "Building Values," Appendix 4.

19. RBF, *Diary*, February 23, 1928.

20. RBF, "Lightful Houses," 21.

21. Ibid., 22.

22. Lightful was the name Fuller first chose for the name of the company in the manuscript. Throughout the manuscript, "Lightful" is crossed out and "4D" replaces it.

23. Fuller and Marks, *The Dymaxion World*, 21.

24. Joachim Krausse and Claude Lichtenstein, eds., *Your Private Sky: R. Buckminster Fuller, The Art of Design Science*, exhibition catalog (Baden, Switzerland: Lars Müller Publishers, 1999), 80.

25. Wong, "Geodesic Works," 34–35.

26. Christian Øverland, "R. Buckminster Fuller's Dymaxion Dwelling Machine: A New Way of Living" (M.A. thesis, SUNY Oneonta, 1998), 26.

27. RBF, "Lightful Houses," 22.

28. Ibid., 3–4. In 2007, a $50,000 automobile would be about $614,552.63 (www.bls.gov).

29. Ibid., 4–5.

30. *Manuscript 28.01.01, Folder 9.* The note is on the outside of the folder and not in Fuller's handwriting. Its author is unknown.

31. "Labeled Cover of Copy #155 of 4D Timelock," R. Buckminster Fuller Papers, Stanford University, M1090, Series 2, Box 20. The notes are in an unknown hand.

32. RBF, *4D Timelock* (1972), xi.

33. Ibid., 6. Emphasis in original.

34. Ibid., 8.

35. Ibid. $45,000 would be close to $553,097.37, and $800 about $9,832.84 in 2007 dollars (www.bls.gov).

36. Ibid., 7.

37. Ibid., 10. He is using conventionalized to mean stylized or abstracted.

38. Roger Babson, "There's Magic in the Air," *Collier's Weekly* (April 7, 1928): 8–9, 50–52.

39. RBF, *4D Timelock* (1972), 13. Emphasis in original.

40. Ibid., 13.

41. Ibid., 16. Emphasis in original.

42. Ibid., 17.

43. Ibid., 20.

44. Ibid., 21.

45. Ibid., 22.

46. Ibid., 24.

47. The abandoned patent application was added to *4D Timelock* when it was first reprinted in 1970.

48. RBF, *4D Timelock* (1972), 1. According to Dietrich Neumann, Brown University, the first sentence is taken from subchapter VI; the last two sentences are from subchapter X. These are found on page 173 and page 176 of the 1981 paperback edition of *The Seven Lamps of Architecture* published by Farrar, Straus and Giroux (Dietrich Neumann, Brown University, Providence, RI, to the author, July 11, 2000).

49. Ibid., 1.

50. Ibid., 28.

51. For a transcription of the *4D Timelock* reference list, see Lorance, "Building Values," Appendix 5.

52. RBF, *4D Timelock* (1972), 33. In 2007, they would earn about $12,292.05 (www.bls.gov).

53. Ibid. In 2007, they would earn approximately $1,229.11 (www.bls.gov).

54. Ibid., 35.

55. U.S. Copyright and Trademark Office, Washington, DC, to the author, New York, NY, January 20, 2003.

56. RBF, *4D Timelock* (1972), 48. L. J. Stoddard, Cleveland, OH, to RBF, Chicago, IL, May 28, 1928.

57. Ibid., 50. Bruce Barton, New York, NY, to L. J. Stoddard, Cleveland, OH, June 8, 1928, *4D Timelock* (1972), 50. Stoddard forwarded Barton's reply to Fuller with the disclaimer: "The enclosed came today as well as prospectus No. 55 returned. Sorry — but all in life is not a bed of roses" (Stoddard to RBF, June 11, 1929, *4D Timelock* [1972], 50).

58. Ibid., 48. Gamaliel Bradford, Wellesley Hills, MA, to RBF, Chicago, IL, May 28, 1928.

59. RBF, Chicago, IL, to John T. Boyd, New York, NY, June 15, 1928, *Chronofile*, vol. 34 (1928). Grammar is original.

60. AHF to Wolcott Fuller, August 10, 1928.

61.   A number of the pages Mrs. Nelson translated into French are among her husband's papers in the Paul Nelson Collection, Avery Library, Columbia University, New York, NY.

62.   See the correspondence between RBF and Scribner's Manhattan office in *Chronofile*, vol. 36 (1929). Fuller knew by the end of 1929 that Scribner's would not publish the book, although he insinuated it was still a possibility until 1932. (See *Chronofile*, vols. 37–43 [1930–1932].)

63.   "Draft of Invitation to Co-operative Lecture," *Chronofile*, vol. 39 (1931). It is unknown if this invitation was sent or if the lecture was given as planned. There is nothing further in Fuller's papers, and the author was not permitted to research in the archives of the Architectural League in Manhattan.

64.   Charles Pearce, Harcourt Brace and Company, Inc., New York, NY, to RBF, New York, NY, February 9, 1933, *Chronofile*, vol. 44 (1933).

6 PROTOTYPE

1.   RBF, Chicago, IL, to L. Pierce, Boston, MA, July 9, 1928, *Chronofile*, vol. 34 (1928).

2.   RBF to C. W. Fuller, July 16, 1928.

3.   AHF to Wolcott Fuller, August 10, 1928.

4.   Fuller and his three siblings owned two rental properties in Cambridge, MA. In 1928 Fuller transferred his share to Anne (*Chronofile*, vol. 34 [1928]). Then, in 1929 they were sold for $26,500 (approximately $325,712.89 in 2007 [www.bls.gov]) and the proceeds were equally divided among the four owners (*Chronofile*, vol. 36 [1929]).

5.   Hatch, *Buckminster Fuller*, 91.

6.   AHF, Lawrence, NY, to RBF, Chicago, IL, July 13, 1927, *Chronofile*, vol. 29 (1927).

7. RBF, Buffalo, NY, to AHF, Lawrence, NY, July 31, 1932, *Chronofile*, vol. 41 (1932). Fuller never considered that his wife could have felt selfishly betrayed if he consumed her money while attempting to get the house into production. Fuller tended to find selfish betrayal something others did to him, not what he did to them. His single-mindedness reflected his mother's warning to Hewlett not to let Anne marry Fuller because he was "irresponsible, thoughtless, and selfish" (Hatch, *Buckminster Fuller*, 47).

8. "Dymaxion House Chronology," Hamilton Extracts, box 49, folder 6, no date, [1]. For a complete transcription, see Lorance, "Building Values," Appendix 6.

9. Ibid.

10. Fuller and Marks, *The Dymaxion World*, 21.

11. Marshall Field & Company, "Announcement for Exhibition of the Dymaxion House," April 1929, *Chronofile*, vol. 36 (1929).

12. Various written and telephone correspondence between the author and Tony Jahn, Marshall Field & Company archivist, between June 1997 and August 2003. The author was not permitted to research in the archives.

13. Fuller and Marks, *The Dymaxion World*, 21.

14. Ibid. A variation of this story crediting the creation of "dymaxion" to two advertising men is found in Snyder, *Autobiographical Monologue/Scenario*, 54.

15. Mary Reynolds, Chicago, IL, to RBF, New York, NY, May 4, 1933, *Chronofile*, vol. 44 (1933).

16. RBF, undated, unaddressed draft of letter, *Chronofile*, vol. 34 (1928).

17. Chamberlain to RBF, October 24, 1928.

18. RBF, Chicago, IL, to Paul Nelson, sailing from New York to Paris, August 11, 1928, *Chronofile*, vol. 35 (1928).

19. See various correspondence between Atwood and RBF in volumes 42–50 of the *Chronofile* (1932–1934).

20. RBF, Chicago, IL, to C. W. Fuller, New York, NY, February 4, 1929, *Chronofile*, vol. 36 (1929).

21. It is unclear when Fuller began to give a twenty-five-year period of development for the house. One of the first instances was in the autobiographical essay to Joe Bryant (RBF, "Letter and Essay to Joe Bryant," 5).

22. Theodore Morrison, "The House of the Future: Dymaxion House Designed by Buckminster Fuller Embodies the Principles and Advantages of Scientific Housing," *The House Beautiful* 66, no. 9 (September 1929): 292–293, 324, 326, 328, 330.

23. Ibid., 292.

24. Page 65 of *Pencil Points,* January 1929, *Chronofile*, vol. 33 (1928).

25. Page 607 of *Pencil Points,* September 1928, *Chronofile*, vol. 33 (1928).

26. Arthur Holden, New York, NY, to RBF, Chicago, IL, June 15, 1928, *Chronofile*, vol. 34 (1928). Emphasis in original.

27. "What the Offing Holds," *New York Herald Tribune* (November 11, 1928): 10, *Chronofile*, vol. 34 (1928). After the design of the Dymaxion House model was finalized in early 1930, Fuller received two letters about European designs similar to it. In the summer of 1930, William Crane, Jr., wrote Fuller about "a young architect from Odessa, Mr. Seigfried Ebelling" who "had a model and plans of a cylindrical shape metal and glass apartment house and on which he was anxious to get American comments" (W. M. Crane Jr., New York, NY, to RBF, New York, NY, July 18, 1930, *Chronofile*, vol. 37 [1930]). In March of the following year, Herr Schäfer sent a letter of inquiry to Fuller noting: "We were informed by Mr. Robert L. Davison, Director of Research, that you have developed a very interesting theory of low-cost construction which is similar in principle to the Rasch Brothers apartment houses hung from a mast" (Herr Schäfer, Internationaler Verband für Wohnungswesen, Frankfurt-am-Main, Germany, to RBF, New York, NY, March 3, 1931, *Chronofile*, vol. 38 [1931]).

28. Loretta Lorance, *Buckminster Fuller — Dialogue with Modernism, Part 7*, http://dsc.gc.cuny.edu/part/part7/articles/loranc.html (Spring 2001): 8–11.

29. RBF, "A Tree-like Style of Dwelling Is Planned," and "Toward a New Architecture," *The Chicago Evening Post Magazine of the Art World*, Part III (December 18, 1928): 5.

30. RBF, *Manuscript 28.01.01, Folder 9*.

31. RBF, to Rosamund Fuller, August 11, 1928.

32. Morrison, "The House of the Future," 293.

33. Banham, *Theory and Design in the First Machine Age*, 326–327.

34. Le Corbusier, *Towards a New Architecture* (New York: Dover Publications, 1986), 247–248: "Modern achievement . . . replaces human labour by the machine. . . . Servants are no longer of necessity tied to the house: they come here, as they would a factory, and do their eight hours; in this way an active staff is available day and night."

35. Orson Fowler, *The Octagon House, A Home for All* (New York: Dover Reprints, 1973).

36. Hatch, *Buckminster Fuller*, 24.

37. RBF, "Mass Production of Houses in Factories," text of address given to the City Club Forum, Tuesday, May 28, 1929, *Chronofile*, vol. 36 (1929).

38. R. G. McPhail, "How Many Outlets? Modern Electric Equipment Demands More of Them as Well as Better Planning," *Building Age* (June 1929): 94–95, and "Consider the Refrigerator When Planning Homes," *American Builder*, vol. 44, no. 5 (February 1928): 120–122.

39. See J. A Ryan, "Efficient Slaves of Intelligent Masters; Proper Care of Electrical Appliances," *National Safety News*, 20 (October 1929): 116, 126, and "Electric Servants Accomplish Many Household Tasks," *Dun's International Review* 53 (July 1929): 31–34.

40. Mrs. C. S. Peel, "At the Ideal Home Exhibition," *The Queen: The Lady's Newspaper and Court Chronicle*, vol. 163, no. 4237 (March 7, 1928): 38–39.

41. Deborah S. Ryan, *The Ideal Home through the 20th Century: Daily Mail — Ideal Home Exhibition* (London: Hazar Publishing, Ltd., 1997), 55–57.

42. See C .A. Coffin, "C. A. Coffin's Vision of Future of Electricity in the Home," *Forbes*, vol. 18, no. 3 (May 15, 1926): 12, 124, 126–127; "Consumer Possibilities of the Residential Customer," *Journal of Electricity*, no. 57 (October 15, 1926): 300–302; and Sophia Malicki, "Utility Women Help — Abstract," *Electrical World*, no. 91 (June 9, 1928): 1223–1224: "A utility company should be the community household management center. It should answer the plea of housewives for a place to which they can turn for advice. . . . The fact that women need to place a higher value on their energy and time brings a direct responsibility to the utilities for a liberal portion of education in standards of health and decency." One approach was for electric companies and appliance manufacturers to sponsor symposia in the use of their products. See, for example, "Women from Fifteen States Attend Pioneer Course in Electrical Equipment Economics at Iowa University," *Public Service Management*, no. 42 (May 1927): 139–140.

43. Mrs. Christine Frederick, "Selling Small Electric Appliances: Sound Sales Arguments for National Electric Week — Contrasting New with Obsolescent Cleaning Methods in the Home," *The Electrician*, no. 99 (November 11, 1927): 590–591.

44. AHF, Woodmere, NY, to RBF, New York, NY, September 12, 1929, *Chronofile*, vol. 36 (1929).

45. RBF, Chicago, IL, to Henry H. Saylor, New York, NY, May 9, 1929, *Chronofile*, vol. 36 (1929).

46. "Announcement of February 1930 Dymaxion House Exhibition at the Architectural League," *Chronofile*, vol. 36 (1929).

47. Fuller and Marks, *The Dymaxion World*, 18.

48. Undated, unidentified clipping, *Boston Evening Transcript*, *Chronofile*, vol. 36 (1929).

49. RBF, "A Tree-like Style of Dwelling Is Planned," 5. In 2007, the cost per ton would be equivalent to $6,145.53 (www.bls.gov).

50. Morrison, "The House of the Future," 328. The price would be about $36,873.16 in 2007 (www.bls.gov).

51. Ibid., 238. The monthly cost would be close to $61.46 in 2007 (www.bls.gov).

52. Albert T. Reid, *The World's Strong Man*, cartoon from unidentified source, *Chronofile*, vol. 28 (1926–1927).

53. Inez Cunningham, "Fuller's Dymaxion House on Display," *The Chicago Evening Post Magazine of the Art World* (May 16, 1930): 10.

54. Russell Walcott, Chicago, IL, to RBF, Chicago, IL, May 29, 1928, *Chronofile*, vol. 34 (1928). Walcott sent Fuller a note exclaiming, "You see that Leonardo had a part of your scheme worked out as far back as 1515!" Included was the following excerpt from Edward McCurdy's book *The Mind of Leonardo da Vinci* (New York: Dodd, Mead, and Company, 1928): "Changed arrangement (mutatione) of houses seems in some details almost to anticipate the conditions of standardization consequent upon modern mass production: Let the houses be changed and arranged in order, and this will easily be done when they are first made in parts on the open places and then the framework can be fitted together on the site where they are to be permanent (From Leonardo's notebook)."

55. RBF, *4D Timelock* (1972), 39.

56. RBF, New York, NY, to Eugenia Walcott, Barrington, IL, September 10, 1929, *Chronofile*, vol. 36 (1929).

57. RBF, Woodmere, NY, to H. W. Corbett, New York, NY, April 4, 1930, *Chronofile*, vol. 37 (1930).

58. *Chronofile*, vol. 37 (1930). The 2007 equivalents are $1,258.54 and $629.27 (www.bls .gov).

59. R. C. Sacketter, Advertisers Incorporated, Detroit, MI, to RBF, Woodmere, NY, April 26, 1930; Fuller responded on June 30, 1930, *Chronofile*, vol. 37 (1930).

60. Mrs. Helen Hodgdon, Medford, MA , to RBF, Chicago, IL, May 29, 1929, *Chronofile*, vol. 36 (1929).

61. G. B. Olmstead, Brooklyn, NY, to RBF, Chicago, IL, September 4, 1929, *Chronofile*, vol. 36 (1929). Emphasis in original.

62. RBF, Woodmere, NY, to Mrs. Rothwell Hyde, Kailau, HI, July 2, 1930, in reply to her letters of January 8 and April 9, 1930, *Chronofile*, vol. 37 (1930).

63. RBF, Bridgeport, CT, to Richard Reed, Lancaster, PA, May 16, 1934, *Chronofile*, vol. 50 (1934).

64. Fuller and Marks, *The Dymaxion World*, 22–23.

65. RBF, Woodmere, NY, to G. Keeble, Carnegie Institute of Technology, Pittsburgh, PA, April 3, 1930, *Chronofile*, vol. 37 (1930).

66. RBF, Woodmere, NY, to Henry H. Saylor, New York, NY, April 4, 1930, *Chronofile*, vol. 37 (1930).

67. RBF to H. W. Corbett, April 4, 1930. Emphasis in original.

68. J. C. Folsom, A Century of Progress, Chicago, IL, to L. Levinson, *Shelter*, Philadelphia, PA, December 14, 1932, *Chronofile*, vol. 42 (1932).

69. L. Levinson, *Shelter*, Philadelphia, PA, to J. C. Folsom, A Century of Progress, Chicago, IL, December 12, 1932, *Chronofile*, vol. 42 (1932).

70. J. C. Folsom, A Century of Progress, Chicago, IL, to RBF, Bridgeport, CT, March 10, 1934, *Chronofile*, vol. 49 (1934).

71. RBF, Bridgeport, CT, to J. C. Folsom, A Century of Progress, Chicago, IL, May 12, 1934, *Chronofile*, vol. 50 (1934).

72. Lewis Mumford, "Mass-Production and the Modern Home," *The Architectural Record*, vol. 67, no. 1 (January 1930): 20.

73. See *Chronofile*, vols. 38–41 (1931), for information about Fuller's work for the Pierce Foundation.

74. See *Chronofile*, vols. 41–44 (1932), for information about Fuller's work at *Shelter*.

75. Deborah Dependahl Waters, Museum of the City of New York, New York, NY, to the author, Long Island City, NY, March 11, 1998.

76. See *Chronofile*, vols. 73–86 (1940–1941).

77.   Donald Deskey, New York, NY, to RBF, Bear Island, ME, August 7, 1930, *Chronofile*, vol. 37 (1930).

78.   RBF, Bridgeport, CT, to Mr. Parsons, Yonkers Chamber of Commerce, Yonkers, NY, May 15, 1934, *Chronofile*, vol. 50 (1934).

79.   *Chronofile*, vol. 64 (1939), and "Dymaxion House Chronology," Lorance, "Building Values," Appendix 6.

80.   RBF, New York, NY, John McAndrew, Museum of Modern Art, New York, NY, February 15, 1939, *Chronofile*, vol. 63 (193).

81.   Telephone conversation between Pamela Wilson, managing archivist, Time, Inc., New York, NY, and the author, January 24, 2003. On the advice of legal council, Ms. Wilson refused to send written confirmation that the Dymaxion House model had been thrown away.

7 END PRODUCT

1.   RBF, "Letter and Essay to Joe Bryant."

2.   See RBF, "A Tree-like Style of Dwelling Is Planned," 5, and "Builds Unique House to Sell by the Ton," *Chicago Daily News* (April 1, 1929): 2.

3.   See "Unique Dynamic House of Arboreal Design Will Solve Future Dwelling Problems—Inventor Claims Harmony with Nature," *The Harvard Crimson*, vol. 95, no. 76 (May 21, 1929): 1, and Morrison, "The House of the Future."

4.   Cunningham, "Fuller's Dymaxion House on Display," 1.

5.   Mme. X, "Buckminster Fuller Explains His New Housing Industry," *Chicago Sunday Tribune* (May 18, 1930): Part 8, 1.

6.   Fuller and Marks, *The Dymaxion World*, 11. See chapter 2, note 31. For a more detailed discussion of Fuller's forebears, see Conrad's dissertation, "Buckminster Fuller and the Technocratic Persuasion." He devotes part of one paragraph to Fuller's mother's family and about fifteen pages to his subject's paternal ancestors.

7.   "Draft of Philadelphia Art Alliance Press Release," *Chronofile*, vol. 42 (1932). Fuller was from Milton, a Boston suburb, although it made sense to use the better-known city.

8.   Ibid.

9.   RBF worked for *Fortune* magazine, and Bryant worked for *Time* magazine. Both were owned by Time, Inc., and housed in the company's Rockefeller Center headquarters. The essay is divided into *Dymaxion House*, thirteen pages; *Dymaxion Car*, nine pages; *Miscellaneous Observations*, five pages; *Personal*, five pages; *Family & Career*, twenty-two pages; and *The Book*, three pages.

10.   RBF, "Letter and Essay to Joe Bryant." The monetary equivalents are as follows: $50 in 1919 is close to $607.45 in 2007; $55 is about $668.19; $80 in 1922 is like $1,000.84 in 2007; $50 in 1927 is around $603.96 in 2007; $700 is about $8,455.40; and $22 is almost $265.74.

11.   Fuller admitted that he deserved to be "fired" from Harvard, but he shifted the blame onto factors beyond his control:

> *My father died when I was quite young, and though my family was relatively poor I had come to Harvard from a preparatory school for quite well-to-do families. I soon saw that I wasn't going to be included in the clubs as I might have been if I had been very wealthy or had a father looking out for me. . . . I considered myself about to be ostracized or compassionately tolerated by the boys I had grown up with. I felt that my social degradation would bring disgrace to my family . . . I became panicky . . . went on a pretended "lark," cut classes, as was "fired." . . . I went to work and worked hard . . . reports went to Harvard that I was a good and able boy and that I really ought to go back to college; so Harvard took me back. However, I was now considered a social maverick, and I saw none of my old friends; it hurt too much. Again I cut classes, spent all my year's allowance, and once more was "fired." (Buckminster*

> *Fuller,* Education Automation: Freeing the Scholar to Return to His
> Studies *[Carbondale: Southern Illinois University Press, 1962]: 4–5)*

Fuller may have been an outcast as he claimed, but it is unlikely poverty was the cause. After all, there were uncles and family friends to sponsor his memberships. One must wonder why Fuller thought dismissal from Harvard was less embarrassing than not being accepted into clubs.

12. Fuller probably contributed to his dismissal from Kelly-Springfield. On April 5, 1922, he wrote letters to C. W. Young, the company president, and E. O. McDonnell, the friend who recruited him, about dishonest distributors in New York and Boston. According to Fuller, parts were removed from new trucks and then installed in old trucks. They then sold new trucks with bad parts and old trucks with new parts. There is no response in Fuller's papers from either Young or McDonnell, which makes it impossible to establish a connection between his disclosure and his dismissal (*Chronofile*, vol. 22 [1922]).

13. *Chronofile*, vol. 23 (1922)

14. Allegra Fuller Snyder, Pacific Palisades, CA, to the author, January 29, 2003, and www.timeanddate.com/calendar.

15. Geoffrey H. Movius, ed., *The Second Book of Harvard Athletics, 1923–1963* (Cambridge, MA: The Harvard Varsity Club, 1964), 142.

16. Anne noted: "Bucky had very good talk with Mr. Deffenbacher, owner of Virginia about leaving our bill unpaid. It will be alright. He told Bucky all his troubles & Bucky is going to see . . . if he can help him in any way & thereby cancel our bill" (AHF, *Diary*, December 5, 1927).

17. RBF, *4D Timelock* (1972), 41.

18. Sometimes the period of silence is given as longer, almost two years. Hatch explains that Fuller spoke to Anne and Allegra, but no one else, during this period.

19. RBF, *4D Timelock* (1972), 20.

20. Rosen, *Wizard of the Dome*, 46–47.

21.   Muller is last mentioned by name on March 8, 1928. There are other references to bids Fuller was preparing on Muller's behalf on March 12, 16, and possibly 17.

22.   RBF, *Diary*, February 1, 1928.

23.   Fuller and Marks, *The Dymaxion World*, 2.

24.   There are ninety-six pages in the *4D Timelock* manuscript (ninety pages of text, one page for Christopher Morley's poem "To a Child," and the five-page reference list).

25.   RBF, *4D Timelock* (1972), 76.

26.   RBF to Alfred and Pauline Fuller, January 9, 1928.

27.   RBF, to AHF, July 31, 1932.

28.   Ibid.

29.   Fuller and Marks, *The Dymaxion World*, 22–23.

30.   Dan P. McAdams, *The Stories We Live By: Personal Myths and the Making of the Self* (New York: The Guilford Press, 1993), 12.

31.   Ibid., 11.

32.   Ibid., 12.

33.   Many of the significant events of Fuller's private life were never made public, such as the 1932 letter he wrote to Anne from Buffalo about their marriage problems. Although he and Anne never divorced, Fuller had numerous affairs after their return to the East Coast from Chicago, which are documented in the *Chronofile* but not publicly disclosed.

34.   McAdams, *The Stories We Live By*, 301n1.

35.   AHF, *Diary*, March 8, 1928.

36.   See Bertrand Russell, *Education and the Good Life* (New York: Boni & Liveright, 1926); Bertrand Russell, *Selected Papers of Bertrand Russell* (New York: The Modern Library, 1927); and Bertrand Russell, "The Training of Young Children," *Harper's Monthly Magazine* 155, ser. no. 927 (August 1927): 313–319.

37.   AHF, *Diary*, March 8, 1928.

38.   Bertrand Russell, "A Free Man's Worship," in *Selected Papers of Bertrand Russell* (New York: The Modern Library, 1927), 7–9.

39.   Fuller codified the official version of his activities in the 1920s by 1960 when the semi-autobiographical *Dymaxion World of Buckminster Fuller* was published. He gave a more mystical adaptation twenty years later in *Buckminster Fuller: An Autobiographical Monologue/Scenario*.

40.   McAdams, *The Stories We Live By*, 12.

INDEX